T0158634

EX LIBRIS

VINTAGE **CLASSICS**

The Princess and the Dairymaid

LADY DIANA COOPER

Lady Diana Cooper was born on 29 August 1892. She married Alfred Duff Cooper, DSO, who became one of the Second World War's key politicians. Her startling beauty resulted in her playing the lead in two silent films and then Max Reinhardt's *The Miracle*. In 1944, following the Liberation of Paris, the couple moved into the British Embassy in Paris. They then retired to a house at Chantilly just outside Paris. After Duff's death in 1954 Diana remained there till 1960, when she moved back to London. She died in 1986.

LADY DIANA COOPER

Trumpets from the Steep

VINTAGE

2 4 6 8 10 9 7 5 3 1

Vintage
20 Vauxhall Bridge Road,
London SW1V 2SA

Vintage Classics is part of the Penguin Random House group of companies
whose addresses can be found at global.penguinrandomhouse.com.

Penguin
Random House
UK

First published in Great Britain by Rupert Hart-Davis in 1960
This edition reissued by Vintage in 2018

penguin.co.uk/vintage

A CIP catalogue record for this book
is available from the British Library

ISBN 9781784873028

Typeset in 10.4/13.5 pt Adobe Caslon Pro by Jouve UK, Milton Keynes
Printed and bound by Clays Ltd, St Ives plc

Penguin Random House is committed to a sustainable future
for our business, our readers and our planet. This book is made
from Forest Stewardship Council® certified paper.

MIX
Paper from
responsible sources
FSC
www.fsc.org   FSC® C018179

Dedication

With this and my two earlier volumes I have received more help than I can decently acknowledge. Most of my benefactors will have to remain anonymous, but I feel I must say a special word of gratitude to Flora Russell for allowing me to print so many of her brother's inimitable letters, Martin Battersby for letting me decorate my three books with the epics he painted on my walls,* Cecil Beaton for recording so many events in my life and giving me freedom to use the results, and Laurence Whistler for permission to reproduce his brother's letters and drawings.

Norah Fahie has typed and retyped my pencil-scrawled manuscript, repairing my spelling and supplying punctuation. But for her endless care and patience I should never have got into print, and without the loving and ruthless badgering of Jenny Nicholson I might never even have put pencil to paper.

To all these kind friends, and to Rupert Hart-Davis my dear publisher and nephew, I dedicate this last volume.

JULY 1960   DIANA COOPER

---

* Refers to the designs on the endpapers in the first editions of the autobiography, which were taken from murals in the author's house at Chantilly.

Contents

Illustrations

1
Talking through Armageddon

In 1939 the writing so long scrawled on the wall was translated into many languages. The birds of ill omen no longer screeched but perched gagged in the still trees. The voice of Cassandra sank to a whisper. The lull waited for the hour when strife must be hailed, calculation and logic forgotten. We must summon up all our courage and magnify it, and behave well.

To go or not to go to America became our own particularly burning question. When he resigned from the Government after Munich, Duff had signed a lecture-contract for a year ahead, and now October 1939 was here and so was the end-of-the-world war. Duff, irked by his independence and seeing no niche for himself at home, favoured this useful mission to the United States, yet the idea of leaving England in wartime made him hesitate. The oracles he consulted gave diametrically different but not equivocal answers. One augurer felt confident that Duff, a resigned Minister, would shortly be back in office, for already the Government looked rickety; another said that America would resent propaganda. Friendly American journalists like John Gunther and Knickerbocker urged us to go. Winston wavered, unable to admit the Government's instability. Lord Cranborne cried 'Forward!' while Lord Salisbury murmured 'Back.'

My optimistic husband had been to some army manoeuvres in his anachronistic Second Lieutenant's uniform. He had wound his puttees tightly round his elegant legs, filled his water-bottle, brushed up his kitbag, and packed it with his few troubles. He had marched off to a field-day, looking as portly as a Secretary of State and jumping with surprise when the Generals called him 'Sir.' By evening he saw that the army held no future for him. His helmet

now must make a hive for bees, but a lingering hope urged him to appeal to Colonel Mark Maitland of the Third Battalion, Grenadier Guards (he who twenty years before had shouted Duff off to war from Waterloo). The Colonel dashed his last hope. Now only the Prime Minister's approval of his absence remained to be asked.

The interview was an unhappy one. Mr Chamberlain naturally had no words of sympathy or regret. Duff was surprised at this lack of courtesy. I expected it, but what we did not anticipate was Mr Chamberlain's suggesting that in a few weeks' time, when 'things get pretty hot here, a man of fifty might be criticised for leaving his country.' Ever since I have maintained that the Prime Minister advised Duff to 'go for a soldier.' I can find no corroboration in Duff's memoirs. I expect that he suppressed or forgot the advice, or else I am guilty of a conscious and vengeful lie that I have come to believe. After a hum and a haw the Prime Minister grudgingly agreed to Duff's going to the United States if he promised to say nothing that might smell of anti-German propaganda. As if Duff was going to talk through Armageddon about Keats or Horace or the Age of Elegance.

The die had been cast in fateful September. John Julius's day-school in London moved to a less congested county, and together with his familiars he became a boarder at Westbury in Northamptonshire, the best solution for my peace of mind and his untroubled development. In October, with a trembling hand in Duff's, I boarded the American S.S. *Manhattan*. To Conrad Russell I wrote from Southampton:

> The platform was Frith's *Paddington Station* – people with all their worldly goods (nothing so pathetic), the guitar, the clock, the old rugs, cricket bats and toy engine. Mine (had I taken any) would be my wax face by Jo Davidson and Queen Victoria's picture of Mother, your diamond dolphins and what not? The Frith scene made me see ourselves as Ford Madox Brown's *The Last of England*, and such conceits as these have kept my spirits well up.

It's a brilliant day. No balloons up. I'm equipped with luminol and a beautiful bottle of old brandy brought by Raimund to the station. I feel that this is the first time I have been part of real life. I was going to say 'except when John Julius was born,' but even that wasn't very real. Artifice, science and drugs veiled the reality. My mother's death was real enough, I suppose, and one mustn't see only horrors as real life. Wandering in sun-bathed Somerset perhaps is real too.

There's a man sorting at least five hundred gas-masks on the platform, some of them with snouts protruding from their cardboard confines. They are stacked in a disorderly pyramid, and these (the lost 'Mum's,' 'Dad's' and 'Sis's') are the residue of *one* train-load only. *Priez pour nous.*

We sailed unexpectedly south to Bordeaux. It added two days of terror to an uneasy state of mind, inclining neither to the devil nor the deep sea. We both felt uncertain if we were right to leave all we held dearest to the devil, yet riding the deep and treacherous sea in throes of fear I felt, in a complicated way, less cowardly. We were favoured with a cabin to ourselves in a figurehead position, with a shower that gave an unsaturating trickle of nearly-cold water. Black-outs in belligerent waters, no *Lebensraum*, as all the spacious saloons and ballrooms had become tightly-packed dormitories. We had nothing to complain of above sea-level except a Jonah-woman, who had been in the torpedoing of the *Lusitania*. I hated her, for she told me insensitively that when she had heard Duff was on the ship she had tried to cancel her passage. This put new and gruesome ideas into my head. On a neutral ship, with Old Glory fluttering at the masthead, could armed U-boat captains surface alongside and claim Duff individually as their rightful prey? I remember wondering distractedly at night how to counter this grim menace. There was a benison of nuns on board, Jonahs in themselves to many faint hearts, but revered by me (who had my own Jonah). I saw the sisters as a potential salvation, for at the first alarm I would have Duff's moustache off in a trice and

3

borrow a nun's habit for his disguise. They would refuse if I prepared for the eventuality by asking the loan in cold blood, but with the sea-wolf baying at the door they would surely come to our rescue.

I confided all my fears, not to Duff, who would have despised them, but to the Captain himself over a cocktail, asking him what he would do if the claim were made? He answered that he had not made up his mind. This was hardly reassuring.

Dreadful rumours, many unfounded, came through a radio at its most confused and raucous worst. The sinking of the *Repulse* was one to depress us unnecessarily. We passed no ship but were expecting S.O.S.'s hourly. Never did I look forward more to seeing good Ellis Island and the Statue of Liberty, so unexpectedly green as grass, and at last the skyline in early morning light, its towers unsubstantial as a dream, a sight that always robbed me of breath. I wrote to Conrad:

Ambassador Hotel, New York   *22 October 1939*
    We landed in thick fog, so there was no sky-line to see,
    although I was up by 6.30 so as not to miss it. The good Dr
    Kommer was on the dock and so was my old chum Iris Tree,
    but I didn't feel relief or pleasure or anything at all. My
    heart's dead in me. The fog lifted and I could see without
    thrill how marvellously beautiful this city is, and how much
    more beautiful than ten years ago. Duff is in a perpetual
    swoon about it, and is as happy and *sans souci* as a colt.

Mr and Mrs William Paley were the first to welcome us and give us confidence, although we had met them but once in Scotland. He was the young and successful head of the Columbia Broadcasting Corporation, physically a little oriental and very attractive. Together they lived in a Colonial house on Long Island. This luxury taste slightly depresses me. The standard is unattainable to us tradition-ridden tired Europeans. There was nothing ugly, worn or makeshift; brief and exquisite meals, a little

first-class wine, one snorting cocktail. Servants were invisible, yet one was always tended. Conversation was amusing, wise-cracked, light and serious. A little table in your bedroom was laid, as for a nuptial night, with fine lawn, plates, forks and a pyramid of choice-bloomed peaches, figs and grapes. In the bathroom were all the aids to sleep, masks for open eyes, soothing unguents and potions. In the morning a young, silent girl, more lovely than the sun that blazed through the hangings, smoothed all and was never seen again. We felt like a couple of Slys in *The Taming of the Shrew.*

It was difficult to be in New York in those early war days (labelled 'phoney' to one's superstitious horror). The change back to normality was too sudden. I felt ashamed of everything, ashamed of some scrimshanking English people pretending nostalgia for home, ashamed of the 'Keep out of it' attitude of many highly intelligent Americans, although sympathising with them full-heartedly. News was plentiful and splendidly biased, though presented in small grey print. It told chiefly, I remember, of bitter hatred of Germany, and of how London and all England would be stormed. I think that Hitler was abhorred as much as in Europe, and they all seemed anxious for the repeal of the Neutrality Act. We moved in journalistic circles with Hamilton Fish Armstrong, Mrs Ogden Reid of the *New York Herald-Tribune*, the famous Dorothy Thompson and the brilliantly successful Henry Luce. The conversation was always above my head. The Tripartite Agreement, the Treaties of St Germain, Trianon and Sèvres were argued, and I do not remember once opening my mouth.

We visited the World's Fair and even that did not suit me. Nothing did. Duff savoured all and everything. He could not be drawn away from the Surrealist exhibition arranged by their leader, Salvador Dali. It took a lot of beating. I wrote:

The entrance is between a lady's legs, and when you get in it's dark except for a dimly-lit tank full of organs and rubber corpses of women. Ceaselessly a beautiful living siren, apparently amphibious, dives slowly round her own bubbles,

completely naked to the waist. She fondles the turtles and kisses the rubber corpses' mouths and hands. In the dark I could see Duff's face glowing like a Hallowe'en turnip. I infinitely preferred the Hall of Medicine, where you can see a foetus (genuine) brilliantly lit in spirits and glowing pink (not green) from the word 'Go!' to the ninth month, in nine close-ups. You can see livers and kidneys pulsating, transparent men and women with pounding hearts, pools of v.d. bugs greatly exaggerated in size, and real babies in incubators, snug and warm and calm, unconscious of their doom and greatly to be envied.

When I first came to New York and so adored it, I was busy from the first day, absorbed in the theatre, with no time for Society, and a new and loving escort ever waiting. This time I have nothing to do, only Society to pull against and a sleepless broken nervous system. Where it was all new blood, in myself and others, it's today old, old. It will be better when we start travelling.

So we went to Washington. Lord Lothian was our Ambassador and no better appointment could have been made for those days, since he was a spirited, giggling, disarming envoy, loved by Americans. I imagine that he had orders from his Government to discourage Duff from laying the Allies' point of view before his lecture audiences. We stayed at the Embassy and felt happy there. The Ambassador told us that next day we were to go to the White House at five o'clock. This took a load off my mind, as Kommer's suspicious nature had warned me that sabotage might be used to prevent an interview.

Five o'clock was the time to meet my President face to face. I was shaking with hero-worship and trepidation. 'He'll say he has met you before,' Lord Lothian had said. The White House is all it should be, not a palace but a charming country house of the date I love (1805 or 1810) with a bit of

Second Lieutenant

Minister of Information

Retour d'Egypte about it. We were shown into a good-sized room with a lot of tea and cigarettes going on, and a helpful lady-hostess-secretary and a couple called Davies. The President sat on a little seat-for-two ('love-seat' in the trade) and said as foreseen: 'Lady Diana, come and sit next me. I haven't seen you since Paris 1918. You wouldn't remember it, etc.' Of course it was true, although I remembered only the occasion, not the man. It was during the Peace Conference, when I had been sent away from England to detach me from Duff.

I was ridiculously nervous. Duff was far away talking to a middle-aged lady and I was wanting all the time to change places with him but didn't know how to. Roosevelt ran the party. He talked all the time and seemed completely leisured and serene and all I pictured, devoid of nonsense, talking immediately about the triumph of repealing the Neutrality Bill, his hopes and his fears. What fun it was drawing lines down the Atlantic with a pencil. His 'belt of chastity,' he said. He clearly despises neutrality. We were there about an hour and then the aide came in to say: 'The Secretary of State wishes to see you.' I suspected an arrangement, and the darling said: 'I'm afraid I must go – at least *I* don't go.' So we all said goodbye, clearly having outstayed a bit, with promises of another visit when we return, which is quite soon, and as he said to Duff: 'I admired so much what you did in 1938 in the light of later events,' I should think that he means to see him again and alone, but the talk I want to have with him can't be had at a tea-party nor yet at a lunch for six, but only in a crowd or *à deux* in a buggy.

Duff had been disappointed by the restrained applause at his first few lectures, but I remembered that we were not at an election meeting, loud and harsh with cheers and brickbats, nor yet in England where most of the audience have had a 'couple' to get them to the lecture. These listeners were old cold-sober professors

with their wives. Anyway the overfilling of the hall was encouraging. One learnt as these first days passed how divided people were for and against neutrality. Though many felt, we thought, a little ashamed of the attitude adopted and over-adopted of 'We won't be dragged in,' their fear was well established. Nor could one be surprised or unsympathetic.

After long waiting I got my first letter from Conrad with the local news for which I was famished:

Mells   *20 October*

I plod away on the farm and think of you and miss you terribly. There's not much ground for feeling cheerful. Look at it how I may, the separation is utterly beastly. Today I listened to our propaganda in German. I never got it before. It seemed very well done; lots of bits out of *Mein Kampf* and examples of German deception in the last war. Old Hitler said in his last speech (the one where he escaped blowing up) that he never felt in the last war that he was 'engaged against a superior foe.' It's what I always felt. I always had a sense of the immense efficiency, strength and bravery of the German army, though I always thought that we'd win because of our 'don't know when we're beaten.' The German Freedom Society, according to the *Standard*, has distributed a million copies of Mr Duff Cooper's 'Manifesto to the German People.' Have you heard about this? Total surprise to me.

Lady Horner is no better. The war is killing her wish to live. If one is 85 it might be wiser to die now than to live on another two or three years. On the other hand there are two Miss Horners aged 90 and 97. They don't go to bed until 1 or 2 in the morning, and I'm told that if you pass their house about then you'll see lights and hear a lot of chuckling and low quiet laughter coming from their room. I wonder if it's: 'Stop me if you've heard this one!'

Our separation has begun and it will extend for 120 days at least, but I won't indulge in mopeyness and self-pity. What

prayers there are will be for your safety of mind and well-being and happiness. When we walked down the Savoy corridor in the early hours this morning, a corridor fragrant with memory of high jinks, I thought of Lady Wolseley saying that when Sir Garnet left her for active service (which was very often) she always said goodbye exactly in the same way as when he was going round to the club to see the evening papers. They were two turtle-doves.

A new life now began, with the Pullman car as home and haven from the storms and doldrums, the feasts and fasts of lecture life. In the letter-diaries I read that mobility and action soothe and stimulate nerves frayed by keeping one's end up, and one's country's end up, by night-clubs and by lack of confidence. The worn nerves had produced some inexplicable skin-disease that lowered my resistance. A famous German dermatologist told me that he had often had suicides among his patients. He put my head in a steaming-machine and under X-rays and ultra-violet rays, and gave me injections, instructions, unguents and tea-leaves from the teapot. I came out of his treatment-room with a scarlet face and white rings round the eyes where spectacles had protected them from malignant rays. His ointment was for a darkey make-up and smelt of dung. It humiliated me. The cure seems to have been complete, though the Massa Bones night-make-up was continued until I got on to a bottle labelled 'Less dirty and milder' and once in the train everything pleased.

We were on our way to Stanton and Washington, where Duff again saw the President, this time alone and off the record, admitted by a side-door, while I mouched round, occasionally eating a waffle in maple syrup or buying a paper to read inevitably bad news of the sinking of English destroyers and hideous threats.

Conrad wrote in November:

Why does censorship drive people (i.e. censors) demented? We read that Queen Mary went shopping in a West Country

town, and a photograph of Lady Astor's children at Cliveden was rubber-stamped 'Not to be Published.' I presume because the picture might reach Germany, on which German bombers would leave for Cliveden in order to kill Lady Astor's children. Insanity can go no further. Tommy Lascelles writes, dating his letter 'Somewhere in England,' and the postmark is Sandringham plain as a gate.

I go regularly to Maurice [Baring] at Rottingdean. He is fair. Spirits good. There are lamps in the train going down, but I come back in a completely dark train, last night alone with a woman (sex guessed by light-coloured stockings).

The *Daily Mail* had a competition on 'What part of the war do you mind most?' To my surprise 'Women in uniform' came first and 'Black-out' second or third. Some people simply put 'Unity Mitford.' The thing that I mind most, which is shortage of animal feeding-stuffs, came sixteenth. 'Evacuees' didn't come as high as I expected.

Seven and a half years of my grown-up life have been wars, and always, always England's failure. It was Stormberg and the Black Week, Tugela, Magersfontein, guns lost, unpleasant white-flag incidents, the retreat from Mons, Gallipoli, Passchendaele and backs-to-the-wall etc., etc. Here we are still going strong, but never once in seven and a half years did there come the news of a brilliant victory, nothing like Waterloo, and Jutland was far from being like Trafalgar. When we had allies it was Caporetto or Tannenberg or 'Mutiny of the French Army,' yet we seem to win in the end. I'm afraid you'll mind coming back from the whirlwind gaiety of America to this sober serious melancholy life. Wars make it impossible to be happy.

My cat Goebbels passed away yesterday after an illness of a few hours. It's rather strange and may forbode something. As you may remember, I called a cat Austria and it was murdered by its own father. I've been woodcutting all day with Brixey and old Monty. A great deal of politics talked.

They are very anti-Chamberlain as the man that got us into the war. 'He's too old' and 'He's too soft' they say. 'Eden and Duff Cooper knew what was coming' and 'We ought to have had Eden and Duff Cooper there to stop Mussolini taking Abyssinia, then there'd have been no more war.' This last opinion rather surprised me, and it's always 'Eden and Duff Cooper' who are named together as representing a particular attitude. Their only way of showing disapproval of Chamberlain is voting Labour next time.

I went to Frome, where I took an oath holding the Bible in my right hand and saying 'I swear by Almighty God' etc. and in the end I only swore by Almighty God that I didn't know that I ought to pay American income-tax on my Celanese shares. It seems blasphemous.

As our progress continued we learnt what we should have been taught beforehand: never to dine with the lecture-promoters before the lecture. They are hospitable to a fault. They will wish to entertain you royally, but dryly as a general rule. They allow plenty of time, and that is the snag. The lecturer is too nervous. Neither Duff nor I were mills that grind on water, and small talk had never been Duff's long suit. It is not mine; I can babble of green fields for ever, but the babble is not worth listening to and nervous energy is wasted. We were growing wise in the profession, to accept no preliminaries and put the shoulder to the unpredictable wheel after the performance, never before.

I wrote to Conrad:

At Cincinnati the Union Jack and the Star-Spangled Banner streamed bravely from our window on the twenty-fourth floor. The town has changed from cottage to palace since I was here fourteen years ago. The great cities concentrate on stations and hotels; these take the place of the baths in a Roman community. Here the station is as always of marble and crystal, mosaic and silver, as warm as one's bed

and on such a scale that the entire town couldn't crowd it. There you can eat and read, buy a hat or boots, medicine or *Pravda*, be photographed while you wait, be ill and retire to the Invalids' Room, have your snack of oysters and stout in the taproom, or muffins-and-maple, shirred eggs, cookies or cheese, palm-hearts and lettuce and pineapple in the coffee-shop, or tenderloins, hash and brown potatoes, yams, chicken à la King, Bourbon, Scotch or Benedictine in the restaurant, all iced or piping. You can put a coin in the door and it will open and allow you to wash and dress in cleanth and artistic surroundings. It no doubt has a tasteful mortuary. The hotel does all this and more, and costs more. I prefer station life. By the way there is never a sight or a sound of a train until you *leave* the station proper. At the hotel you can buy the motor-car that is generally on show in the vestibule. I should think they would let you try it out in the corridors. You choose your music with a dime in a slot, melodious or hot, Hungarian or Hawaian. On every floor there are ballrooms, and dancing starts at noon. You can be shaved or shod, pedicured or dentally fixed, operated on or laundered, while you wait. One of these Baths of Caracalla hotels was a town, with at least two Conventions going on, and swarms of Elks and Kiwanis and Rotarians.

We seemed to dart around as unsystematically as dragonflies. Our organiser, Mr Colston Leigh, appeared in our eyes a most whimsical madcap. But rests were allowed, and with reason, or he would have killed his paying geese. It was an exhausting fatigue. My diary tells of perpetual returns to New York, Washington or Chicago, with brief spells in rich homes.

In these delightful houses hung with blessings it is often nearly impossible to write a letter, not for me who write with a stub on my rounded knee as the train cavorts, but for my

patrician lord it's more difficult. Educated, business-trained Americans don't have a writing-table in the whole house. Staying with the Paleys, Duff said that he must write some letters and the footman was asked to find all the necessaries, as if one had asked to make toffee on a wet afternoon. Again at another house in Chicago the answer was: 'Yes, of course, only the pen is such a bad one. That's why I never write letters. The pen is so frightfully bad,' as though it was irremediable, like the central heating in our country.

How came I not to write to you about the Chairman of our lecture in Toronto? The Lady-in-Command told us on arrival how lucky she felt herself, and for that matter us, in having secured him as Chairman. He had been gravely ill, but was back on his feet and he would turn the prettiest of speeches, brief, witty, succinct, all the facets. She was right. He said his piece to perfection and sat down two paces behind Duff, who was alone on the platform with his chairman. Within five minutes he was unmistakably drowsy; within ten he was in a logged sleep. Before they got used to it the audience tittered dreadfully, which poor Duff could not understand. No cheek-on-hands dumb-show from me in the front row would have explained the situation. The chairman remained to the final applause snoring, mouth cavernously open, slumped over his chair. He woke to clap loudly.

Conrad wrote in December:

I listen to Haw-Haw, the German propagandist from Germany, in English. I don't know what it is meant to accomplish. Not being an idiot I've never thought England or the English perfect, so isn't it very good for us all to know our faults? Then we can try and improve. We all ought to know about the Opium War and our failures in India and Ireland, the Black and Tans, the disgraceful surrenders in

South Africa, the non-payment of the American debt, slums, low wages and unemployment. It can surely be only a benefit to have all this brought to our notice. I suppose Germans can't stand hearing of their own faults. Hitler must be a demi-god or nothing, whereas we are quite aware that Chamberlain is a second-rate old bungler that we've got to put up with for the time being. The papers all advertise when to hear Haw-Haw.

Lady Dufferin's pet goldfinch was frozen to death in her bedroom. This is a remarkable thing to happen to a British bird.

How dreadful your life sounds! We are happier in Mells. But Miss Gamble who keeps the general shop has said that she thinks Hitler is in the right. It has deeply shocked my carter and he said darkly that it wouldn't surprise him if Miss Gamble found her windows broken one morning. So minorities are persecuted and Mrs Baker (aunt to Miss Gamble) said she believed that the Second Coming of Our Lord was at hand. He would appear as soon as the first bomb fell on England. Lady Horner sent Mrs Baker a message telling her not to talk such rot.

The Vincent Sheeans came into our lives with a Christmas explosion of joy and goodwill. With them we hung over the radio for *Graf Spee* news. With them we heard that she had gone up in flames off Montevideo. Good news was so rarely come by that this glowed exaggeratedly bright. I groaned because America in the first flash called it 'a Viking's end' but rejoiced that later, on learning of the Captain's disembarkation, they labelled it 'ignominious suicide.'

Conrad wrote at the end of December:

Mrs James of Sutton [Conrad's general servant] has been ill and her morale is zero minus. Everything is too awful and her tearful complaint of the war is: 'It isn't like an ordinary

war – not like the last war at all.' She means the retreat from Mons and the long casualty lists, I suppose.

Both my refugee boys have gone lousy. They had no lice when they came. Now the village heads are crawling and there is a delousing parade so many days a week in the barn. Mrs James told me about it and burst into tears. I had to say quite sharply: 'Shut up! Everyone has lice in wartime.' She said she had had the most miserable Christmas of her life. I said: 'I can well believe it; about a hundred million have.'

A rest interval in January took us to Palm Beach, where friends had arranged an extra lecture for our benefit. Barbara Hutton, frail and beautiful as a sea-shell, gave us shelter from the fearful cold of Florida.

Zero in Alabama, magnolias and gardenias under snow, but in Barbara's house tuberoses that brought me all Venice – youth, escapades, d'Annunzio and Longhi – in a whiff. In the garden pattered her little Danish son, game and sturdy for three, followed by a big white French governess, English nanny and a burly detective in pale-grey flannel, growing fat and flabby in his unmanly occupation.

I had to sleep under my fur coat. They've shut the schools in Florida as it's too cold for the children, too cold to have Duff's lecture in a tent as intended. So it was given at the Everglades Club and the hurricane gave the unenthusiastic guests no excuse for defaulting.

I notice a distinct change in the Press and general attitude in this country. It isn't much, but it's clear that the feeling is leading away from the Allies. Our old fool who won't allow propaganda here and says: 'Leave it to Hitler and let the rugged truth talk' would change his orders if he could see the rugged German lies doing their work so successfully. Germans make speeches and write letters to the papers proving the war unnecessary and kept going by England. They write articles on

15

the slavery practised on Indians by a tyrannic Empire masquerading as a democracy. Only Duff is here to reply against a powerful organisation. They are violently anti-war. It hasn't died down at all, and won't until the Allies' true troubles begin. Duff answers the commonest question: 'Why did England wait so long before seeing the danger and protesting with force?' by saying that it was because of the dread of war, and that there is no more dangerous state of mind for a country. The theory that anything is better than war will inevitably land you into one. That gives them pause.

Jacksonville

Shaming departure. In front of the Quality the big brown oubliette bag containing night-necessities, coats, boots, books, bottles, a radio, Duff's slippers (embroidered with roses and a D.C. in forget-me-nots), buck-basket linen, a half-bottle of whisky etc. got a jab in its canvas back and split, spread and started gushing out its intimate contents, headed by Vincent Sheean's collected works. Duff's 'vanity case,' designed and planned with tender care and great expense in ivory and scarlet, also gave out. So two pieces are scrapped, thank God!

Mark Hopkins Hotel, Barbary Coast   February 1940

Good old George Gordon Moore, ranchless yet unwhitened by age, met the train and we dined with him at a Babylonian hotel with dance music to stun you. Moore is like a mammoth truffle, black and of no known shape. There's no diminution of vigour. Twenty-five years ago it was just the same – a war and Moore screaming against the band, and my listening to hotly-whispered words of love, not one of which I could actually hear. You might say he has 'a wild originality of countenance' while not at all resembling Byron. Another pleasant shock from the past was dear Sister White, ex-matron of the Rutland Hospital, she who brought me nightly

to my dressing-room in old *Miracle* days hot chicken-wing
smothered in mushrooms under a cloche.

We had been asked to stay in Los Angeles by Mr and Mrs Jack
Warner. I had fought it, fearing the high standard of clothes and
up-to-the-markishness. Duff, on the other hand, was yearning for
the 'stars.' We compromised and I went, on the condition that we
should spend a long week-end lost in some desert wilderness. But
when the Sunday came we were too happy to move, overwhelmed
by friendliness and wallowing in luxury. The house was beautiful,
so was the hostess, and our own Rolls Royce had a better Ronald
Colman at the wheel. Our rooms, bathed in sunshine, had a private terrace furnished with sofas, tables, cigarettes, books and gin.
Lying on my bed I had only to press a button to find my room
flooded by a Beethoven or Tchaikovsky symphony, not presented
to me by Wrigley's chewing-gum but coming from the tennis-
court where Jack Warner was playing.

I tried to straighten my possessions and conceal the dirt
and deficiencies from the simpering maid who has been given
to me. She whipped away every stitch as soon as my back was
turned to have it washed or cleaned (there is a private
laundry). The walls are covered in Chinese paper, the twin
Chippendale beds are under a single Chippendale canopy, the
carpet is rich and white, every piece of furniture is a museum
piece. The lamps are Ming and the sheets embroidered from
hem to hem. An on-time clock on every table, a lordly dish of
fresh fruit, a table of forty magazines of this week or month,
flowers in profusion, a large orchid for this evening in a box,
two white fur *couvre-pieds*, even stationery and pens, a radio
too (of course). The ravishing dressing-room is made of
unpolished flesh-coloured wood and is completely cupboard.
There is no part of the wall that does not open on to shelves,
hooks, racks, jacks, hangers and presses. The drawers of the
dressing-table are filled with cotton-wool, tissues, aspirin,

pins of all shapes and sizes. The bathroom is the size of a drawing-room and includes separate showers, with new rubber caps hung in them, separate lu-lu with cupboards within easy reach when seated, filled with a wide selection of the most intimate necessaries. Other bathroom cupboards hold all drugs, strapping, soaps, unguents and a big bottle of French scent to refill the bottle and spray on the dressing-table. My plan for the desert is collapsing.

In the evening we went, while Duff lectured at Long Beach, to the Russian Ballet. They were giving, amongst others, the surrealist Dali creation. The male dancers are naked but for black trunks with large lobsters as codpieces. After this to a night-club and our first view of the stars at play – Marlene Dietrich, Joan Crawford, Charlie Chaplin and Olivia de Havilland. The dance-club got me down a lot, and once home I became a great nuisance of groans and despair. In Hollywood I always feel an undesirable alien.

16 February

However, I woke bright and better today. Mr Warner sent me down his osteopath, a very fresh young man who, when I asked him if he got tired on his job, said no, he always had a strong rye whisky between treatments, which kept him going. I don't think he did me any good, but as everything is free in this house I won't miss a trick. I talked to Aldous Huxley on the telephone and tried hard to get Laurence Olivier and your Miss Leigh without success, so we ordered our Rolls and drove off to lunch on top of a far hill, Palos Vendes by name. We ate out in the sun, staring hard at the Pacific, and I felt I could face things better. The birds sing when I wake. When dressing starts Mrs Warner sends her *coiffeur* down to me. I admit he improves me, but I'm embarrassed. I feel he is criticising my scalp and my comb and the unicorn's vestige on my forehead. He will take no payment.

Duff's fiftieth birthday. He never groans at the passage of time. I can't think why. The night before the Warners threw us a star-scattered party. It was a bit of an orgy, none the worse for that, and we enjoyed ourselves hugely. I started in a fine pink brocade Molyneux dress, but Mr David Selznick told me that my breasts were too flattened and that people were complaining about them, and could I change? So I went back to the old Central European peasant's dress and took a new lease of deep-bosomed life. This morning after being woken betimes by Anne Warner's enchanting child of five singing 'Happy Birthday, Mr *Coo*per,' I feel fine. 'The climate looks after you here,' as George Gordon Moore used to say as he gulped down another demijohn of alcohol. We lunch with adorable Vivien Leigh in her caravan. There had been galaxies of kisses the night before, and now we had a birthday bottle of champagne and more kisses, and back to pack, for we must leave these glowing fleshpots of Ming and jade, these beds of Chippendale and asphodel and moly, for the desert and the war. I witnessed a fine battle between very 'sound' Elsa Maxwell and a hideous Hitler agent, who turned up at Elsa's hotel to book a room and got an avalanche of insults from Elsa in front of the manager and clientèle. 'I'll have you run out of the State of California,' she said. I never hoped to hear the phrase. She will be as good as her word.

Duff and I agree that we could live in California. It has a radio quality of having the world in this little space. You can tune in and live your day in whatever country, art or grade of intelligence or idiocy you feel inclined for.

In the train

Hard reading and looking up every minute for a squint at this amazing desert. It goes on and on. I picture the

Mormons crossing it. Mountains, rocks, canyons, no habitation, no animals, an occasional eagle; grey as shadow, with grey vegetation and our own dissolving grey smoke wreathing it. Occasionally there is a contorted grey cedar growing out of rock, and it looks like Hades, drawn by a scholarly Chinese of the fourth century. At other times the valley opens wide and it's snow and blue skies and pyramid-shaped rocks and architectural geology, looking for all the world what it should look like – a Masonic Victorian print. I look up to the sky for an eye in a triangle. Soon it will be Nebraska and then Iowa, and then Illinois. We turn the clock's hands on an hour every day. There's a lecture at Chicago, another next day at Louisville, Kentucky. The police came to see us at Salt Lake, as threatening letters have been received about the lecture at Louisville. I mustn't think about it.

Louisville

Duff's threatening letters weigh upon me, not unduly, but imagine my nerves when at 7.30 a.m., that dark hour of arrival and Press photography, we were met by a posse of 'tecs and a couple of big cops carrying bludgeons! We hopped into a police car along with the 'tecs and whizzed through the streets shrieking like a million banshees. I enjoyed it very much.

It's a nice place and the hotel was most tasteful. The police had us well in hand. The two 'tecs sat in the room next ours with the door open and their eyes on the elevator. At five Duff was escorted to a radio station to do a local broadcast, and said that he'd be back in half an hour. The boys took him off to find a mint julep and he returned an hour late. I'd worked myself into a hysteria of terror lest he had suffered at the assassin's hand. A lecture that evening followed by a very successful reception, which ended in the night-club of the hotel with dancing and carousing, everyone a bit lit and the boys each warning me about the other's tipsiness.

It's nearly over. Three good letters from you this morning tell me what to expect. The coal-and-foodstuffs muddles pass belief. I suppose wartime has always been the same in all countries. Well, I'm coming back to it all, and I don't care a pin about coal or light or food. But I do care about fear and alarms and excursions, death in all forms, hidden weapons, germs and gasses, and getting both ends to meet. I must try and find a profession. Kaetchen suggested that I write him news of London weekly in my own inimitable style and that he will publish it. I have promised to try, but I doubt its working, especially as a letter is made amusing by the stories of muddle, mistakes, cattishness and gossip, none of which would help our rough island's cause.

The tour draws triumphantly to its close. I must bid goodbye to light and security, and look forward to darkness and fear.

The old song refrain was:

> *Fancy me and Mrs Stubbs*
> *Joining all the ladies' clubs,*
> *Fancy us forsaking pubs*
> *At our time of life.*

Iris and I saw ourselves as these jolly old girls and on a night of blizzard and rain in New York I thought I would go and bid her farewell, perhaps for ever.

I packed Duff off to a smart dinner, put on the old squadron cap, a tarpaulin jacket and my rubbers, and set out to walk down to 11th Street, where Mrs Iris Stubbs lives below stairs. On the way I bought some raw hamburger steak, a pound of butter, some bread and some fat raisins. Getting late, I hopped the subway for the last lap. What fools foreigners

look from ignorance! In the station there is a turnstile with a slot for one's nickel and several other odd slots. I pop mine in and wait for a ticket to shoot out. It doesn't shoot out. I peer and press things and shake, and finally have to appeal to a stranger who thinks I'm dippy and tells me to walk through. He passes on while I'm still trying to explain that it's all different in England.

Iris lives underground in a room that is 50% charm and the other 50% Zola. There we threw back a schnapps and started off in the downpour to find places gentlemen (you are an exception) wouldn't look for. Tonight it was discovery of an Armenian restaurant where we dined sumptuously enough on vine-leaves, lamb, raisins, curds, honey, almonds and heady white wine. Afterwards, already very late, a vain hunt for anywhere with a dim light. Just fancy! Back to the pubs with Mrs Stubbs!

New York   *9 March*

They forgot to call us at 8.30, so we woke at 10.30 by good luck. Imagine the frenzy and scramble. Somehow it was done without time for tears, though many were shed as we steamed out of port, the band playing and the crowds waving their loved ones away. I'd hoped to see the *Queen Elizabeth*, which caused a tremendous sensation by arriving out of the blue, like the *Mayflower* unannounced, but she was not in sight.

On Board

I don't sleep at all. I never shall again, I fear. Is it due to deep-lying fear that takes control at night, though well in hand by day? I fear it is. One gets tired of reading after three hours. I try reciting old poems to myself and I reconstruct the *Enchantress* trips, or look at my own eyelids, which makes me think of nothing, or make the mental effort of relaxing, which is done by pretending that you are sinking through the bed. Nothing works.

Gibraltar

Darling Conrad, reading old English papers I've just learned of Lady Horner's death, and so long ago. One doesn't see English papers at best for two weeks after publication, and as it isn't *news* in America it's not unnatural that we didn't know. I've seen a few details that I hope to be true, i.e. that she died in her sleep. Well, well, she was like a fine tree, strong and beautiful in youth, and in age magnificent, a great shelter. I knew her first as Mark's kind mother; that's a long time ago, and now is a good time to be cut down. Poor Katharine, what a lot she will have to shoulder. How desirable the convent will look to her as she flounders through wills, trusts, mortgages, mortmains, mergers and all the insane laws that follow on death. Only you will be of help.

Naples

Vesuvius letting off very little steam. Somewhere in a Pass the dictators are kissing each other. God help us all. Just landing. No time for farewells.

Paris

No sign of war in Paris, no delays or substitutes. Heavy meaty and buttery meals in abundance. The Government fell with a thud as we arrived. Conversation at dinner stuck to who would be who tomorrow. Most are for Paul Reynaud. Henry Bernstein considers him a man of such value that his Premier-power should be kept for a tougher time. He has a mistress in a boater called Madame de Portes. Not my type – beastly strong.

I walked the streets, very unlike London, hardly any sandbags. Those that there are protect whimsical objects like glass fountains, while splendid monuments must take their chance, and the black-out's a blaze. No reassuring balloons pattern the sky, no robot aerial guard, gasoline is rationed.

The Ritz barman told me that they feed the cars alcohol. Motor and man drink from the same tap. Business as usual at Molyneux. Patterns are chosen subconsciously when talking of Sumner Welles or Rumania. Suzy, the ultra-fashionable hat-shop, is the same chaotic monkey-house it always was, a welter of ankle-deep débris, straw, feathers, spangles, flowers, buckram and elastic. Clients sitting mesmerised before cruel looking-glasses, Sumner Welles at last forgotten while cunning workwomen pull roses and bows over their right eyes. Very unlike New York, where surroundings and service are designed to soothe and lull and glide you into easy buying of the mass-produced. God help her who wants her own idea carried out. Here a creation must be born with labour-pains. To secure an impudent little lid needs a desperate tussle in a tropically-heated battle-room heavy with the smell of stale scent and hot hard work. Screaming like a jay among jays, I bought three. They ought to see me through my war. The French think that we are smug. We think we're better prepared than they are. The Americans think us phoney. What is to be done about mankind?

In London Conrad's letters awaited me:

Mells   *25 March*

Your lovely telegram has come. I shall see you tomorrow. If I seem boorish and insensitive don't misjudge me. It will be better when I have been alone with you for hours. I've hated this separation more than I've ever told you. I would much rather be dead than live without you.

The Ides of March are come and gone, and with them the anniversary of the death of Julius Caesar (perhaps the greatest man that ever lived) and also finis of Czechoslovakia. The pig's pen is being dug for victory. As I was digging I thought seriously about the Resurrection. I find it quite impossible to

Conrad in the Home Guard

The refugees: Kaetchen, John Julius and Nanny Ayto

believe in it, and yet after two thousand years the persistence of the belief is very strong. I dare say I am the only person in the whole parish who feels any strong inability to believe in the Resurrection. We are all bewildered in a maze on a sea whose chart is lost.

2
The Last-Trump Capital

We were homeless in London on our return from America to face the real war. Those days became so charged that I find it insuperably difficult to calendar them. Childhood is stamped on the fair face of one's uncluttered memory as clearly as morning, and a heart beating with love, enterprise and procreancy seemed recordable, but when I come to armies clashing in the dark, to destruction, to the rulers and their strength, shortcomings or ambivalence, their relations with Duff, or even the impression that they made on me in those noisy years, I am lost in a rabble of stampeding thoughts that can never be rounded up.

'What will she do when she gets to the interesting years?' asked Vincent Sheean. 'To Winston? To de Gaulle? To the things that matter?' 'O my dearest Jimmy,' I felt like saying, 'what more can I do? Friends and critics ask of me what is beyond my power. I'm only a narrator, a recorder of what mine eyes have seen. I can't speculate, conclude, judge or even write character-sketches. Scorn not the saga: don't shoot the narrator. We all dip into the Creevey papers for cheerful gossip, and into Hickey's memoirs, less for his journeys than for his weakness for claret and women. And who would not rather read in his diary of how Pepys pinched the housemaid hoping not to be seen, of how Nell Gwynn was prettier than he had thought as she dressed in the shift-room cursing because the pit was not fuller, or hear of the clergyman's slip of tongue when he prayed God "to preserve to our use" not the kindly fruits of the earth, but "our gracious Queen Catherine," than hear of his arguments in "the Office" or read his history of the Navy? It is for you, my ever-pink-and-white boy, who with Winston got me somehow through the blitz, for you, for historians, journalists and

modern recordings to uncover the motives and measure the ebb and flow of the tides that stormed against us, while I tell of the clothes, sulks and smiles of the characters I knew, and of my own quakes and quiverings, sunlit heydays and many triumphs over Giant Despair. I can't cope with more.'

My letters shall be my staff and scrip, for they are undeformed by memory. The first I find, written to Kommer, is clearly propaganda and meant to be quoted to his prophets of defeat in the United States.

London   *Late March 1940*

We were welcomed here like people returning from the Promised Land of Utopia. A million questions, flowers, more questions, birth and death announcements, more questions. So often on return from foreign adventures one has to bear with cruel disinterestedness: friends have not registered one's absence; one's narrow escapes and aesthetic thrills fall on ears listening to home chatter, and one reluctantly suppresses the photographs and press cuttings. But here was a new experience. 'What did you do?' 'What did they say?' 'What do they *really* think?' 'Do they think us phoney?' 'Are they on our side?' 'Why is the betting going against us?' 'Why do they send us food?' Fortunately, magnificent accounts of Duff's lecture-tour had reached home. Friends from all parts of the United States had written. The New York and London caution-mongers have been disproved by heartwarming reports of future contracts (offered but not signed), so no breath need be wasted blowing Duff's trumpet.

A great deal of our welcoming took place at the Savoy Hotel, where we had decided to perch until I could divest my house of its battledress. The Savoy was selected because now more than ever is the Grill the one place in London. Without music and apparently without closing time, you are certain always to find bits of the Cabinet there (for where else can late supper be eaten?). Workers off their shifts, actors,

writers, the Press, Mayfair's hostesses who have abandoned their private houses and still want to entertain – they are all grazing in the Savoy Grill. Friends move from table to table – here a cup of soup, there a glass of wine.

By living in this great hotel one need never wrestle with the black-out, which is blacker than ever – no gleams to guide one, no Dursley lanterns, if you know what they are.* Who, *who* is so fond of the black-out that it remains? Sandbags have greatly diminished, civilians have discarded their gas-masks, but the nightly eclipse still wraps us round with death in its darkness.

We little thought in September last that spring would see us so unscathed. With thousands of others I thought and feared that London would be a smouldering heap, disease on the march, many friends widowed, confusion worse confounded, the Apocalypse, the Legion of Anti-Christ still to be faced and fought, perhaps even in our land. Instead the cities are strong in protection, guts and gaiety. The newspaper stories deal with hardships of winter, not of war.

The theatres boom. The movie I saw the other night showed Hitler and Mussolini gesticulating in their ridiculous fashion through snow on the Brenner Pass. I automatically started hissing, but my protest was drowned by hoots and shouts of laughter. The higher the goose-step, the more the two chins thrust themselves forward, the more tickled the audience.

Evelyn Waugh, now an officer in the Marines with as smart a little moustache as Errol Flynn, has never been so happy. Edward Stanley is one of four officers in a minesweeper. They bag as many as fifty in a week. He reads Shakespeare to the captain over tumblers of hot toddy,

---

* Gentlemen, when escorting ladies out to dinner on dark nights, would pull out the tails of their shirts and walk before to show the way. So says Mr Kilvert, who wrote his diary in the 1870's.

between catches. I have never seen a man of thirty so childishly high-spirited.

Last night to the Admiralty, where I went to dine with Winston, my dearly-loved First Lord. O what a change was there since my day! Did you ever see my bed? It rose sixteen feet high from a shoal of gold dolphins and tridents; ropes made fast the blue satin curtains; round the walls Captain Cook was discovering Australia. Now all has suffered a sea change. The dolphins are stored away and on a narrow curtainless pallet-bed sleeps the exhausted First Lord. My gigantic gold-and-white armoire holds his uniform. The walls are charts. On the top floor, where I had hung chintz curtains spotted with red and blue seahorses to amuse my little boy, the Churchill family is installed. It makes a delightful self-contained flat with dining-room, bedroom, kitchen and their own lovely pictures. Winston's spirit, strength and confidence are a beacon in the darkness, a chime that wakes the heart of the discouraged. His wife, more beautiful than in early youth, is equally fearless and indefatigable. She makes us all knit jerseys as thick as sheep's fleeces, for which the minesweepers must bless her.

Bognor   *Later*

I am back in Sussex for my child's holidays. Always faultless in my eyes, he delights me and the urchins of the Lodge with his songs – 'Hang up the washing on the Siegfried Line' and 'Run, rabbit, run.' The relief here shows even more than in London. Since October my cottage has been dense with child-refugees. Even digging on the sands these poor mites had gas-masks to hinder them. The Stately Homes in my radius were all gutted of their fine trappings and turned into maternity homes for mothers from crowded areas. Aubussons had given place to linoleum, and rows of hospital beds were the only furnishings. Heirlooms, pictures

and their own children had to make way for cradles, charts and nurses. In the brilliant sun of last September, exhausted and cumbersome women lay panting in last-word Fortnum & Mason garden chairs, staring at turquoise bathing-pools. They were not happy. They learned of new pests, like wasps. They yearned for their street of neighbours and familiar surroundings, however squalid. One mother said that she could stand anything but the trees; they really got her down.

Now all is restored. The carpets spread, 'cushions within the chairs and all the candles lighted on the stairs.' Sir Joshua's children are back upon the walls, and the living ones play hide-and-seek behind heirlooms. True, all these may within twenty-four hours turn again into grim hygienic wards, but we are thankful for today.

Last April, I remember, the spring wrung my heart. It seemed like a child that had to die. Today either conditions or custom allow us a much robuster spirit. We 'Dig for Victory,' we camouflage our houses dizzily from ladder-tops. Our fine motors are jacked-up for the duration in the garages of the still-rich, and we buzz about in grotesque little seven-horsepower motors. Mine is called Dodgems and is almost a teetotaller. When I send for the plumber to deal with some appalling sanitary disorder, two little boys of about ten arrive with a lot of jacks, jigs and jemmies, diagnose the trouble and bustle off to the next job. In fact it is the children's spring.

There is truth in these letters, but there were other moments as true and far less debonair. Gloomy lethargy clogged my limbs and mind. I sought out the doleful, the dejected and the apprehensive; these, because of contrariness, I thought I could encourage, but I felt that, like a leper, I should carry a bell and mutter 'Unclean' before the buoyant and optimistic.

We settled or rather camped in Chapel Street, with outings to Bognor. One dead-of-night Duff received a message from Winston, who, having been summoned to France for a conference,

would not be able to address the Royal Society of St George. He asked Duff to take his place. Duff accepted, conscious of the responsibility of making such a speech at such a time, but it was one of the best speeches of his life. This was the peroration:

Once more St George is mounted on his charger. He has never ridden in a nobler cause. He has as his opponent, or his quarry, the foulest monster that hell ever spawned. Germany has assumed many ugly shapes in her past – under the perjured pervert Frederick, miscalled the Great; under the mountainous bully Bismarck, with his treble voice, his sly and shifty diplomacy and his forged telegrams; under the vain, crippled Hohenzollern, himself the servant of the half-crazy Ludendorff, who so hated Christianity that he worshipped Odin and Thor – but none of these previous manifestations of the soul of Germany was quite so repellent as the little gang of blood-stained, money-making murderers who now are urging on the hordes of barbarism to the destruction of civilisation.

Yes, St George is once more in the saddle. Have we not met him countless times of late throughout our countryside and in the streets of our cities? At this very moment he is going, laughing gaily, into battle by sea and land, high in the heavens and deep under the ocean waves. Either he will return with the laurels of victory on his brow, or else he will sleep well, his duty done and the name of England graven on his heart.

The audience was electrified and I felt myself on St George's pillion, clinging to his cloak, galloping to kill the dragon and rescue England. I must forge myself a sword, ride out the storm and stop funking the fray.

Conrad was working manually on his Somerset farm for twelve hours a day, and was to work eighteen before the effort finally killed him. His letters continued:

I have started Nevile Henderson's book. He says on page one that he does not doubt that he was specially selected by Providence to go to Berlin in order that Peace might be preserved. The book is called *Failure of a Mission*. So who muffed it – Providence or Henderson?

I feel sick at heart about Norway and the Prime Minister's vulgar and idiotic comment: 'Hitler has missed the bus.' The less Mr Chamberlain talks about missing the bus the better. Will people never realise that the Germans are clever and brave and well-organised? Their army is the best in the world and their air force ditto. Making foolish military mistakes and muddling incompetence are English and not German characteristics. God help us!

Then I remember that we've never in all history done anything quite so idiotic as to entrust our country to a Führer or a Duce. Nor to a Stalin, nor to a Pétain. We get pretty good stinkers to govern us every now and then, such as Charles I, James II and even in our day, Mr Chamberlain. But it's out you go! Other countries don't seem to do this so easily. The French still greatly admire Napoleon – certainly the man who did France most harm.

Disastrous April was upon us. I can remember moaning as I re-pasted my numberless orangery windows with sticky anti-blast tape, wondering what to do next. I could always sticky-tape the windows of our Bognor cottage, still packed with discontented refugees from London's East End. And then what? Find war-work? I shrank from becoming a V.A.D. They were now to be paid and regimented into their rightful menial rank in the hospitals and not be allowed free run of the wards as I had been in 1914. Besides, on paper I was too old. I must wait on events as phenomenal and sudden as earthquakes and waterspouts, that would give me no choice and no weighing. The inevitable only would direct.

Disastrous April brought the fearful fiasco of Norway, the horrifying stories told by eye-witnessing friends of defeat and chaos. England's banks were pale with primroses, and I remember at sight

of them thinking of those trudging the Norwegian snow who must be dreaming of these carpets. There was the shining day of Narvik when *our* Admiral Whitworth (he whose life-jacket in the *Enchantress* storm had been laid on his bunk like a boiled shirt while I was praying knee-deep in the débris of my cabin) became the hero of the day. Little countries in fell swoops were avalanched and temporarily obliterated. We knew that our turn must come before the irresistible invaders blasted their way towards France. There was too much, too much, and weaving through the alarms was the conviction of Parliament and the people that Winston Churchill must take the helm of our scandalised ship. He must shoulder our hopes and our efforts and imbue us with courage, or the ship would sink. With nothing yet to do, with irons waiting for a fire, I slunk round my fine London house, happy in that Duff would be part of this essential activity, one of the plotters and builders, and that he would be certain and relieved that the time was at hand.

And now in April my flawlessly beautiful niece Isobel, with all the insouciance of her youth, said to me blithely at a party: 'Papa has got pneumonia.' The word in those days to my foreboding mind spelt death, and though at that ugly time I thought of death's calm as nearly enviable, yet for those who love and are left, war has no terrors. My brother John died too soon, long before life could pall. He left unwillingly his archives, his archaeology, his excavations and his collections of mediaeval tiles, his birds, his enthusiasm for nature and sport, his five children and his darling wife. He was the first of us four children to die, and my sorrow was fierce and isolated among the many sorrows.

It was May and Whitsuntide when the juggernaut's car bulldozed through Holland and Belgium, and on the same day Winston became Prime Minister of England. The phoney war had ended, and now we must wait for them to *fahren gegen Engelland*. Duff was made Minister of Information and felt himself to be the ideal choice. The American tour had confirmed his views on propaganda and the way it should be organised. So he was happy in spite of having to announce a succession of appalling calamities that befell us

33

on the battlefields and on the seas. I had been gladly pressed into a Y.M.C.A. canteen in Parliament Square, while Conrad became in the first week of the shooting war a Local Defence Volunteer, along with a quarter of a million other bumpkins. He wrote:

Mells   *16 May*

I hope that you are calm and cool. It is easier in the country. Employment is a boon. Fears may be liars, says poet Clough. I heard Duffy at six o'clock, quite excellent and dreadfully moving.

I've enlisted in the Local Defence Volunteers against the *Fallschirmspringer*. It was done in Mells fashion, leaning over the gate in shirt-sleeves chatting with P.C. Marsh, our charming constable. He pointed out that as I should only have a rifle and the German a machine-gun, it was really a suicide club. I said grandly: 'O, I don't mind that!' My corps would be called the *Fallschirmspringer vernichtungsarme*. Ask Raimund. It's Cincinnatus called from the plough. I don't think it is right to give this job to a man in his grand climacteric. I've always hated soldiering and seem fated to go on and on until the grave. It was monstrous that I should have ever been in command of a squadron, and worse that I should have gone to the trenches in my fortieth year. Three of my boys (Mouldy, Feeble and Bullcalf) have just been in to report. England doesn't change much.

27 May

I went to a meeting of Section Commanders today. Most looked too old to have been in the 1914–18 war. Major D is almost a Lord Cardigan type, deaf as an adder. Disagreement from me can do little good. I spent from 1915 to 1918 in profound disagreement with Lord Haig on the uses of cavalry, but it didn't prevent him maintaining five divisions (about 20,000 sabres of cavalry). All now argue that Haig was wrong, and Yours Truly right.

The carter said today: 'I'm glad Duff Cooper went to America. He's long-headed and a wiry little chap too.' The signposts are being taken down here. It strikes a terribly serious note.

In early June Duff went to Paris on a mission. I was as usual in a pitiable state of tension when he left, to be made ten times more frantic the following day by a series of extraordinary accidents. I needed some money and asked my faithful Wadey to fetch it for me from Drummond's Bank. In normal times it would not have struck me to suggest the taking of my passport as a proof of *bona fides*, but times were out of joint. So she made the inevitable search, and finding it she found also a letter addressed to me between its leaves. She brought it to me calmly enough, but the sight of Duff's writing, coming, as it seemed, out of time and space, made my blood run cold. What I read made it colder. The letter was viatical. He felt certain, he said, that he would not return. He had walked in the garden that morning, at peace and surprised by his calm and his thankfulness for life and love. I must not over-grieve; all was ordained. It was a letter that as I read I felt he would never have written without complete conviction, yet presentiments (let alone fearful ones) were not for him. Or had he in the past concealed them for my serenity's sake? Now he had written his words in my passport, that I might not open for years. Without a thought for anything but his succour, I grabbed the telephone and asked for Mrs Churchill at 10 Downing Street. 'Listen, Clemmie, listen to this letter! You know how unlike Duff it is! O Clemmie, what shall we do?' Completely sympathetic, she answered: 'How awful! I'll tell Winston at once. He'll send out some Spitfires. Don't worry too much.' They were surely sent to escort the aeroplane back from Paris. On Duff's safe return I was forced to admit my interference. He would have scolded me more roundly had he not been as astounded as I had been by these astonishing coincidences. Did I save him? An astrologer would have warned him of the unpropitious occasion. In astrology there is room for precaution

and obstruction; the disaster is not inevitable. One can dodge the stars in their courses. What guided my hand and his on that same day to a laid-by passport? Were the German marauders there in wait, and did the Spitfires give them pause? It was very strange.

So Duff came back to me, and together we fought on. We had left Chapel Street. It was too big and too difficult. Pictures were taken from the walls, china and such treasures as I possessed (also junk) were packed and sent to friends' country houses, where they stood a better chance of survival. We moved into a top-floor suite in the Dorchester Hotel: from its high windows one could scan nearly all London beyond the green sea of Hyde Park, sprawled out for slaughter, dense with monuments, landmarks, tell-tale railway-lines and bridges. How red would the flames be, I wondered, when our hour struck? (They proved to be *less* fiery than I feared.) It was liberating to be houseless, and the high Dorchester was sunny and airy. A picture of my mother and one of John Julius were all that distinguished it from any other hotel room. One could see from the eighth floor whether the Ministry of Information was still standing. The high white building became symbolic to me, like Dover's cliffs.

The labour of a house-owner with rationed food and fuel, blackout and wardening, was gruelling. Everything was gruelling, and there was always so much to carry – a tin hat, a gas-mask (which one was advised to wear for half an hour daily but never did), a ration-card, petrol-coupons and a useless identity card. When parking one's car for as much as five minutes, one was ordered to remove the distributor-head, rotor-arm or some unknown part. At night we travelled without lamps and stopped at traffic-lights reduced to a red or green cross, thin as a match. By day captive balloons were gay and gave a touch of carnival; the boarded shop-windows were sad but sensible. Already the sandbags were sprouting fresh grass and budding willow-herb. The weather was radiant, as it so often seems to be in catastrophic times. One night we groped our way into Max Beaverbrook's house to learn what seemed the worst of all news. 'How black can you take it?' said a friend as I came in. The Channel

ports had gone. Now were we truly naked to our enemies. Italy was against us too, bitter but expected news.

Conrad wrote:

Mells   *10 June*

Ernest says: 'It's Duff Cooper who keeps us going.' He also says he's always had a very poor opinion of the King of Italy – 'a Nazi at heart he is,' and he says: 'The Pope's about the best of the Italians.' They talk about the Pope just as we might, and about 'old Stafford Cripps' and 'What's he doing with old Stalin?' Everyone is called 'old.'

When my neighbour read about the Germans dropping parachute troops in Holland, he said: 'Kind of damned silly thing they would do.' That's the English officer's attitude. The Germans are silly incompetent people and the German army opera bouffe. You have to have been at Eton and Sandhurst to know anything about fighting. O God, help us! Chores in Frome, and I left a tin marked 'Teat Ointment' on the counter at the bank and had to go back and ask the cashier: 'Have you seen my teat ointment?'

I had taken on the earliest shift at the Y.M.C.A. canteen. It suited me, always mindless of what time I get up, being a bad sleeper and a bad dreamer. There was good cheer at 7 a.m. when the tired night-shift left, and the watchers, wardens and early workers came in for a splendid breakfast of porridge, eggs and bacon, butter and jam, with unstinted tea and sugar. Rationing did not exist in that hospitable Central Hall, run by my old friend Juliet Duff's efficient daughter. Later, when the blitz began in its full ghastly force, it was to be my happiest refuge. Many of my fellow-workers had husbands and sons in France, and I used to marvel at their control, courageous smiles and energy through the desperate Dunkirk days. How did they manage to be so good, I wondered, and how did I manage to be so bad, with Duff by my side at night and in a massive office all day? Perhaps we all thought

the same. We all looked the same, all awful, with blue overalls and tied-up heads. The work was, though not heavy, fortunately against time.

Without reason the English felt better after the fall of France. I know I did. It was a challenge, which is always invigorating. Insane that it should have been so, but we had Winston to stiffen our sinews and teach us how to war. 'We're better on our own,' we said, and the new strength and independence showed in the faces and morale of all the people as they waited for their triumph or destruction.

After Dunkirk we talked exclusively of parachutists, of how they would come and deceive us by being dressed as nurses, monks or nuns with collapsible bicycles concealed beneath their habits. An English uniform would have been a better disguise for the expected invaders. Orders and suggestions overwhelmed us. We must stay put (how does one do it?). We must not spread alarm or dismay (I must therefore hold my tongue). We must fill our ginger-beer empties with an explosive prescription, label it 'Molotov Cocktail' and hurl it at the invading tanks. We were advised to feed the enemy's cars with sugar to neutralise their petrol. Place-names were obliterated on roads and stations. Barricades of wagons and tree-trunks were successfully obstructing our own movements. We must 'Be like Dad and keep Mum' (very funny, we thought), and the children must not have kites or fireworks. We had killed our black-widow spiders when war came, and now the Zoo's Home Guard were trained riflemen. To have been hugged to death by a bombed-out bear would have been an anti-climax. One zebra only got a run for his money and streaked round Regent's Park pursued by the Zoo's secretary, keepers and the public. We had all given our weapons, binoculars and dainty opera-glasses to the Home Guard. In June the ringing of church-bells was stopped, so that they might ring again for invasion. It sounded a topsy-turvy order. Their silence, and the darkened houses that betrayed no cheer or welcome and were no longer symbols of shelter, affected me acutely.

A difficult suggestion that had a foolish appeal for me was to equip one's car with an all-covering armour of small pebbles between sheets of tin. This naturally never materialised and I was disappointed. Buckets of water must stand everywhere possible, to be stumbled over in the dark, and one's attic must be emptied of inflammable contents, which meant everything. The Local Defence Volunteers, now called the Home Guard, were increasing in millions. The Americans formed a detachment in our uniform, with red eagles on their arms. Mr Kennedy, the United States Ambassador, was said to disapprove, but we approved wholeheartedly. I do not remember the bombing of London being prepared against with the urgency that was given to invasion precautions. The German aeroplanes came over England, singly at first, then in squadrons, and soon was to be fought the Battle of Britain. We knew that this battle must first be won, and then would be time to think of what would fall from the sky, and orders for shelters, camouflage and improvised safety-measures begin in earnest.

The scheme for evacuating children from London had been disappointing in its results. The wives and children who had been sent to spend their phoney-war days in the country had dribbled home, and now, when the danger was truly great, they were reluctant to be sent back to what they had detested. But a scheme for a children's exodus to Canada and the United States was shaping on both sides of the Atlantic. I was desperately anxious for John Julius to go, but I do not know if we would have sent him had not Mr Kennedy offered to take him and many other children in his neutral ship. So off the dear boy went with Nanny Ayto in charge of him and some other children. I felt tremendously relieved to think of him at a Canadian school, calm and unafraid, with Kaetchen to guard him, and Bill and Dorothy Paley to enliven his holidays in America. I expect we were scowled on by the Prime Minister for this move; he deprecated what he called 'the stampede from the island.' Not for him the services of the 'little ambassadors,' and not for the King and Queen, who kept their Princesses by their side, but John Julius was meant to have a year's schooling abroad,

probably in Switzerland, so had he not gone he would have stayed in London *because* of the bombing, which seemed grotesque. With the children went all the gold in England to be banked in Canada. We were stripped for action. I wrote to Kaetchen:

London   *2 July*

Here is my child and here is Nanny armed with £25, and now they belong to you for the duration. He shall go to some Canadian school. Establish him in Long Island with the hospitable Paleys until the term starts and overlay them with my gratitude. Never have I put more in your dear gesticulating hands, never have I taken your order 'Use me' more literally.

If we are killed you will know best what to do for his good. If a miracle ends this war victoriously for us, then what a glorious jaunt he will have had! If a miracle subjugates and occupies this land beneath Hitler and we are in prison or Duff is fled to Ottawa with King and Council, he might, if here, become a hostage to force Duff's hand or mine. It is for this reason, not because of bombs, that he leaves. You'll be glad to hear that my spirit is unexpectedly high, but of course I am very unhappy. Perhaps this citadel island will have fallen before this reaches you and all will be over. If it is, you know that I am certain no one ever had a better friend than I had in you and no one loved you better.

London   *10 July*

Please, Kaetchen, do not let my little boy get spoiled by riches; buses not taxis, drug-stores not restaurants, and not too many cinemas. He is a very good child and will give no trouble, I am confident. If you see him in any way fresh with Americans or if he is not perfectly mannered, reprove him with all your might. Do not let him be loaded with presents; keep your own hands from your pockets. Nanny will buy him

clothes cheaply – from Bloomingdale's please, not at Saks. You must be tolerant of my idiosyncrasies and conform to them. I feel very strongly that it must never be said that English children are living on charity, so I would like my suggested money arrangements done almost legally immediately. Who would have thought you were to be a father so soon? I like Doll Iris's influence on John Julius, so ask her to see a lot of him. Keep me in his mind a bit and teach him to admire Duff. Tutor him hard in American history and current events (war and peace). I'd like him to be braver than most and not to be taught 'Safety first.'

I started a diary for John Julius. I would read my letters to Duff, who, as head of the Censorship Office, never thought that they would pass, but my words seldom got blue-pencilled, whereas Duff's letters, models of clarity and simplicity, often came back cut into lace by the censor's scissors.

London   *5 July*

    I'm going to try to write to you every day even if it's only a scrap and even though it's about things that won't interest you a great deal. That way there will be a record of these hideous days, and I shall feel I am in touch with you, and you with me.

    Your emigration is holding up the smooth working of Parliament. I send you some cuttings about it. The blow hasn't fallen yet. Invasion is always to be next Tuesday or next week-end. However it is calm in London Town and people go about their work and play with strong bright faces, and the inhabitants of the little houses that are blown to a fine powder drink a glass of ale on the ruins and stick up flags left over from the Coronation. I saw this on a newsreel. It's an answer to our dear American reporters who say: 'You don't *realise.*' One realises all right if one's house falls on top

41

of one, but one smiles apparently, so why not smile before it falls? Great excitement as I write. The telephone rings and it is St George's Hospital telling me to come and give my blood. I'm thrilled and only hope I shan't go green in the face and sweat with cold fear when the moment arrives.

The other day a man was stopped by a sentry saying 'Halt!' He stood stone-still and the sentry said: 'Halt!' again. 'Well, I have halted,' said the man. 'Why do you say "Halt" again?' 'My orders,' said the sentry, 'are to say "Halt!" three times and then fire.'

6 July

I went to [censored, but it was Rottingdean] this morning to see poor Maurice. He is half the size he used to be. A bright blue budgerigar sits on his shoulder always chattering into his ear, pecking his cheek and making little messes. He claims that Dempsey (that's his name) talks. I doubt it. I wasn't allowed to drive along the front where the camouflaged six-inch guns are.

7 July

It's rather lovely living at the Dorchester. No débris (if you don't know what débris is, ask Kaetchen), but Chapel Street was terribly full of it – mine and Noona's * and plaster dropping from the ceiling. Here I feel as free of possessions as a bird – just the clothes I am wearing, the book I am reading, the letter that has to be answered and a few preparations for sudden descent into the shelter. Wadey is definitely going to dress, but I shall put on a dressing-gown with a zip and have my nightcap on, and some black smeared off my eyelashes on my cheek. Wadey suggested that I should wear a particularly comic robe that I bought in America and when I said: 'O no, I'd look too funny' she said: 'I didn't think you minded that.'

---

* John Julius's name for my mother.

A day of rage, no lunch, then débris-righting at Chapel Street. Exhausted and hungry I bought myself a strawberry ice-cream at Gunter's, also a strawberry tart in a paper frill, and took them to the house of Jimmy Sheean so that I might eat them in company. There I found a German. Now all yesterday I had been wrestling with the police and with the Prisoners of War department under which internees come, in a great struggle to get some unfortunates liberated. My heart bled for the poor alien anti-Nazi women whose husbands have been torn from their sides, and who are as demented as I should be if Papa were torn from mine. However, after half an hour's talk with the German so-called anti-Nazi man, I found myself wanting to imprison him and all his kind for ever. He felt so violently against us for daring to intern him or any anti-Nazi, and could not see that even though the innocent suffer temporarily we cannot risk a lot of Fifth Columnist spies and Nazi propagandists, sent as refugees to this country by Germany, being at large weaving thickets to tangle us. I left the house furious.

The internment order by which aliens were dashed willy-nilly to non-existent camps and to distant countries, segregated from their wives, posted to Ultima Thules or to watery deaths was a harsh measure and, in the fearful early days of Fifth-Column predictions, it was done so quickly and so disorganisedly that it became a scandal. In the afternoons therefore I employed myself, generally unsuccessfully, arguing with the Home Office, War Office or Scotland Yard. I used cajolery, blackmail, braggadocio or bootlicking in my efforts to have men and women traced or put in prison or taken out (or kept out), or children sent to New Zealand or found in Canada. Thank Heaven, one of my rare successes was to keep Emil Kommer, Kaetchen's brother, out of internment. Innocent as an English child, it was still a miracle that he did not find himself ground-sheetless on a Cumberland moor.

Bognor *11 July*

When I got back to Dodgems today what did I find but all the air gone from the tyres! I bawled for the policeman whom I saw walking away rather fast. He came back sheepishly and I asked him what had caused him to be such a brute. 'You should lock your doors,' he said. 'If you will look at my doors you will see that they have no locks. It's a 1909 model,' I said with pardonable exaggeration. 'Try and start it,' I went on, 'here is the ignition key. Get in and try to start it.' I had been to all the pains of taking out the distributor, which means diving half oneself into the engine and covering one's clean summer dress with oleaginous black muck. He apologised and looked guilty and ashamed, but that didn't help me. I had to telephone a garage and get a man with a pump, and there was no vengeance that I could take upon the policeman.

London *12 July*

Another day of rage. I woke up to find my letter to you, written a week ago, returned to me by the Censorship Office because I had denied a rumour, which is what we are told to do. The rumour and its denial are also in the newspapers. The Censorship comes under the Ministry of Information, so I am the boss's wife and had written my name outside the envelope. I shan't do that again because I suppose they think they will not be considered thorough if they let my letters pass. You will get my last letter with large black-outs. I hope you will guess what the words are.

I had got a berth on a ship for another little refugee boy, my sister's butler's son, and poor Kaetchen looked like being pressed into Pied Piperdom. I never ceased belabouring him.

As regards my own boy:

(1)   I've just remembered kidnapping and don't *you* forget it!

(2)   He's quite keen on Latin. In America and Canada it is not taught until boys are fourteen or so. Encourage him to keep it up on his own. Half an hour a day, and someone to correct his exercises.

(3)   I suppose French will be forgotten and I don't see how it can be helped unless he goes to Montreal and catches a Louis XIV accent.

(4)   Another sad loss will be his piano. Do you think that a syncopating negro could be found in the village where J.J. could repair thrice weekly and have jazz or classical music lessons? That would fan his keenness.

(5)   Encourage intelligent books and not futile idiocies and comics.

Poor Kaetchen, what a job it is! I am longing for a calming letter about finance, non-kidnapping, guarantees of disciplinary upbringing, economy practices and non-spoiling.

Conrad had written to me:

Battle of Mells   *5 July, about 1 a.m.*
I was woken up by machine-gun fire just overhead. Then out of bed and take a peep. There he was, a fiery cresset i' the sky just above us, lamenting heard i' the air and strange screams of death. At one moment I feared he would fall on us, but he turned, leaving a trail of fire. He descended in a parabola across the sky, and when he fell, he fell like Lucifer, never to hope again. Alan Plummer, Mells Home Guard, took a prisoner. Another came down and broke his leg and a third gave himself up. The fourth is still at large or was possibly burnt up in the Messerschmitt, for such it was, or perhaps he's dead in a wood.

45

And I to John Julius:

London   *21 July*
Papa is having a rough passage in the Press. They got it into their hysterical heads that he wanted to put a stricter censorship upon them. He never did, but they went off the deep end and have attacked him on everything, on the Silent Column and on your going to the United States. Now that it is all settled and they know that they are not going to be muzzled and never were, they all think that their abuse and baiting have gained their point. It's a hard life, politics, and one must have all the things that 'If' tells you to have. Papa has most of them and is unaffected by bludgeonings, but your poor Mummy has none of them and is not unaffected.

I've just come back from the hospital minus a pint of my rich blue blood. I was shown into a fine empty ward and led to a bed surrounded by screens. Now, being an old hospital bird, I know that screens are put round beds only for the gravest cases and herald death. So they gave me a bit of a gasp, but having just had a nip of brandy I was feeling in good heart and in good tongue. A young doctor came and pinched my forearm, and another one, a bit older, said: 'How are her veins? Nice and big?' 'No, I'm afraid they're very small,' said the younger doctor. Now funnily enough I was glad they were small, in spite of the fact that being small they would less willingly release their blood. It sounded more charming, more graceful, more delicate – finer workmanship. Next they gave me an injection (with a hair-needle that doesn't hurt) of novocaine that numbs the spot. Then into my frail flesh was jabbed a needle the size of a skewer which turned into a rubber tube that ran into a pint bottle. They wiggled round for a long time to introduce it into the vein. I had to open and shut my hand (gimme, gimme, gimme) to expedite the precious flow. Blood is used for people who are desperately weak, collapsing or dying. I give this adventure in full, knowing how you enjoy anything gruesome or queasy.

I found Maurice in high spirits today owing, he said, to being in acute pain. His blue budgerigar was pecking hairs out of his ears and talking to him incessantly. The visit passed in a flash. We both felt so gay, sipping sherry and nibbling chocolates and arguing about the Pope.

Last night at about 1 a.m., when Papa was asleep and I was reading, a gentlemanly voice on the telephone said: 'I'm speaking from Hoxton (a sadly poor quarter of Greater London) and a great many parents in Hoxton would like to come and see you because they resent your having sent your son to America.' I said I would be delighted to see them and what day would they come? He chose a day and let me choose the hour. 'Before 6.30 a.m.,' I said, 'for I go out then.' I thought he would gasp a bit and sure enough he did. He wanted to think that I wasn't called until noon.

25 July

Another voice bawls into my ear at 7 this evening that it is speaking from Deptford, and that parents in Deptford would like to come and have a look at me too. He knew about the man from Hoxton, so I said: 'Do you know that I was afraid he could not have been sober, ringing me up at that hour?' 'Not sober!' yelled the voice, 'Mr Wingfield is a teetotaller! He thought you were at the theatre.' 'Why not call me before the theatre (which I was not at) or next morning?' I said that he could bring the parents. Both men suggested bringing fifty strong. I said I didn't see how a hundred adults were going to get into my small room but they could try, and there was always the passage to surge into. I don't know what I shall say to them and I'm really shaking in my shoes, as I stutter and stammer, gobble and gulp if I have to speak to more than two people at once.

Papa is still attacked daily with great malice by my oldest demon-friend Lord Beaverbrook. He announced to a dinner-party of his own adherent yes-men, and to two

outsiders who blabbed, that he was not going to stop until he got Papa and the Minister for Air (Archie Sinclair) out of office. Papa weathers it well but it makes me sick and ill and sleepless all night and yawny all day. We always knew that the Ministry of Information was a hideous shapeless chaotic mess and a lot of people are being sacked. One can only hope the new ones will not be worse.

Rex Whistler and Caroline came to dinner last night, Rex with a tough military moustache. He says that there are not so many hairs, but each one is as thick as a hedge, so they make a brave show. He was funny about his agonies as an inexperienced subaltern in the Guards. He was told suddenly to form his men up and march them to church. Every order he shouted produced greater chaos, soldiers scuttling in opposite directions, forming sixes and sevens instead of fours (or is it threes now?). At last he found himself isolated in the middle of the parade-ground. One day's more experience would have taught him when in doubt to say 'Carry on, Sergeant-Major.' Standing in a row to be inspected, he realised that he had forgotten his collar. The Colonel inspecting felt this so apoplectically that he was robbed of speech, which did not return to him until he came to the next officer, who got the full blast of blimp rage for having a loose shoelace. Poor Rex, he's not suited to the life. He can't paint, so he has no money at all. The little pay accorded to him by a country at war has to keep the wolf from his mother's door. This is a sad bore at the bar, and Rex likes a bar as much as you do, and drinks of a strengthening nature more than you do, and now the tired youth has to pretend to like a glass of rain. He has had to lay his pencil down for saluting. I always thought his pencil was part of his hand, a sixth finger. He wields it still when off the square and decorates the messrooms and draws for his soldiers pictures of their kit and kitbag, to pin over their beds so that they can't idly forget.

I just turned on the radio and by ill luck got the news in Welsh. It was so funny, like this: 'Llanfair dufcooper pwelliwin gegeroth dufcooper sinscreillio gogooth dufcooper.' Torture too, not knowing what they were saying about poor Papa. Poor Papa indeed. The papers get worse every day. He made a very very good speech in the House. I went to listen. He counter-attacked the Press, which is bound to have the result of more mud in Papa's eye, but things will be better after this outburst, I am sure. Perhaps invasion will put it right.

There are two schools of thought in England about the invaders' reception. Shall every man and woman shoot to kill, poison, trap, snipe and stab in sleep every Hun they come across, or shall only the Army and Home Guard deal death? I'm for the former method of ending the war, though whether my courage would stand up to the end I can't say. I think that the majority feel my way. Papa told us of a man he had seen, an English aviator who had been obliged to bale out (i.e. jump from his aeroplane with a parachute) over Kent. As he got near the ground he could see only rifles and shotguns pointing out of every hedge. Tortured by fear, he guided his parachute in the limited way one can to the bang-centre of a cornfield, hoping that would give him a little time. But no! On landing there was an old farmer a few yards away drawing a relentless bead on him and a soldier following up. He had a horrible feeling that something was behind him and flashing an eye round saw a burly man with a large iron railing in his hands, just about to crown him with it. He managed to convince them that he was a friend and not a foe, but the farmer was so disappointed that he kept his gun aimed at the unfortunate and went on saying: 'I'd like to shoot your bloody head off!' I dread to think what would have happened to a Polish hero. Another poor airman falling in a home ditch found an old woman with a scythe bearing down on him. Dame Death, no less!

Your godfather Lord Beaverbrook yesterday was made a member of the War Cabinet. From the hour of his promotion he changed his tune about Papa. Orders from his boss, no doubt, to cease bludgeoning a colleague. The sheepish Press will take his lead, and so the assault I hope is over.

The deputation of Hoxton and Deptford mothers never came. I fussed a good deal from 6.30 on, but by ten I felt safe from the visitation. It's been a good day. When Papa came in he brought a letter from an unknown Colonel who wrote: 'Your wife has been the victim of a hoax. The secretary of the man who rang up and purported to be from Hoxton is a swine of a *nouveau riche*.' Now I am dying for the hoaxer to ring me up again, and I am going to say: 'I am rather upset by what happened. I feel I ought to warn you of the danger you are in. What at first I took to be a joke, as you must have realised when I said I thought that the Hoxton man was drunk, has now become, through my talking and laughing about it, a rather serious matter and is quite out of my control. All Mr Cooper's telephones are naturally tapped by Scotland Yard and I have every reason to believe that they have traced you.' In other words 'Scram!'

Today in the *Sunday Pictorial* there is a Duff Cooper ballot – a coupon to be cut and sent back to the editor. There is a picture of Papa as a debauched criminal and the coupon says: 'He gets £5000 a year for being Minister of Information. Do you think he should hold the office? Yes or No.' Now only cross people who hate you or are indignant fetch a pair of scissors, cut it out and buy a stamp and send it off, and those women who are in love with you, but they are very few. The large majority, who are quite satisfied with you and think that the Press is making a fool of itself always and anyway, just dismiss the idea and of course don't look for the scissors. So today I started buying *Sunday Pictorials* at the street-corners. Never more than four or six could I get. Suddenly at St Pancras station I found 240, so I shamelessly

bought the lot and shall send them scissored and enveloped to friends to send in. It probably won't make any difference, because by next Sunday Hitler may be here, or interest may be quite dead, or anyway they don't play fair. For all that I enjoyed collecting them on a Sunday. It was like digging for gold – so many disappointments and then striking a seam.

I lunched with the Cranbornes and dined with three journalists – Jimmy Sheean, Helen Kirkpatrick and one Robertson, representing *P.M.* here. We went to the Players' Club and to the Savoy and then to a flat. We jabbered and drank until the small hours. Papa meanwhile was jabbering and drinking with sixteen English pressmen, chiefly editors who had been abusing and insulting him, guying him and spitting ink in his face for the last ten days. This get-together meal was arranged in the height of the fight by Frank Owen, editor of the *Evening Standard*. They all told Papa what a good chap he was, and that they approved whole-heartedly of the 'snoopers' and that all newspapers use the method. All of which makes me think most journalists exceedingly low.

Conrad wrote in August:

Our parade (Lord Birdwood reviewing) was very successful. I got through the drill as well as most or better. I think that the men enjoyed it. It's extraordinary to find oneself in the ranks, with the General saying: 'Well, my lad, what were you in private life?' 'A farmer, sir.' 'Were you wounded in the war?' 'No, sir.' 'It's always you big chaps who escape.' And then at the Fall Out of officers one doesn't fall out. But O that I should be doing this at sixty-two! The Field Marshal said that the Norman Conquest was two thousand years ago, and that Buonaparte's invasion was defeated by the elements. Was it? I thought it was the Battle of Waterloo.

Bang, bang, bang! goes Jerry.

I must go out and pen the sheep. It's the first time I've ever penned sheep. It sounds so romantic. Then I change into regimentals, then high tea and patrol until midnight. I've been given a bayonet and belt, a fine pair of marching boots (size ten), chevrons to denote my rank and the silver badge of the Somerset Light Infantry (Prince Albert's Own) to wear in my cap. We have Jellahabad as a superscription. We did simply wonderfully there in 1841, but of course you know that.

In the afternoon I took the cows on the green and read the Analects of Confucius.

My letters to John Julius continued:

The London raids have begun, as usual less bad than I anticipated. It happened on a day when I could almost have welcomed a bomb to destroy me utterly, because at five minutes to midnight I had said, to please Desmond MacCarthy, that I would broadcast in a programme called 'And So to Bed,' in which people whose name is at all well-known read and comment upon a favourite verse or piece of prose. I settled that I would give them 'The Battle-Hymn of the Republic.' It pleased my own American love-complex. I thought that twenty lines and the five verses would last five minutes all right. Papa wouldn't or couldn't help me, so I sweated blood to put twenty lines together. When at last I thought it could go at that, I found that by reading slowly it took just two minutes. I tore off to the shutting London Library and got a life of the authoress and against time dug out of the two fat volumes two episodes that I hoped would pass muster. At 11.45 I was at the BBC with my pathetic script rustling in my moist hands. No sooner had I got to my studio on the third floor, when there was what is called a blue light – almost the red, which means

'Take Cover,' so down we went to the basement studios. I swear to you that I was longing for the light to turn red, in the belief that such trivial talks as mine would give way before government directions. The light wouldn't change, so I was for it. I don't know how it went. I think not badly. Anyway I didn't boggle or splutter, and my tongue, though too big for my mouth, did not twist. Papa, listening at home, said it was all right, but Wadey asked me what programme I had been in. I told her, and she said that she had listened to the news at midnight but had not heard me. I said she must have. She said no. She had heard a woman talking about the war, but it wasn't me. I let it go, but of course it *was* me. I suppose that the old rasp was quite unrecognisable. All to the good!

The second raid took place when I was asking to see a man at the M.O.I. about getting some rooms in the actual building for me and Papa to live in, and he said: 'I'm afraid that's the warning.' The whole million souls who inhabit the Ministry trooped down to the basement where the big boys conduct business as usual. One dreads curiously enough (once reasonably safe) not bombs but boredom, and the fear that it may last four or five hours. There were tin-hatted decontaminators, theatres and Red Cross nurses, firefighters, all grades of ARP. Papa was sitting in a soundproof room with his big shots round him and fifty telephones, maps, signals, lamps and gadgets. He might have been conducting a war from G.H.Q. Armageddon.

I got some friends to talk to and was jabbering away when a male voice shouted 'Quiet please!' Silence followed, and then 'All firemen upstairs.' Of course I thought the bomb had hit us. Next order, after the jabbering was again quieted, was: 'This passage to be kept clear for Red Cross ambulances.' Corpses next, I thought, but it was the All Clear, thank God, and so far no news of anything destroyed.

I went to see poor shrivelling, shrinking, palsied Maurice at Rottingdean today. I took my tin hat along. I do not think he will bear the front line much longer. Compulsory inactivity under bombing is not to be borne. He had best take his last patience to Laura Lovat in Scotland, where there will be fewer alarms. The high white cliffs are bristling with guns. I can't see how even the Huns are to scale that height of chalk.

This evening was quite another picnic. At 7.30 the farmer and I were sitting in my room talking, naturally, about guerilla warfare. (The professor of Conrad's Home Guard course at Osterley is an experienced veteran of the Spanish Civil War.) Suddenly Conrad said: 'There goes the raid-warning.' Some people, though sharp-eared, can't hear a bat; it is out of their ear's register. I have that peculiarity when it comes to raid-warnings. I took his word for it and down we went to the lounge. I fetched out the despatch-case with the diamond dolphins, trembling diamond spray, other precious stones, essential papers and passports, £200, powder, rouge, brows and lashes and a comb. But I forgot book, knitting, gas-mask and tin hat. It didn't matter because it only lasted a quarter of an hour, but I was ashamed of my lack of method. The lounge was full of quite gay people ordering tea and cigarettes. A few streetsters came in and many freaks came out of their rooms for the first time. Even the elevator boys said that they had never taken them up. I suppose some went to the shelter, but I think very few. When we all got back to our eighth floor, Wadey pointed out an enormous column of black smoke about ten miles away. I don't yet know what it was.

Our greatest relief these days was to get to the country on Saturdays, leaving the last-trump capital for the Surrey hills or Sussex or (happiest of all) Ronnie Tree's house at Ditchley near Woodstock.

I'm at Ditchley again. Papa met me here. He had been discussing the propaganda of war-aims and the future with Professor Toynbee at Oxford. After dinner the butler came in and said that the Home Guard were being called out. Talk and games continued, and Ronnie Tree went to telephone to Oxford. He came back with as long a face as you can pull without breaking, and said: 'It looks like the real thing this time. The Home Guard is being called out and the church-bells have been told to ring by the code-word.' Nobody seemed to believe it much. Papa got on to the over-calm Ministry, who said that they knew of no invasion. Many parts of the country had had the order and it was a mistake. The London docks had had a knocking about and the raid was still on.

Now I'm in bed and I've broken a valuable lamp, and so that is weighing on me as well as the war. I'll have to confess my clumsiness to the hostess in the morning. O dear, O damn!

A bad-news Sunday. The raid last night, as you will have read, was on a far bigger scale than we have had before – damage, death, fire and I fear much agony. Hannah Hudson, the wife of the Minister of Agriculture who lives at the gate here, has heard that her little house in Smith Square has collapsed. The two maids in the basement spoke to her quite unharmed and unflustered. Chapel Street may be a heap of ruins for all I know, with your little grind-organ and my ski-boots hanging incongruously from a beam. I went to church by myself. It was an Intercession Sunday with prayers against dismay, cowardice and many other things, and I prayed hard, knowing my need of their opposites.

In the afternoon I went to see the Ducal Marlborough baby being christened at Blenheim in the parish church. It

was touching and lovely, and tiny Winston (the baby) was godmothered by Clemmie Churchill, looking most radiant and gay. There was champagne and tenantry on the lawns, and nannies and cousins, and healths drunk, all to the deafening accompaniment of aeroplanes skirmishing, diving, looping and spinning in the clear air, teaching children to be pilots. No alarums or excursions this Sunday evening, although Randolph's wife, straight from Chequers, told me that invasion was fully expected now. I asked Nancy Tree to send me to sleep with a pill. She gave me two black things, like you put down horses' throats. Boluses? I remained refreshingly unconscious until 1 p.m.

Conrad writes: When we went off this morning we were told to stay in uniform if possible, and to take our guns to work with us. So you might picture me minding the cows on the green with a rifle slung on my back, like the Bulgarian peasants we used to see out of the train.

Ditchley   *9 September*

Darling J.J., Another appalling raid on London last night, and it's there that I am repairing today. The days have an autumn nip in them and a later sunrise, cobwebs and dew and a yellowing leaf – all too beautiful and always cloudless, and the senseless inglorious attrition from the sky goes on.

London looked just the same. Conversation is restricted entirely to bombs. Phyllis de Janzé, whose war-work is smelling out spies, has had her pathetic house burgled in the black-out and her furs (her ratcoats, catcoats, stoat and weasel coats) all taken. What *will* the thief do with them?

There are six or seven raids a day. One copes with them fairly well. People say: 'You know there's an unexploded bomb in Montagu Square or Buckingham Palace?' or 'Lansdowne House has gone. Hadn't you heard?' One could bear it better if one could see any end to it. Of course it's there (the end, I mean), but one can't see it yet. Is it the

beginning of an invasion scheme or is it just to break our spirit? It won't do that.

It's not really the place to sleep, the eighth floor of the Dorchester. I never close an eye, but Papa sleeps like a baby in a pram, cheek on hands. One hears those vile machines and the whistling and thuds, and then one starts waiting for the next and counting the watcher-of-the-sky's steps overhead. I cannot bear to look out of the window. There always seem to be great fires ringed round. The All Clear goes when light comes, and at last one sleeps for an hour – and then one looks out on to the next day and there are no fires, and one cannot believe that so much can have gone on and so much yet be standing and unchanged.

There was a big row tonight between Papa and me undressing and in different stages of nudity. Our gun was banging away outside and the thuds were hideous to hear, and I said that we *must* go down to the basement. I had meant to all that day, and had taken precautions to stop argument such as 'I haven't got a suitable dressing-gown' by buying him a very suitable shade of blue alpaca with dark red pipings. 'I think you're too unkind,' I'd say, pulling off a stocking. 'We *can't* go down; I'm too tired. Besides it doesn't make any difference where you are.' I was beginning to cry and give in when the guns gave a particularly violent salvo and the look-out man popped his tin-hatted head in at the door saying excitedly 'You are advised to take cover.' This was a break for me and it settled Papa, who then donned his Tarnhelm outfit with the slowness of a tortoise, and down we went. I had arranged with the management that if I achieved my purpose we could have two rest-beds in the Turkish bath. So there we slept in hygienic comfort and, to my mind, greater security. The dynamo makes a nice *Enchantress* or Clipper noise, so that you hear the bombs less, and our own big Hyde Park gun doesn't blow your head off as it does above ground. Still we are encouraged by its bombast because

we feel it is some kind of answer and the noise is said to exhilarate.

Last night we dined with a lot of French – Mademoiselle Eve Curie, Monsieur Palewski, airman and politician, all violent de Gaulleites. The guns, bombs, orchestra and jabber deafen and bewilder, and the more you try to escape the danger and noise of war with light music, food and wine, the more you think of the East End, the homeless, and the fires raging nearby. While the Huns are turning London's heavens into hell, they are not doing much harm to our factories for war-production. Therefore unless resistance breaks (and there is no fear of that) they are wasting their pilots, ammunition and confidence. Eve Curie told me that she had been on a tour of provincial ARP shelters with Lady Reading. All the little children of five have Mickey Mouse gas-masks. They love putting them on for drill and at once start trying to kiss each other, then they march into their shelter singing: 'There'll always be an England.'

Thousands of mothers and children are being got out of London each day, but even now they are unwilling to go, and act very strangely when they get to the outer country. At Mells, for instance, ten or twenty women arrived at noon, who had been all night in the train and four hours in a church at Frome in the early morning. The first thing they asked Katharine was: 'Is there a Lyons here?' When she said 'No' they gasped and said: 'What, no Lyons! How often does the bus go to Frome?' 'Twice a week,' she said. Well, believe it or not, no sooner had they swallowed their dinner than half of them walked the four miles to Frome to get back to streets and see the shops. Another twenty arrived at Daphne Weymouth's and asked for shelter. Although her house is packed already with evacuated crippled children, she said she would manage somehow and tore off to the local town to buy

Rex Whistler

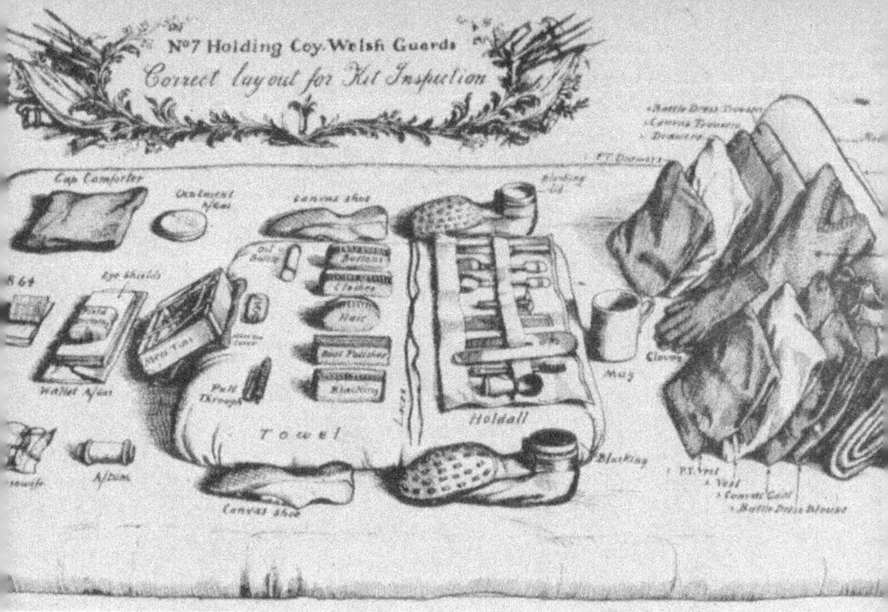

No 7 Holding Coy. Welsh Guards
Correct layout for Kit Inspection

Two drawings by Rex Whistler

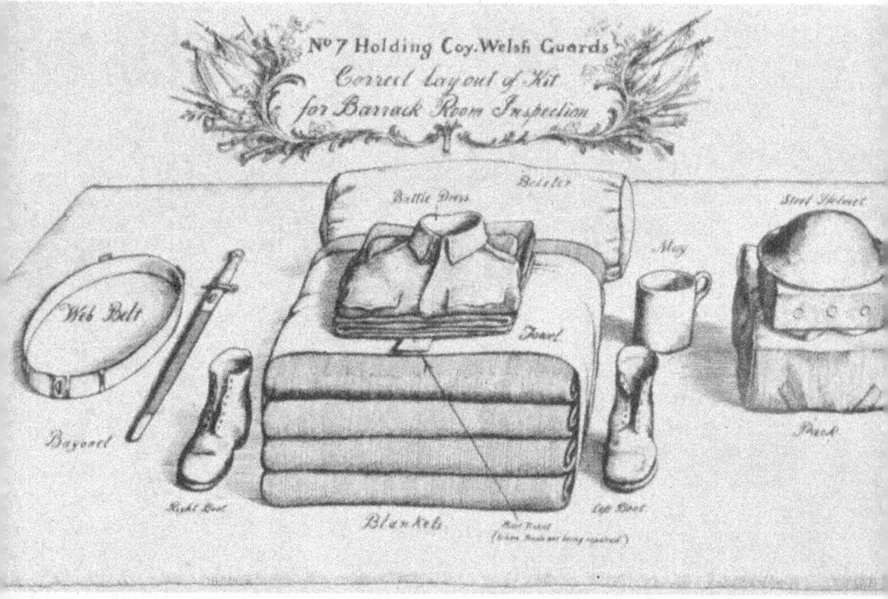

No 7 Holding Coy. Welsh Guards
Correct layout of Kit
for Barrack Room Inspection

them blankets, pots, stoves, etc. £20 she spent, and when she returned staggering under her load, they had gone – vanished, and no word left of explanation.

I wrote to Kaetchen on 23 September:

Darling Kat, You little know what you say when you tell me to write for the papers. I am not, as you know, made of the stuff Londoners are made of. My instinct is to flee. I cannot report on scenes in shelters. There are hundreds of keen, nerveless people out all night pursuing fires and demolishment. But for you I will tell of a day in London last week, when my canteen closed for a term.

At about 7 a.m. the first siren would start up. Wade would be calling us with the tea and very bleary eyes, and I would have been asleep for an hour after coming up from the depths. The odds are that I would be too exhausted to care, and that the All Clear would go an hour later. Sometimes I feel that it is madness to remain on our roof floor, but I know it is useless to shift Duff away from his shaving, so I resign myself to sweat. At 8.45 Duff goes off to his Ministry. There, I know, he sits beneath a Selfridge-sized plate-glass window which will kill him if a bomb drops half a mile away. Is he better there? Or now, since the siren has gone again, is it worse to be in a car or already in the Cabinet which (if at Downing Street) is a target made of lath and plaster? He won't carry a tin hat or gas-mask, so I have to see that both are in the Dorchester suite, the car and the M.O.I., but I can't sneak one into the Cabinet Room.

Meanwhile, apart from thoughts, civilised morning life goes on identically. *The Times* is there for one's waking. Other papers are there by 8.30 or 9, letters a little later. The telephone buzzes on through the raids, with friends relating night-adventures and narrow shaves. I plod on with little zeal and little success to get internees liberated. I try the

Office of Works to get Duff's Ministry windows wired. I ring up Lord Moyne, Lord Camrose and all the rich I can think of to give me old mattresses, blankets and pillows for basement-shelters to house the workers. I get up wearily at last. The water is boiling, the sun always brilliant, service prompt as usual, messages, flowers from Moyses Stevens (now glassless but just as artistically decorated). I paint my face in the same way, dress as smartly (but against the grain) and buzz off to the Ritz for a drink with one or more of the boys. The Ritz is a little empty compared to the Dorchester. Conversation: bombs only. In the afternoon: more chores, *Evening Standard*, radio. The balloon-barrage turns from silver to gold, and at seven the black-out starts, the siren wails, and I wonder why Duff is not back and try not to telephone for news of him. Bath, evening clothes, for we semi-dress for dinner much more smartly than we would in days of peace. I have a serviceable get-up, black to the ground with a black lace top over pink and long sleeves with shoulder-puffs. We call it *La Maison Tellier*. I have too several diaphanous shirts worn with the same skirt and the saucy flowered crowns with veils (bought before Paris fell) to hide sad traces. Then down to the luxury-liner restaurant, reminiscent of S.S. *Titanic*, jam-packed now with passengers and crew that one knows too well. Dinner to the accompaniment of a band playing as loud as it can to drown the storm of the Hyde Park guns incessantly booming. At 11, a little lulled by Chianti but utterly unexhilarated, we walk down to the Turkish bath, stepping over hundreds of hotel-mates dossed down on mattresses, some with dogs that bark as you pass, some snoring, some reading with a torch. The Turkish bath is not so safe, as it's not under the main building, but it has cubicle-privacy, a cot, blankets not sheets, a light apiece, and above all deadened noise. The passages in the middle floors are lined with sleepers, but our floor is, I think, deserted by all. I feel comparatively calm in my

subterranean cubicle and sleep with the help of a pill. The cleaners arrive at dawn, and with the dawn the All Clear, so up one trudges to one's proper bedroom and it all begins again.

Still it is endurable and my greatest terror is being forced by Duff to leave the city. It is so utterly unlike what I imagined the raids on London would be. I thought of a bigger, suddener attack, with the whole population blocking the roads, Ministries evacuating to their pre-arranged dispersal-stations, frightful dislocation, worse perhaps but not so much worse than this cold-blooded waiting for destruction. Most people don't see it so. They have confidence in a defence being found. 'This is only a phase of the war. We'll stick it out all right.' There is not a street that does not show some assault. The curtains flap dismally out of Londonderry House and most of the big Piccadilly houses. I try to avoid the places where the cruellest gashes have been inflicted, but one has to take the way that cut-off streets, encumbered with bombs ticking to explode, allow. Two Berkeley Square houses are non-existent except for one tall wall from which waves a long red stair-carpet like a banner. Our Ministry took it full in the middle of its high head but stood up to it. It's the older houses that collapse completely. Queen Anne's Mansions are cleft in twain. The Dorchester has had incendiaries on her deck, but Jim from the crow's nest puts them out with sand, or has done until now, though he's always on my floor-telephone saying how hot things are getting. I wouldn't be a Jim Crow for a V.C. The wind has been blowing Armada-strength but has now dropped. *Qui vivra verra. Dum spiro spero.* I'll close now with those two platitudes.

I cannot have shown my true colours (chiefly yellow) and some wave of a panache must have been left, or Conrad would not have written:

I think your spirits wonderful. Mine are awful. I wonder you can bear me, but you are always gay, witty and the life and soul. I know that it is done by an effort and as a duty. I'm lost in admiration and so totally unable to be as you are.

Nor would I have written to Conrad had not Duff and I in our hearts been deeply dejected:

Duff is anxious to live in the country, and so am I if we survive. He seems depressed. He thinks that Winston hates him now. He is both bored and worried and dislikes facing doom (who doesn't). All these weaknesses are frighteningly unlike Mr C.

1 October

Darling J.J., All my supports are leaving. Jimmy Sheean has gone. H. G. Wells has flown to America. Knickerbocker and Somerset Maugham do the same tomorrow. Our first funk-hole, the Turkish bath, is said to be a death-trap, so we are in the reconstructed gymnasium. Eight nice Little Bears' beds behind screens, all the camels, horses, bicycles and rowing-sculls removed. Unfortunately it has a hollow wood uncarpeted floor, three swing-doors with catches on them and the room is treated as a passage. I never get a wink, but Papa is the proverbial log. The second night a great improvement took place. We had sheets, a table and a lamp. No one else had a lamp. There was a carpet to muffle the many fewer footsteps. Conversations are conducted in whispers that take me straight back to childhood and to you – Sir George Clark asking Major Cazalet if he knows what the time is etc. No one snores. If Papa makes a sound I'm up in a flash to rearrange his position. Perhaps Lady Halifax is doing the same to His Lordship. Between 6 and 6.30 we start getting up one by one. We wait until they have all gone. They each have a flashlight to find their slippers with, and I see their monstrous forms projected caricatureishly on the ceiling magic-lanternwise. Lord Halifax

is unmistakeable. We never actually meet. Sometimes the All Clear goes in the middle of the night and some idiots trudge to their upstairs beds and get comfy, only to be woken an hour later by the siren and down they have to trudge again. I wish, I wish it was all over – Hitler defeated, the lights up and the guns still.

Today we moved down to the fourth floor and I shall feel safer in the daytime and I shan't hear our Jim Crow's pitter-patter. At night I feel quite secure in the gym and sleep like a log. It's certainly more pally in the Underground, where families go in about five p.m. with bedding, babies, buns, bottles, and settle down to community singing, gossip, making new friends, exchanging bomb-stories etc. I should rather like it, but can you imagine Papa's reaction if he had to join the party?

I walk across the Park now at 6.45 past the Achilles statue. The railings are all down and the ground is deep in leaves that have fallen fast this year. Mr Coombs, Papa's political agent, took me to see the ruins of Pimlico today and spared me nothing. I was happy to talk to the people and hear their stories and wonder at their serenity, and stand aghast at their sincere desire to stay in London and not be evacuated, but I didn't see why I should have to look at the craters and ruins. Mr Coombs appeared to think that it was a treat, and probably you would have thought the same. The truth is that I don't like realities, John Julius. I like dreams, shows, plans for the future, storybooks, music and jokes. Best of all though, I love you and Papa, and you are both realities, so my argument collapses.

In the midst of our uplift over the Italians fleeing in Greece came the news of Lord Lothian's death. I'm ashamed

to say that my second thought was: might Papa be given the job? What a vista of hope and light I floated down! I should (just to begin with) see you again as a bachelor and not as a man with a beard and family; I should come out of the darkness, out of the fear; the shame of leaving others to face what I was missing would be mitigated by being *ordered* away. I must not write of the hope nor think of it, as the odds are much against it. No use planning whether to take Wadey, or if I'd be well advised to take the old brown boots, or whether to have my hair permanently waved this side or that. Enough, enough!

I wrote to Conrad:

I am grief-stricken. Euan Wallace is dying. Alas, poor Captain! He led a happy, healthy, abstemious life. How little it pays! Take Lord Lothian. Orangeade and Christian Science quite vanquished him. An untimely end indeed. Perhaps Duff will be sent to Washington. I am torn by conflicting hopes. I'd like of course to see John Julius again before he's married, and I think that Duff would do well and get the credit for the United States coming in, which I know they will do, but I should hate to desert you, to say nothing of the Fighting Temeraire England. I see that a name has been submitted. I hope it's not a Munichois. Halifax would be branded an appeaser. Bobbety it would kill, and Betty is not the ideal, as she probably still sees them as rebels. I've suddenly thought of George Lloyd. He's the Goschen – 'I forgot Lloyd.' Winston loves him. He's an Eastern expert, but we know East meets West.

London   *20 December*
   Darling J.J., I cried with laughter over Papa's censored letter. It was like something you cut out for Christmas

decoration. I never write to you without his telling me that my letters are unintelligible to a boy of eleven, or to an adult for that matter, indecipherable and censorable, so my triumph over him is complete. They seem to me to be as clear as a nursery rhyme, not that a nursery rhyme makes much sense, but one knows them since childhood and you've known me since childhood and before, so we must hope you like to get a bit of news from this dear island. Not that you can get much, for Papa tells me nothing. It's been a grievance for twenty years.

The proud city has had another easy week. The joy I should have taken in the relative calm was utterly marred by your dear Papa waking up on Wednesday, after a healthy dinner and good sleep, with a temperature of 103. You can imagine my fuss and to-do! I of course feared for his life, and also was greatly upset to think that he would miss the Christmas week at Ditchley, that we had greatly looked forward to as a restorative and delight. I thought of the weeks at the Admiralty when he had tossed with influenza-bronchitis from dolphin to dolphin, until my courage fainted. However, with intensive cosseting, two nurses, physicking, heating, sweating, cooling, plus a lot of praying and purging, we have thrown the germ off (I trust) in four days and we shall go to our Christmas on Sunday. One good service this disease has rendered to Papa is that it has kept us out of the gym, and I must steel myself after Christmas to sleep above ground.

So Lord Halifax is to go to Washington instead of me. I suppose there will be a prejudice against him because he was a Munich man, but America will like him very much when they know him. He has infinite charm and his predecessor had a worse reputation for appeasement when he was made Ambassador, yet he made a very good name for himself and was much praised. His only fault was to let the Huns have all the propaganda in the United States to themselves.

We've got here, thank God! You should have seen the
party leaving the Dorchester – Wadey staggering under
sordid paper-parcels, last-minute sponges, slippers poking
out, two tin hats, two gas-masks, guns, ammunition, a white
Christmas tree in a red box, another Ministry red box, big
boxes, little boxes, fur gloves, a terribly intimate hot-water-
bottle of a poisonous green, and Papa himself twice the size
of M. Michelin, in two coats under his fur coat, a muffler
round his throat, another over his head and ears, a hat on top
of that and only one bright little blue eye goggling out.

I wish he could have a real holiday. He has not had a week
except for flu since France fell. He's tired, poor boy. Winston
never is, but he does all his work from bed and sleeps after
lunch in pyjamas, works again from his bed, gets up for
dinner and feels like a daisy at 2 a.m. when others are
exhausted. Clemmie seems blissful. She can't understand
those who write from the United States in pitying vein.
'Why are they sorry for us?' I quite see why they are.
Clemmie, wife of the greatest of living men who finds
himself beyond his life's ambition and knows that he can save
us and triumph, exults in his unswerving confidence and is
less to be pitied than some poor gnomes whose husbands
have thankless jobs that they hate, or whose sons are fated.

I have asked Mr Wendell Willkie to dine with us. Will he,
I wonder? I met him once. I shan't know what to say because
what will be on the tip of my tongue will be: 'I'm so glad
they didn't elect you President.' It is great fun, though,
hearing people's impressions of London when they first
arrive. They vary a great deal, some thinking it a complete
ruin, others noticing nothing unusual, just depending of
course on their characters (like you and me). You would
never notice any disasters and I have double vision of them.

You will be glad to hear that I have slept my last night in the gymnasium. Papa had one more. After Christmas I became resolved no longer to expose him to derision by dragging him underground. On a convulsive boisterous night, seeing my sufferings, he tried to drag me down, but I had learnt pride and would not now budge. He said that he would bolt down himself so as to lure me to comfort and sleep, and thus it ended with him down and me up.

London was excited and electrified by the Wendell Willkie visit. He went down into the Underground at night and down like a dinner with the crowds. They shout and cheer and say: 'Tell them we can take it!' and 'Send us everything you can!' and this elephantine figure, with a painted-white tin helmet, seems to amuse and impress them. I gave a dinner-party for him (only ten of us) in a private room at the Dorchester. He had a gentleman along with him, whom we had stayed with in Minneapolis, called Mr Cowles, whom I also liked very much. Willkie was treated like a king and film-star rolled into one. The newspapers told us what he ate for breakfast and what size boots he wore. Now he has gone. I waved him goodbye last night and I pray God he will give a good account of us and our country, our needs and hopes, when he comes to testify to the Senate.

It was at Ditchley that the Prime Minister used to spend full-moon week-ends. He travelled down to the house, one of the most beautiful in England, with his staff and detectives, his maps, intercoms and operators.

19 February

Great excitement last week-end! We went to Ditchley where Winston was staying. Golly, what a to-do! To start with, the Prime Minister has a guard of fully-equipped soldiers. Two sentries are at every door of the house to challenge you. I look very funny in the country these days, in brightly-coloured

trousers, trapper's fur jacket, Mexican boots and refugee headcloth, so that on leaving the house I grinned at the sentries and said: 'You will know me all right when I come back.' However, when I did return the guard, I suppose, had been changed. I grinned at what I took to be the same two soldiers and prepared brazenly to pass, when I was confronted with two bayonets within an inch of my stomach. They no doubt thought that I was a mad German assassin out of a circus.

Winston does nearly all his work from his bed. It keeps him rested and young, but one does not see so much of him as in the old Bognor days. There is also a new reverence for so great a leader, and that creates an atmosphere of slight embarrassment until late in the evening. Also instead of old friends the guests included people called D.M.O. and D.M.I. (Director of Military Operations and Director of Military Intelligence) and an enchanting king of the Air Force, Sir Charles Portal, with a wife whom I used to play with as a child because she lived at Denton near Belvoir. Brendan of course was there, and Venetia, also Winston's wife and beautiful, animated daughter Mary.

Then on Sunday a flood of Poles rushed in – President Sikorski, the Polish Ambassador and some other sledded Polacks. After lunch the little procession, headed by Winston, followed by the upstanding Poles and brought to a finish by your exceedingly reluctant and rather sleepy Papa, walked off to a private room for a conference on Polish publicity. It took an interminable time and when at last it ended and the Poles were due to move home, the Prime Minister suddenly thought that the President should have a guard of honour. Secretaries and A.D.C.'s went tearing round trying to find the Captain of the Guard, but he was sleeping or walking and could not be found, so Winston himself finally routed out some rather raw, inexperienced soldiers, who had never formed a guard of honour before.

Meanwhile the patient Poles were sitting on the doorstep waiting for their guard to arrive, and the President said: 'Mr Churchill is so great a man that we must let him do what amuses him.'

I tried to remember things that the Prime Minister said that would interest you, but my brain is like a sieve and I can only think of one thing which I thought very touching and disclaiming of his power. When I said that the best thing he had done was to give the people courage, he said: 'I never gave them courage; I was able to focus theirs.' He also talks glibly of the war in 1943 and 1944, which causes me to tingle with terror and tedium. We had two lovely films after dinner and there were several short reels from Papa's Ministry. Winston managed to cry through all of them, including the comedy.

I carry a dowser's twig that guides me to a Folly. I remember stumbling with high-heeled shoes through a pathless wood in Victor Rothschild's park at Tring, catching in brambles, sinking into sloughs and suddenly coming upon a disused avenue with at one end a crumbling, classical, pedimented house submerged in umbrageous and dripping trees, at the other an obelisk. When I found it by chance that memorable day, my heart leapt and visions of what it could be filled my eyes and thoughts. Duff and I could commute from this sanctuary. I would find work in Tring, cook and keep a few animals, a hive of bees and a vegetable patch. Victor would surely put it in order, for historically it asked to be preserved. He would let it to me, and I would furnish the three rooms. The idea obsessed me for a time. Victor listened and smiled, teased and cat-and-moused me, but finally agreed to grounding my folly-in-the-air. My passionate prayer answered, I planned the minutest details of good sense, beauty, war-duties, drains and vegetable plots. Then something went wrong. Victor could not have known what a bitter dispossession it was (on a par with Eden), but its loss bred a new fancy in my heart and head. Why

should not our Bognor cottage become an eccentric farm of bees, goats, hares and guinea-pigs? The seed once sown grew apace and by the end of February it looked likely to produce a good sensible harvest of bread-and-butter and *brioches*.

I wrote to Conrad:

> If the folly fizzles out we shall try to commute from Bognor. I'd have to farm a bit. Could I keep hens, a cow, utility rabbits and get goats in for cheese? Could I feed a couple of piglets on refuse? Why not on whey? An expert here says: 'Folding units for fowls induce cannibalism.' Is one to believe that? Would you spend a night and most of two days a week with me once I am at Bognor? If only invasion doesn't interrupt us!

London   *3 March*

It's almost settled. For Easter Papa and I will be at Bognor, I hope. I went down yesterday for a few hours accompanied by Wadey. We borrowed a utility van and piled it high with all we have got here, plus stores, gramophones, radios, saucepans, books, pictures etc. and bumped down on wooden seats to the little house. There is a gun and strong-point at the gate by the wood. There is another at Barrack Lane corner, and all the prom is dense with wire and concrete. No getting through any of our back gates. Sentries armed cap-à-pie walk up and down. The same thing goes on as far as the eye can see. I've sold Dodgems. I'm quite unhappy to let it go. I gave £22 a year ago. It's had a gruelling time and I'm getting £35 for it. Not bad! I wanted to buy a small van so as to be able to cart myself, my swill, goats, swarms of bees, fowl-pests and pigs-in-pokes, but vans are as rare as radium and cost as much, so I've bought a boring 1935 Vauxhall. It has cost £85 and if the war goes on, as it must for a year at least, I shall sell it for double if I'm still kicking.

Papa says that he is tired, a thing I've never heard him say before. He sometimes used to say, with a view to upsetting me: '*Ich bin so müde, Weibchen,*' which is what the Prince Consort said to Queen Victoria when he began to die, but the way he says it now wrings me. I hate it. I wish, I wish I could see you. Send me all the snapshots you can of yourself, or I may not recognise you, darling, darling.

20 March

My London Dorchester sojourn has two weeks at most to run. Then for the beaches! Meanwhile it's preparations. I've bought two expensive bee-hives, a butter-churn and four goats. I study the *West Sussex Gazette* for advertisements of sales of farm-implements. I read leaflets from the Ministry of Agriculture about all the awful things that can happen to livestock – mastitis for the cow, red mite for the hens, Isle of Wight disease for the bees. Nothing can happen to the scapegoats on their blasted briared waste-land; they are pagans and worse than devil's cattle. A lady in Bagshot is going to teach me to milk them, and then with the trailer I'm buying to replace Dodgems I should be able to transport pigs, bee-hives, garbage and even people on mattresses if necessary. We've got no money at all but that matters least. Always remember that, poor pauper. You are good and sweet and write lovely letters often, and I am indeed a lucky mother to have so grand a son. Don't be influenced by people in bad ways. Don't do things I should think common or mean, underhand or cruel, because it's easier or because someone else does them. Be like Papa in courage and straightness, and don't forget to love me.

3
The Good Earth

Duff was exhausted and unhappy. He felt himself impotent and frustrated. 'Frustrated' was the current word, and it was surely coined in the M.O.I. The Ministry was the butt of the Civil Servants and the Press. Duff was unused to the feeling of defeat. His successor, Brendan Bracken, alone was successful in this office, for he had the ears, eyes and heart of the Prime Minister, whose love of that dear and remarkable red-headed man caused Winston to give him unfailing support and attention. In Duff's day Winston thought propaganda of no importance, because it would not win the war. It bored him.

Since, in April 1941, no dissolving of cloud lightened his darkness, and conscious that resignation should not be an action of convenience, Duff agreed half-heartedly to live in our coastland cottage and commute to London. I was hilariously happy. I longed to get away to the green fields, nightingales and lambs. The Folly's loss was forgotten, for now, occupied by Hutchie's son Jeremy and his wife Peggy Ashcroft, it no longer beckoned, pleading emptiness and neglect. A year's tension and the clashing and pounding of city life, at all times wearing even without the addition of high explosive, had brought me to a state of sluggish dejection. Now I felt as full of spirit as the month of May. It was exciting to leave the stalwart bulwark of the Dorchester and settle on the Bognor beach regardless of invasion. Lethargy, I knew, would float away like gossamer. Wadey and a gardener and his wife were to run our lives and the lives of a dense concentration of animals. The unheated little house, because of its small rooms, could be stoked up to fever-point. Half of it could be closed. Refugees still groused in the lodge. Holbrook's unaccommodating pomposity no longer

there, his cramped built-out bed-pantry should be my dairy. I had my car. I should be lonely at first, but the Gothic Farmer would put in two days a week and teach me to make cheese and to clean sties. June would be twilit at midnight because of double summertime. The birds would sing me encouragement and the grass invite my flocks to graze; the bus would come to the door at the convenient time. The war itself looked less disastrous. Money was short (another reason for leaving the luxurious hotel) and so was material for what was to be my profession. I wrote to John Julius:

Bognor   *April 1941*

Papa commutes. He likes it very much and he catches the 7.45 train in the morning and gets back at eight or nine according to how busy he is. I like being in the country a hundred times better than in London, but I miss you, my darling. On Sundays we go over to Bosham and have lunch at the Ship Inn Club. The water laps the houses at high tide and there's a little bar after your own heart. When I was younger than you the theory was that the best sunbonnets were made at Bosham, and also that King Canute's daughter was buried in the church. Off Selsey there is a cathedral under the sea. It once stood on dry land but the sea claimed it. They say that on rough nights you can hear the bells pealing.

Bognor   *8 April*

Darling Conrad, the next *Tag* dawns. There will be exciting arrangements to be made. Buy pullets Monday. Could you try and stay two nights, as I think Duff will not be able to come back ever on Tuesday on account of late Cabinets? Gardener Jones has already built me an outside fireplace on which to bubble my trouble for the piggywigs. Collect me any utensils you can. If you hear of a second-hand henhouse for twelve, buy it. They should be going cheap, as many people are killing off. Cream-skimmers and hobnails

for my clogs are out for the duration. Butter muslin can only be sold in squares for fear we cheat and dress in it. Sweet farmer, help me with my farm! Help me until it hurts, as Willkie says. I'm sure you will.

There is no such pamphlet as 325 Manual of Cheeses with Improvised Utensils. The Ministry of Agriculture disclaim it. They have sent me No. 122 Smallholder Cheese. I sent for dozens more manuals on fowl-pox, fowl-pest, white diarrhoea in chicks and many other fascinating subjects. Far from improvised utensils my pamphlet tells me to get quickly a table six feet by two-and-a-half feet with raised sides and ends, lined with tin sheeting. For a coffin?

10 April

Darling John Julius, I have to do all the marketing as there is no more delivering. I enjoy it enormously, not that there is any choosing and no pinching of chickens' breasts, no picking out brown eggs or settling which biscuits to buy. You just take what you are given and like it, but there's the big excitement of suddenly seeing a bunch of leeks or some mushrooms and falling (no, pouncing) on the find. Mr Parfrement sold me his old henhouse for thirty shillings and said: 'I hope you'll give me all the patronage you can. I can supply any fish you want as well as meat and poultry.' 'I always do,' I said. 'I noticed you had a parcel from Ragler's in your car,' he said. I went as scarlet as a turkeycock and mumbled something about it not happening again.

Goats evade me; they are unprocurable. I've telephoned all over the country to famous herds and scoured every village and farm in Sussex. Mrs Owen, the goat-wife, has two milky animals and I go daily to practise my hand at 'stripping' the udders. I can do it quite well now, but I feel I'll never get goats. There was quite a struggle to find laying pullets, but by dint of walking into every farm between here and Chichester, I bought six from a very eccentric farmer. He

complained of being half-asleep and he wouldn't give me any guarantee that the hens would lay eggs. I liked his lack of salesmanship, so the next day I went to collect them. He complained again of my having woken him and we popped the panic-stricken six into my shut car. They were fluttering all round me as I drove home, clucking and making messes and obstructing the view of the road, but an egg was laid in the car and three more appeared in the egg-nests before night. Wadey and I were thrilled. I collect pails of disgusting scraps from neighbouring houses, boil them and then with my hand break the pulp up small and mix it with rationed meal. They gobble up the muck and it's a great pleasure, as we had only three old foreign eggs the first week. When Conrad brings me another six hens I hope to have eighty eggs a week and sell them easily. The pigs are being bought before I write again.

18 April

I'm still delighting in the novelty of farming. The goats still eluding me, I have settled to buy a cow, also four piglets called the Hutchinson Family, expected tomorrow. I spent a happy afternoon with Conrad fertilising the field with ammonia phosphate, so that it should grow richer and greener for my milk to be more plentiful for my cheeses. The whey will fatten my four little pigs. They are to be crammed into the goathouse and have a pen round them and never be allowed to take an unnecessary step, for fear of losing an ounce of weight. Yesterday I went to Bosham for my bees, to be told by the bee-man that they too were unobtainable. Everyone is going in for bees and goats, and I had been thinking how clever I was to cultivate stock that no one else would be likely to want! Then six more laying pullets arrived at the station in a crate, and I went to pick them and Papa up at 8 p.m. I packed them into the dickey and Papa into the seat, and looking at my petrol-gauge was horrified to see that

the tank was almost dry. I knew that the only garage was shut and so we had to risk it, Papa in an agony of sweat and fuss. Of course it gave out a little short of the house, and I had to break it to Papa that it meant carrying a crate of hens as well as walking home. He took it with a pretty good grace, and off he staggered. The crate was tolerably heavy and covered with sticking-out nails. An army lorry came blustering towards us, so I hailed it, which made Papa scream with shame and put the hens down, so I told him to leave it to me and walk on, which he was not at all loath to do. I asked the young soldiers to give me a drop of petrol to get me and my birds home. They said they were sorry they couldn't. I said that I'd give them a coupon. They said no, it was strictly against the law. I said that they couldn't leave a lady in distress and that I'd have to leave the car in the road with its lights on all night, blocking the way if there was an invasion. They said they agreed and that they'd break the law if I gave them a tin, and had I got a rubber tube? I gave them the tin and told them that I didn't happen to have a rubber tube on me. They backed their tank into a side-lane and fiddled for a few minutes and started to come back by the ditch like people ambushing. At that moment an officer passed leisurely on a push-bike. On seeing him they both lay flat on their stomachs concealing the give-away red tin. He looked round but, thank God, didn't stop, and they hurled the tin into my window and tore back to the lorry, and were off in a flash. I was saved and after putting the juice in and struggling to get the crate in, I arrived triumphant with the car and fowls, so now we've got twelve birds laying eight or nine eggs a day. I sell them to the people who give me their shell-egg coupons and their scraps, which encourages them to eat less so as to get more eggs.

We had a nasty raid after the dreadful London one. I was all alone, as Papa stayed up that night. Conrad was here. The noise of planes and distant guns and occasional thumps was

kept up all evening from nine onwards. At ten we went and looked out of the best-bedroom windows towards Portsmouth. It was as bright as day with what are called 'chandeliers' (clusters of incandescent lights that the Germans drop to illuminate their targets) and a steady white-green brilliance that came from I couldn't make out where. I hated looking but Wadey can't keep away from goofing through the windows. We went down and collected Conrad for comfort, and about an hour later there was a new succession of noises which we thought were incendiaries in the garden. We put the lights out and went to see. As I opened the window-door an appalling crash, which was a land-mine at Aldwick, tore the shutter out of my hands. The lights then were as violent at Bognor as they had been at Portsmouth. I couldn't manage to fasten the shutter; the black-out being then incomplete we had to sit on the hearthrug and go on with *The Times* crossword by the light of the fire and one candle. I did not fancy going to bed.

Yesterday came Hutchie, fat and funny. Hilaire Belloc came for a night. He is frightfully decrepit, poor old saint, moves as slowly as a tortoise and is covered with gravy, ash and candle-grease. He can't move or get up without some support, and so always carries a very frayed umbrella about with him. It looks so strange indoors. Noël Coward also came down, fresh from America on his way to lecture for the Red Cross in Australia.

I'm too busy to write. I've taken on more than I can manage and worse is to come. Yesterday I bought a seven-year-old cow for £27. She is called Eighteen or the Princess. She is ugly and tame and heavily laden with milk. I was out collecting my swill when she arrived, but I met the men coming back who told me that she would be sad and dejected for a day or two. Indeed she looked it, but I stroked her and gave her some dairy cubes, and was happy to find that she didn't mind my handling her, as I had imagined insuperable

difficulties when I came to milk her. I put a big nail into the tree-trunk near the little gate that leads into the field, and also a large hook at the height of my knee with a little pail hung on it full of meal. Then, armed with a halter to drag her by, and a sponge to mop her udder, and my fine new pail that can't be knocked over because it weighs a ton, and into which a hoof can't get because the opening is so askew, and my milking-stool, I set off to milk. Nothing would move her from her disconsolate position by the fence, so I gave in to her whim and milked her there with speed and success. She gave over a gallon and a half, and it only took me twenty minutes. Hutchie watched and scoffed a bit. Papa arrived and helped me feed the pigs. All the farmer's daughter has come out in Wadey. She is most keen and helpful and works hard too.

The war was obsessing me less and I was learning to like solitude in restricted bouts. Making the smallholder cheese was the greatest of the new miracles. Life on a farm is miraculous, as is all life and death, but the joy through surprise of the transubstantiation of milk into cheese quite transported me into nature-mysticism. My utensils were improvised all right; one galvanised tub within its larger counterpart, a few six-pound perforated cheese-moulds, two Mexican double saddle-bags, gaudy with tinsel, filled to unliftable-ness with Bognor shingle, which when piled on the mould pressed the desirable trickle of whey from the curd. These and a bottle of rennet and a thermometer could make all kinds of cheese. A cow can inundate a small family with milk, and from one widowed cow's cruse came twenty pounds of cheese a week, a pound or two of butter, plentiful sweet milk for my refugees and ourselves, and enough whey to fatten potential porkers. I loved my cow as the Russian peasant (I suppose) did before her cow was communal. She represented to me life, riches, sweetness and warmth. Dressed as Babushka, I would go, lantern in hand, through the half-light of spring with the birds' first chorus to enliven me from bleary sleep,

straightening up under my inevitable yoke that suspended the queer milk-pail and another pail of dairy cubes. The flickering oil-lamp I would light and hang on a hook in the dark shed while this beneficent beast welcomed me with her soft moo that ejected breath like a dragon's. I would find her ointments and washing-cloths, and there I would sit for twenty minutes or so, my cheek deep in her furry flank, her sweet-smelling warmth enveloping me in content. Conrad, if he was there, would keep me company in cape and fore-and-aft hat, and Desmond MacCarthy I remember once telling me entrancing stories of his adolescence, stories that only the dark, the cow's breath and the strange pure atmosphere allowed him to tell. The twenty minutes lengthened into an hour while the warm milk cooled. I would stagger back under my yoke to the dairy and pour the rich foaming gallons into their appointed tub, skim yesterday's yield, put the kettles on and start miracle-making.

Darling J.J., Conrad came down and together we made a cheese of cow's milk. It's a fascinating occupation, and takes hours of standing with your arms deeply plunged into ever-warming curds-and-whey. As it's winter-cold I'm grateful for the warmth. There's a lot of temperature-ing of the heating water and stirring the milk. Rennet is administered in drops at the proper degree and within a few minutes you notice bubbles rising on the glassy surface. You trouble the surface ever more gently until these same bubbles show obstinacy, then refusal to burst. Stop! The transubstantiation is there and the curd separates from the whey. When this occurs, you take a stiletto-ish knife, and slice and slice the substance while it slowly heats. When it is cooked, granulated and drained, you press it into moulds and press weights upon it. The moulds have holes in them and out trickles the whey.

Ever since my possession of Princess I have felt I cannot be complete without a cow. I had one called Fatima in Algiers and I

have one today in France. Princess was a constant trouble before she got too attached to me, her mistress-calf, to want to escape. How often in that first spring would I come to her with pail and stool under arm, beneath some radiant morning's stainless sky, larks exulting above, a warm sun already up and white hoar-frost underfoot, and find her vanished, the gardener already out in pursuit, the refugees barricaded in for fear of her being at large. Cows find it hard to hide, and I would generally find her at her old dairy-yard, knee-deep in valuable rationed cowfeed, gorging herself to the horns. I would fling a rope over her dear silly head and she would trot home by my side, more agile than I who stumbled along in huge rubber boots as unsuitable for a walk as were my nightcap and greasy face, so that I dreaded being seen by some early-rising acquaintance. The Princess, having no boots, once off the rope would evade me again.

Bognor   *4 May*

Darling John Julius, what shall I do when the goats arrive, which they will do this coming week? Mr Simon Marks of Marks & Spencer found them for me at last – a pedigree one costing 25 guineas which he is giving me, and a good one costing £6 which I am buying. I didn't dare take a peep into the gift-goat's mouth, so didn't ask if they were horned or unhorned. All the whey and buttermilk go to the pigs which have cost me £9.10.0 and which I shall sell again in three months for (I hope) about £40. The goats I shall keep and the Joneses can live on their milk and butter during the winter. The pedigree one can have a kid next spring. The chickens will be eaten when they stop laying. It seems to me that if one doesn't pay labour and doesn't get swine-fever, foot-and-mouth or white diarrhoea, if one scrounges and gets scraps, one is bound to live like an emperor and make a profit.

The evacuees never leave the lodge. I see their dough-coloured faces glued to the windows. I suppose it's the livestock that scares the parents.

I write so seldom because my time is filled. A goat arrived.
Conrad and I went to the station to meet it. Emaciated and
terrified it was, with a gnawed cord about its poor throat. We
lifted it into the car. All our stock travel like the gentry in a
limousine. When I got it out at the stables it gave a sudden
spasmodic dash, backed by supergoatian strength, freed
itself from my nervous grasp and ran like a satanic symbol
across the garden, over the barricades and into the barbed
wire of the defences. I (with the menace of mines in my
mind) pursued it into the wire and rescued it whole but with
its udder lacerated and bleeding. I sent at once for the vet,
who pronounced it only superficial, but agreed that milking
was impossible. He produced a tiny hollow bodkin which
he proceeded to put into the minute orifice through which
the milk is squeezed, and let the liquid flow through it into a
jug. He told me that I must do the same for a few days,
which order paralysed me with fear of bungling the
operation. However I succeeded pretty well. It's better now
and the syringe is put away, but it's still a job that needs a lot
of patience and is not really worth the time that Jones and
I give to it. He has to hold her head and because it's so cold
I still wear the fur jacket, and either she thinks I'm a
billy-goat or she just hates me anyway, but she is always
trying to give me a vicious bite over her shoulder. The
ribald soldiers leaning on the gate roar with laughter when
the cloven hooves leap and upset me and the milk. The milk
is delicious, unrecognisable from the best cow's milk, and
it's dreadful for the Joneses and the evacuees to have to
admit that it's good, and admit it they have to, for fear I
shall give them two separate glasses of each kind and
challenge them to say which is 'musty,' which is what they
want it to be. The Joneses have been awfully clever in saying
that it's only when it's cooked that it's musty, but I'll fool
them yet.

The Pig Family Hutchinson is in splendid fatness and should make me a nice profit and the country some fine bacon. I spend a lot of time asphyxiated by the smell and bent double inside the sty shovelling out their dung, and a lot more time boiling up the swill, which makes my mouth water. The hens are Wadey's pride and joy. One (our favourite, Sussex by name) has gone broody, which means that a mother's instinct for children quite overcomes a bird and as she no sooner lays an egg than we greedies grab it, she gets to a stage of sitting on nothing, hoping to hatch out imaginary eggs and laying none. The thing to do then is to buy her thirteen fertile eggs and let her hatch them out. I did this, and in three weeks hope to have a covey of fluffy yellow chicks.

The success of all successes is the old Princess. She has settled down, crops the buttercups and stands quietly to be milked, tied slackly to the garden gate. She gives me between four and five gallons a day, which makes good durable hard cheese that really will help the country's food in a minute way. I tasted the first one yesterday, made in early April, and I do not think it could have been better or more professional. If all goes well I shall write to the papers and do a broadcast at the end of the season demonstrating what can be done with one acre and a bit of hard work by hundreds of old maids and little families who have got £50 for the initial outlay. But the English are set in their ways, and if they haven't done a thing before they don't fancy it now. They will do anything dangerous. They'll fire-fight and become men and women of warlike action, but gentle agricultural arts have no glamour unless one is born and bred to it. To me it is enthralling. The rotation is fascinating, drawing life out of the rich earth, and that life returning its wealth to the soil by its manure, and the dovetailing of things. The pigs make the field produce more grass, the cow gives more milk in consequence and therefore more whey, which the pigs lap up,

and they fatten and manure the field again. You couldn't call me a drone or a lily of the field that toils not, neither spins. I wish I *knew* more.

For all this activity and happiness (yes, real happiness) in absorption and obsession for the good brown earth, Conrad was to be thanked. He never failed me through this glorious summer, though his own work was hard enough and his Home Guard duties disturbed his nights. Only one night a week he spent at Bognor, and with it two days of labour. In the evening we would eat our *recherché* meal over the fire in the early spring, with a bottle of Algerian wine, Bognor lobsters and vegetables from the cabbage-patch. He would read Trollope or Jane Austen aloud, while I sewed the cheeses into their muslin binders. As summer waxed we would eat outside to the sound of the waves on the beach, unapproachable now, on the other side of the barbed wire and concrete blocks through which the tamarisk forced its feathery pink.

In the first days of April I had seen in a friend's courtyard the ideal small trailer and was told that it belonged to Gerry Koch, who to our sorrow was a prisoner of war. I felt certain that he would want me to use it, so I promptly appropriated the treasure. In the trailer three times a week I would pack ash-cans and make a round of houses, hotels and camps, leaving an empty can in exchange for one brimful of beautiful swill. A friendly baker would give me loaves of stale bread. With these I could keep more hens than the rations for twelve only (issued by law to domestic poultry-keepers) would allow.

In June when haymaking was before us we attached to the little trailer two great chintz (improvised indeed!) horizontal sails (Chinese paravanes they were called) for loading. Off we would motor to the paddocks, tennis-courts and odd patches where hay cut by the owners would be given to us gratefully for the riddance. This way, working until 11.30 p.m. in a Lapland light, we built a neat little stack, big enough for the cow's winter feed. I would

stand on the rising heap while Conrad fed me with swathes. Over all we put a scrounged waterproof sheet and, exultantly tired, ate our Swedish supper at midnight. Conrad wrote in June:

> Going to bed dead-beat. I think being with you at Bognor in hot June weather is as near Paradise as I shall be allowed to come. One has no right to expect Paradise in this vale of sweat and grunts and bearing fardels. Mrs James came in as if it was a tragedy and said: 'I don't know what to give you for dinner. I've only got sausages and boiled beef.' To which I might answer: 'I've also got three-quarters of a ton of cheese, thirty dozen pickled eggs, three dozen newlaid ones, twenty gallons of fresh milk, potatoes, onions, salad and cabbage *ad lib.*'
>
> Christopher Hollis and I hold the watch tonight. My offer to resign my rifle to a younger man is refused, and my offer to resign my Corporal's stripe is also refused. I must be on my guard against ambition; by that sin fell the angels. Have you heard that Lord Hardwicke met his wife leading her cow? He had a squirt in his hand so in a waggish mood he discharged it full in the cow's face. The cow whipped round, knocking Lady Hardwicke arse over tip, and disappeared at a gallop. Now it won't let Lady H milk it any more and its whole temper is altered. Her Ladyship is in a rage with her husband, not unnaturally.

I wrote to John Julius:

> I'm so much happier here at Bognor. I must have been more acutely unhappy at the Dorchester than I realised. The roses are on the verge of blooming, the irises and poppies in flower; buttercups and daisies mask the green fields; the Spitfires and Hurricanes whizz by in the high empyrean, a misty silver formation that from the garden does not look hell-bent.

Bognor after lunch

The pigs
(The scaffolding behind the trees was meant to keep out German tanks)

The bees

Wadey feeds the hens

The Khaki Campbells by my side are preening themselves and making Donald Duck noises. They have no water to swim in, just a basin in which to submerge their heads. It is out of farm fashion to give ducks swimming-space, and yet they have to keep those awful feet. It seems dreadfully cruel, like taking us off the snows but leaving our skis on. It's the first summer day, the first without frost at night. Jones has brought the hammock out, and Conrad and I will rock in it this afternoon and look at the roses bursting hurriedly into bloom and watch the bees making up for lost time. I have two hives now. Did I tell you of acting as assistant to the bee-fancier at Bognor, Colonel Watson, when he came to open and examine my colonies? I had a veil over my face and elastic bands round my wrists, but I forgot my trouser-legs like chimneys. I thought I felt lots of bees crawling up them and attributed the sensation to my imagination, well-known for its activity where horror is concerned. I didn't dare complain to the old Colonel, so I carried on until I was stung in the thigh. I didn't even mind that, but it made it clear that imagination was not all the trouble. So calmly and slowly (for one must do nothing spasmodic or hurried where bees are concerned) I took off my trousers and stood exposed in ridiculous pants, pink as flesh. Looking, I found the trousers lined with bees. It was a Charlie Chaplin scene.

Conrad wrote in early July:

Everything I do with you is always amusing, always just the things I like best, like feeding pigs, paper-hanging, reading about jealousy, picking nettles, making cheese, fetching swill and dabbling about in hogwash.

We came through Southampton, which is terribly knocked about. There was an airman in my carriage who told me that

he had had five homes destroyed in Portsmouth and all his furniture lost each time. Eleven near-relations had been killed. His wife and two children were evacuated to Petersfield, but a land-mine hit the house. As 'she's taken nervous' she went back to Portsmouth. The next time Jerry came he (the husband on leave) sat under the kitchen table with his wife and two children and she was delivered under the table. She was in labour one-and-a-half hours, no doctor and the house all fallen about their ears. The baby is alive and 'a nice little chap.' The man had had eight days' leave.

Do you remember to ted the hay?

I wrote to John Julius:

Bognor   *16 July*

I'm very very fond of you and today it seems a possibility that I may see you before I dared to hope. The Ministry of Information has become well-nigh impossible. It has no powers at all and all the blame. Papa, while thinking it wrong to resign on discontent or pride alone, is far from happy with his position. Today in the papers are rumours of the changes (1) Papa to be Postmaster-General, (2) Brendan to succeed Papa, (3) Papa to be given a post abroad. The first two are absolutely groundless. Papa couldn't even be offered the Postmaster-Generalship; it would be *infra dig*. But the third report has some foundations and it might mean adventure and travel, and even seeing my darling son again. I saw you last in a dim station a hundred years ago.

Meanwhile I try not to think about it, but keep my mind rustic and turn my hay until 11 p.m. Incidentally my hay has no fellows. Last night Conrad and I stayed in the fields until 11.30 and in the almost-dark tried to get the six pigs from the pen to the sty. Three we styed, three we let evade us. Once out these fat little white congested indolences become

energetic liberated young wild boar, and O the hunting and stalking, the struggling and sweating! It ended (just before I passed out) by my grabbing them one by one by the back legs and wheel-barrowing them to the sty, to the accompaniment of such blood-curdling yells and shrieks that I felt all Sussex must wake to the din and brand me an animal-torturer. The Princess has paid a visit to her bull bridegroom. I took her to the tryst. I was less embarrassed than I should have been; bold as brass I was. She was a reluctant bride (her eighth wedding) and bored with the whole performance. It took place, me at the other end of her halter, before most of the licentious Canadian soldiery, cracking their ribs with laughter. All over very quickly, and I led her away with disdain for their ribaldry. We shall hope for a calf next March. Meanwhile if I am transported to another continent, who will tend my Princess? Where are my Moths and Mustardseeds, Cobwebs and fairy monsieurs all? Who will stroke her ears and burnish her silken flanks and talk to her in her own voice (moovoice) as I do?

Aunt Marjorie and Caroline have been staying. It was such a treat. In the war one meets so seldom and Marjorie is such fun. She looks most peculiar, emaciatedly thin, with hair that is neither white nor brown nor pink but a weaving of all three, withal looking very old and suddenly baby-young (no, monkey-young). Caroline was a dream of physical beauty, long classic legs, brief modern pants, Garibaldi shirt, her beautiful sulky yet smiling face very small in a Zulu shock of hair. I am so used to my own appalling appearance, masked with dung and dressed in drab, that these beautiful creatures from their worlds of youth and age left me in middle-aged wonderment.

Spirits exult lately. The Russian fight, the waning of German confidence, the respite of bolts from our blue, the vigour of our bolts from their day-and-night blue. These things have buoyed us considerably, but the longest day is

past and the dread of winter is on your poor mother for one. Still who knows that it may *not* be spent here, and who knows that I may not see my dearest dearest child, if only *en passant*? Keep well, keep good, keep loving, keep truthful, keep brave, keep laughing.

I remember the night in July, me at my most bucolic and contented, when Duff arrived with news so dire that he found difficulty in delivering himself of the whole trust. As usual I found myself less shattered than I might have been. The news that we were to start as soon as possible for Singapore was very dread. This flourishing green isle in the wide sea of misery was to be submerged. The slogans had persuaded me that I was digging and milking, churning and reaping for victory, and that it all 'depended on me.' Now I was asked to take my cowardice into the element that most I feared – the cruel sky. I had been ridiculously happy with the farm. Nature's beauty had ceased to jar upon me, as it had done for two years. Now this content must have a stop. Alternatives arm one. Imagine staying behind. Waiting for news, hearing of the crash or the imprisonment and not being part of it. Then I had Duff's exuberance to protect, at first a little dimmed by causing me qualms and, those dealt with, his relieved spirit would soar and exult, for at last he would be delivered from a long pain. There was very little time, two weeks perhaps, to pack up for the adventure. Conrad would be sad, and I would be the cause.

In Winston Churchill's story of the war he writes:

Nevertheless the confidence which we felt about Home Defence did not extend to the Far East should Japan make war upon us. These anxieties also disturbed Sir John Dill. I retained the impression that Singapore had priority in his mind over Cairo. This was indeed a tragic issue, like having to choose whether your son or your daughter should be killed. For my part I did not believe that anything that might

88

happen in Malaya could amount to a fifth part of the loss of Egypt, the Suez Canal, and the Middle East. I would not tolerate the idea of abandoning the struggle for Egypt, and was resigned to pay whatever forfeits were exacted in Malaya. This view also was shared by my colleagues.

I felt the need for repeating in the Far East the institution of a Minister of State, who, in the closest touch with the War Cabinet, would relieve the Commanders-in-Chief and local Governors of some of their burdens and help them to solve the grave political problems which gathered swiftly. In Mr Duff Cooper, then Minister of Information, I had a friend and colleague who from his central point of view knew the whole scene. His firmness of character which had led him to resign his office as First Lord of the Admiralty after the Munich Agreement in 1938, his personal gifts of speech and writing, his military record as an officer in the Grenadier Guards during the 1914–18 war, combined to give him the highest qualifications. On July 21 he was appointed Chancellor of the Duchy of Lancaster, and succeeded as Minister of Information by Mr Brendan Bracken.

A tropical trousseau must be bought. I had lost my eye for and interest in clothes. Molyneux would deal with this deficiency. John Julius again was a thought to heal, but then I scarcely expected to get across the Atlantic, let alone across America, across the wide Pacific and to land in Singapore. What else, I remember wondering, had Time got up his horrid conjuror's sleeve (if we lived) for Duff and for me?

Conrad wrote on 20 July:

I've seen it in the papers. I never expected anything else once you'd told me. Perhaps you are not off in a great hurry? But that's only drawing out the horror, and I've spent the day numbed and aware that something dreadful is about to

happen. One has no right to expect to be happy in these times, and on the whole we have got through the first two years better than expected, except for the American bit.

My last and sixteenth visit this summer to Bognor will be on Wednesday, and they have been the happiest days of my life.

4

Fiery Portal of the East

'Tremblingly obey,' wrote the old Buddha Empress of China in her edicts. I felt I was always obeying love, duty or conscience, and invariably I trembled as I kissed the rod. We travelled light (my heart alone was heavy) from some airfield in the West of England. I had flown once before on a so-called joy-ride for half an hour in Texas, not out of sight of the runway. The popping corks and holiday joviality of the millionaire hosts had not been an appetiser for future cloud-borne jaunts. I had made a silent oath never again, unless impelled by necessity, to brave the skies. Necessity was here, and here were we, accompanied by Martin Russell, Conrad's young nephew, who had been seconded from the army to act as Duff's secretary at the Ministry of Information. Here also were Conrad and Katharine Asquith to see the last of us. Martin too travelled light, but instead of a heart he carried a capacious saratoga of secret papers. I hoped to be sustained by a bottle of blue pills that Vincent Sheean had given me against fear. I don't remember their helping. We flew south over the Atlantic's eastern coast and in a few hours were at Lisbon in blistering heat, with spirits mounting in thankfulness for recovered earth and the excitement of the unknown. The Ambassador, Sir Ronald Campbell, received us, and the flying-boat was said to be ship-shape, with deck cleared for action next morning.

I reported to Conrad:

> *British Embassy, Lisbon*   *7 August 1941*
>
>   Imagine the anticlimax! We motored half an hour to the Tagus seaplane-port, got weighed, got passed, produced vaccination scars and certificates, swallowed our soothing

pills, got our feet on the scaffold and were suddenly informed that the fourth engine was 'missing' and that the trip was to be postponed for twenty-four hours. My heart sank. I was well teed up and still leaning on the confidence acquired yesterday, and the alternative of another hot day at the Embassy, unwanted and *désoeuvrée*, yawned hideously. It was too hot to sightsee. I had thought Lisbon would be densely crowded with refugees, spies, journalists, the disinherited, the dispossessed, the neutrals, the Jews, the opportunists. I thought the streets would be jammed and the bars bursting and buzzing, but there was no one much about. We felt, as we were so often to feel waiting for aeroplanes, a weight upon the Embassy, not that the Ambassador was overworked. He sauntered round and was kind, but I don't suppose he liked us much. Martin had funny ways that reminded me of my own, so that I hesitated to check him, i.e. picking a piece of long-cold bacon out of the breakfast sideboard dish, holding it high above his upturned face and slowly absorbing it by mouth while talking to the Ambassador. It reminded me of catching Duff's reproving eye as I sucked through my asparagus for the third time while talking to Sir William Tyrrell at a Paris Embassy dinner.

Three heavy days we waited for the plane and at last we took off from the Tagus in a hot hurricane. In seven hours the unpleasant miracle landed us at the Azores – Horta green with rainfall and unsurprising. Then off again for twelve hours to Bermuda. I was new to flying and pretty miserable, strapped in as for the hot-squat, time out of joint, one's head too chaotic to set it right. Jimmy Sheean's azure scarab anti-fear pills perhaps helped, but not to read Virginia Woolf. Duff was better suited with *War and Peace*; it irritated me to see him crying so happily as he read.

When we arrived at the unvexed Bermoothes, an amusing Colonial Secretary took us for a walk in the very empty Sunday dawn streets, not only no motors (by order) but no buggies about.

Martin had not risked leaving the hush-hush suitcase, weighing two ton, with the neutral air-officials, so it had to come along on the tramp, a cruel burden on the poor boy's arm, sometimes carried like a baby (the handle being groggy). I did not think it a particularly attractive island, like Nassau, but then presumably we did not see the enchanted parts – no green shades for green thoughts, no prancing negroes in white boots and crude-coloured muslins gossiping in Parliament Square, which is how I remember my Bahamas.

Up again into the blue after two hours' respite, during which all the mail was opened and censored. It wasn't long before the flat shore of Long Island appeared with its symmetrical blocks of buildings, car-parks, smart properties, each with its green swimming-pool, and then in another few minutes we make a superb landing.

Our progress was detailed for Conrad:

> There was a sort of grandstand with thousands of people packed in tiers, and in the complete density of this crowd I saw the most good-looking little grinning face of John Julius, flanked by Kaetchen, the foster-parents Paley and the Hofmannsthals. We were a long time with doctors, customs-officials etc. and another hour with photographers and movie-men. Then at last I got my dear child in my arms and felt most happy. He really is lovely looking, not grown too much or with a cracked voice, not nasal or spotty or downy-chinned, in fact not wearing spats and married, as I had feared to meet him next when I waved him goodbye at blacked-out Victoria two years (no, one-and-a-bit) ago, but slim and straight and fair as an Angle or Angel. We were again hours in a soundproof room while Duff made newsreel talkies without any effort. The heat was grim and we had to listen respectfully to Queen Elizabeth broadcasting from England, not one scrambled word of which I could hear. At last it was all through and we whizzed off to the Paley home to find Nanny crying with excitement.

In my bedroom I found fruit on a daintily laid tray, and in the cupboard aspirin, witch-hazel, peroxide, a bottle of 'Soporific' bath-powder, one of 'Soporific Rub' and another labelled 'Soporific Nightcap,' some earplugs and an eye-bandage. They are determined to get me to sleep. There are radio sets, televisions and, thank God, plenty of pianos, so although John Julius clearly has no incentive to read a book, he plays for pleasure with a sensitive touch and much facility.

John Julius's treat was a day in Washington:

The news of the Atlantic Meeting had just broken and Max Beaverbrook was due to arrive. We were told we could lunch alone as Duff and the Ambassador were attending a public feast, or a party could be fixed for us. We opted for freedom and a drug-store lunch, shook Embassy dust off our feet, and visited the Lincoln Memorial. I read the famous words on the wall and was as usual deeply impressed by the marble man in trousers who stares out of his shrine at the Capitol and far horizons. From there we went to the Federal Bureau of Investigation, where Mr Hoover's G-men are trained. I'd done it before and knew it would go well with John Julius. He shot at targets shaped like men with tommy-gun and tracer bullets. We both had our finger-prints permanently filed in the Department of Non-Criminals. We read letters dictated to pathetic parents of kidnapped children, and altogether had a wonderful time. We ate an expensive lunch with a mint julep and had an encouraging talk with the 100% American waiter about how Lindbergh ought to be in jail or shot for being pro-German. We looked at the White House and returned on appointment to the Embassy. The turmoil there was most amusing. The arrival of Max always creates pandemonium and fear of consequences. The camera-boys and movietone men were in their legion. Charles Peake looked distraught. I saw Max for a flash in the

passage. He said, as he kissed me, 'I've come over to see you.' I replied 'I knew you would,' and that was all there was to it. Lord Halifax was the only one who seemed detached and calm. He has an attractive little dachshund (typically enough) whose vice is to pull pyjamas from under pillows and bring them to the hall.

We leave New York tomorrow and our China Clipper takes off 26 August from San Francisco. There our Eastern expert joins us. I met him in Washington and was prepossessed. His name is Tony Keswick, about thirty-six years old, and married to a Lindley girl. He is the man Duff most wanted to poach.

Duff went back to Washington and saw the President. He said he was like a child about the Atlantic Meeting. He had so loved the secrecy and giving the police and the press the slip, and sailing through darkness in a strange ship, while his own ship steamed home in a blaze to decoy and confuse. I saw Henry Bernstein, *très bien portant* and obviously having a swell time in a smart apartment, furnished with his own works of art. He is sound as an English bell, and a very good example to the English refugees who bore one's pants off with explanations of why they are over here, how longing they are to be back, and the rest of it. One is at a loss for an answer. Eve Curie too is here. She has been deprived of French nationality, and therefore cannot go to Lisbon, so can't lecture, not having enough straw for her bricks. Considering we offered every Frog dual nationality, I think we might accord a prominent Free Frenchwoman a British pass. Emerald I did not see again, as she went to Atlantic City with Thomas Beecham. It's Blackpool and she thinks it's Cannes.

Claire Luce, a great beauty, alarmingly intelligent and not universally loved, gave me only two bits of information about the Pacific crossing and our mission: (1) that this was the typhoon season, (2) that all women had been evacuated from

Singapore. I feel far, far away and yet I'm not half way to my goal.

San Francisco
    Duff had to make a speech at a big men's lunch, so I walked for two and a half hours through Chinatown, enjoying my liberty and buying as usual a large Chinese straw hat. I tried to buy some airmail stationery, but they only had it in sheets two yards long and quite narrow. A nice old couple stopped me in the street and asked me the way. I told them that I was straight from London, whereat they both seized my hands and wrung them until they hurt, saying 'Mighty pleased to shake your hand. Mighty pleased indeed.'

All the Pan-American schedules had the same snakes-and-ladders hazard of routing in their infancy as today in maturity, so back to Los Angeles we flew and then disembarked on to a rollicking raft (an artificial island) to refill, and there on the raft was my darling Iris Tree and her giant son. She, and only she, had wangled her way, grinning and well-dressed as Lord Fauntleroy. The Pacific lay ahead and those left behind said: 'Good luck.' It used to be said to people bound for the front line. It made my hair stand erect as I climbed the scaffold steps into the China Clipper.

    'The sky's the *limit*.' Tomorrow we should be at Honolulu. I'll write steadily from now on. It helps me in the plane to feel in touch with you. Distance is a great obliterator, as great as Time unless one watches it.

Next day
    At five I woke to a scarlet glow of sunrise and the steward saying we should land in an hour. This was much earlier than I had hoped, and there was a general scramble of dressing behind curtains, legs and arms shooting out of tents,

queueings for the lu and the rest of it. There was Hawaii beneath us, looking as every place does from the sky. Soon we were on the water and landing on to a grove of hibiscus and palms and two honey-coloured hula-girls giving us garlands and tumblers of pineapple-juice. Very lovely, very theatrical. They wore green reed-skirts with dew upon them, and their long hair pinned with blossom. Of course the disillusion came. We were longer at the Customs than their engagement lasted, so we saw them walking away, hatted and shod, just half-caste Broadway girls. A long drive across the island, through furiously active defence-preparations (much building also for Service residents), then through the completely American town of Honolulu to Waikiki beach, some ten minutes out, where our gigantic pink hotel is situated.

28 August

Today I went surf-riding at 8 a.m. with Tony Keswick. What an experience! A beach boy lays you on your stomach on a surf-board, separates your legs and takes his own kneeling position in your fork. He tucks your legs tightly along his calves and proceeds to paddle you out to the birthplace of the breakers. He then dismounts and shoos you off on the back of a wave. One is supposed to stand up, but I did not even attempt it. It is nice – rather – when it works, which is seldom, or when the boy comes along riding you, as he might a dolphin through the foam.

Afternoon succeeded afternoon in forcible feeding of lotus. Claire Luce arrived with heavy news of delay through tintinnabu-lating tee-hee laughter. It was off, it was on. Telegrams buzzed to the State Department from Mr Peck, our fellow-flier and the United States Minister to Thailand. We were marooned and cross. Rows increased. I remember a horrid one with a General who told me that he hoped for America's sake we should fight for another

fifteen years. 'Tough on you, but the best that can happen to you. You're all so soft you don't deserve any better.' Soft! The grey embarrassment of the bystanders was my passive revenge.

Duff was morose. Tony Keswick did what he could palliatively. Martin gave up coming out of his room. Then, at outrageously long last, we were boarding the Clipper with Claire Luce, who rather enjoyed my squirms and encouraged them by saying that the trip was fated. She could hear the engines missing, she said, and followed her pearly-voiced words with her little tsee-tsee-tsee silvery laugh. She was beautifully dressed, to my covetousness, in sand-coloured slacks, jacket and close turban to match. At night she added gold ornaments and a correct bag. Myself I saw as someone at the end of a bank holiday, carrying a multitude of things won at the fair, a hat, a Japanese umbrella, some flowers. Tony Keswick had all the wild and fearful Atlantic, that was bearing his wife and pretty chickens, in his anxious eyes and mien. Duff had finished *War and Peace* and was back at Balzac. Mr and Mrs Peck clamoured for bridge and got it. Martin looked sick and was for ever writing cabalistic signs – chess or algebra problems, or a treatise headed 'Political Warfare.' He was also the only passenger who needed exercise on the aeroplane. It was as though you walked a mile in a small Pullman car. He found difficulty in getting comfortable in his seat, turning round and round in it like a dog in an inconvenient basket.

I learned that to question the staff was useless; answers bore no relation to truth. Arrivals and departures came on this strange journey always as a surprise. To see an island ten thousand feet below, inchoate as an oyster, made me want to cry some word of triumphant relief – Thalassa's opposite.

We first folded our wings at Midway, not the Robinson Crusoe island I had hoped for with three coconut-palms and some spoor, but flat, sprawling and infernally hot, made up of dredgers and oil-tanks. Wake, the next stage, was the same, a blinding coral beach with just-good-enough little grass hotels. The Good Men and Women Fridays marooned there had not only lost all touch

with the outer world but also any interest in it, and concentrated on birds, crabs and cactus-pollination. The passengers would lie in the shallow waters with their heads out, motionless like so many hippopotami; above them screeched the goons circling perpetually night and day. Pan American had disturbed their rest, changed their habits, created suspicion, and they dared not land. On the other hand I remember very adjusted little sitting rats in the brush that I explored, tame with no offence in them. In the brush also I found an escort. He wore the Pan American cap and spectacles. He came from Guam, he said, in faultless school-acquired English. (He told me *en passant* that Magellan had never circumnavigated the globe. He had died in Guam and only his ship made full circle.) My guide's ambition was to be a chartered accountant, his interests were art and politics. He loved England which had produced Shakespeare, author of *The Tragedy of Hamlet, Prince of Denmark*.

Guam came next, infinitely more sophisticated and mountainous with little Bovril-coloured men and huge horned cattle, typhoon-battered Catholic churches with ever-open doors through which shone the candles of the Mass. Manila, the penultimate landing, was complete sophistication, air-conditioned rooms, a President to call upon, but ladies still wore a national dress, Spanish in origin, with a sweeping frilled train. The high transparent and bespangled stick-up sleeves are made of pineapple-fibre. The dyes are bright, the effect dragon-fly. I bought one but it burnt, with so much else, on the quays of falling Singapore. Natives trot around in minute scarlet hansom cabs (driver inside) as delicate as fuchsias and as springy. They carry two carriage oil-lamps and are drawn by sleek lively little ponies.

We left at the usual 4 a.m. next day, boarded our own good Anzac Clipper and spent the most hideous day of the trip. The sky was grim and, for reasons and currents best known to the skipper, we flew for twelve hours one hundred feet above sea-level. This means no air at all, bumps, alarming squalls and blind flying through rainstorms. We lay about like so many living sardines in

a tin on a stove – all dignity, all shame lost, sweating, stinking, writhing, not speaking, not eating, obnoxious to each other and to ourselves. Borneo passed practically unnoticed. It ended, and there was Singapore at our feet, with silver bomber Buffalo planes escorting us in, Commander-in-Chief Brooke-Popham on the jetty and the whole set-up entirely to my liking – liveries of ostentatious gold and white and scarlet on Malay and Indian servants, A.D.C.s, movie-men, gaping coolies, old Indian men with white beards and grubby ordinary European shirts hanging loose, as often as not their turban in hand, allowing their shower of straggly grey hair to fall to their waists. Cantonese men and women in black trousers and gleaming clean white jackets of the chic-est cut, pomaded black hair set with gold ornaments. Rickshaws and their runners looking like clockwork toys.

We drove through this enchanting town, as full of character and colour as one could desire, sometimes like a print in Hickey's diary, sometimes like old Monte Carlo (for that is its chief date, I think – 1860), sometimes like a vision of Peking slums with a population's washing hanging flag-like on rods out of windows, children being bathed in the street, cunning workmen making shoes or gongs or earrings, sometimes like England for a flash with a cathedral and a spire.

Less English were God's acres being mown by the fingers and thumbs of natives advancing on all fours in a serried row and plucking the growing grass-blades. It was the relief of it not looking like Cleveland, Ohio, that pleased me so much.

Government House is as cool as a fishnet and, although it is the size of Welbeck, we can all see and hear each other, which comes of having no doors or windows. My bed stands, mosquito-curtained, in the middle of a room thirty by thirty. For all that I was woken in the night by a downpour of rain on the face, driven in from the Western Approaches, delicious and cooling. It's hot, but not as hot as the halts on our journey.

Sir Shenton and Lady Thomas were kind as could be, and happy in the job, no complaints, anxious to help, discouraging though about getting a house for our Mission. Not a hope – too many Generals, Admirals, Australians in Singapore, no building being done. 'Not an earthly!' But they got me a little Cantonese amah with hands as delicate as filigree, as much gold in her teeth as in her hair, and four words of English: 'Chancellor' (Duff), 'barff' and 'can do.' Officials for dinner, and a lot to learn. Conversation too confident – 'They won't come here,' 'We'll give them a warm reception' – every platitude to be found untrue.

Letters from Conrad greeted my arrival. They must have come *via* Africa.

Mells   *13 August*

It's only a week ago that I stood on the control tower like Dido with a willow in my hand and waved you goodbye as you took the air. There are not words to tell you of the blank in my heart. We had quiet guard. I wore my new inch-thick serge battledress, long winter-drawers, two pairs socks, leggings, sleeved cardigan, kept on my fleece-lined greatcoat, got a good fire going in the small windowless hut, snuggled up close to Les for warmth's sake, but couldn't keep out the cold. I thought of you naked and sweating on your Portuguese bed. This is August in England and cruel it can be.

I'm reading the *History of Greece* by Robertson and am intensely interested in it. The Greeks had trial by jury and there was no judge. The jury settled the sentence too. Unlike us the number on a jury was 201, 401 or 6000. No other numbers were allowed. Then I read about Prodicus, who gave a course of lectures on the whole of wisdom. The course cost two guineas. For those desiring something less ambitious he had a course (also taking the whole of wisdom) which cost tenpence. I shall come to Alexander the Great soon, and then for some odd reason the history of Greece ends, or isn't worth bothering about.

This morning I went to the Chitton workhouse to see old Teddie, my tenant, pensioner and ex-gardener, and the one that only eats duck's eggs from running water. The workhouse master had rung me up to say that old Teddie was very ill and when his mind wandered 'a babbled o' Mr Russell.' The screens were drawn round the bed – heralds of death as I think – and when I said to the nurse: 'I'll only stay a minute,' she said that I could stay as long as I liked. I thought that this meant nothing matters now. It wasn't painful. He talked all the time of crops and gardens. It is cheering to see the care with which the old and impoverished are tended in England – charming nurse, cleanliness, comforts and attention, even spoiling in Teddie's case, as everyone loves him. I shouldn't mind dying in the workhouse. It didn't seem much different from my costly nursing home.

Teddie died this morning. His life bears out your contention about the hooch. He was a perpetual drunkard for sixty years and then died at seventy-six because he would scratch his face with his dirty hands. The nurses worried him not to, but he turned a deaf ear to their counsels and gave himself blood-poisoning.

The carter said several times, 'He was a witty man.' He uses 'witty' to mean 'able,' i.e. having wits etc. I never heard it so used before.

I am very much wrapt up in the *History of Greece* and sometimes I have to look on to see what is going to happen. I'm reading about Lysander now (of Hector and Lysander). I daresay I thought him mythical, but he wasn't and he was a Spartan admiral who won the battle of Aegospotomi.

When Farmer Pony of Eggford (always so called to distinguish him from Farmer Pony of Chantry) cut his wheat

he found the missing German. I mean the one who was missing from the bomber that I saw shot down. He was food for worms when he was found, as you can well imagine. I always thought that he was in the wheat and I am so thankful he was not in mine.

I am reading a new life of Trelawny. When Leigh Hunt arrived at Leghorn to stay with the Shelleys they got off the steamer with six small and dirty little Hunts and a *goat*, also a seventh child *en ventre de sa mère* and born on landing. Byron's bulldog flew at the goat and bit off one of its ears. And when Byron moved about Italy he took 'pet geese' with him. There were more eccentric people then, but few as eccentric as Trelawny.

To Bath, where I saw Mr Miller, my dentist, who did not fail to show me the tiepin given him by the Duke of Connaught and the coloured photograph of the orchids sent him by Queen Mary. I thought it (the orchids) an unusual present from a queen to a dentist.

Two adjoining houses were found for us, standing in green gardens three miles from the town's centre. They belonged to the Government, so why the gloomy predictions? Government House produced every conceivable amenity from another hill G.H. We could all pack in. Tony Keswick, Martin and ourselves in one; our gallant Military Attaché Robertson and Alex Newboult of the Colonial Office would fill the other house, that was also to be offices. Della and Denis Allen from the Foreign Office were due from Chungking to be part of our set-up. Quantities of servants lived in the compound with wives, concubines and children. Their reason for living seemed to be for our comfort and their smiles never faded until the last goodbyes.

We were delighted with everything, including my own pretty improvements. You came in through a Florentine arcaded

approach to an open hall with wide brick stairs that led to the only other floor. On the ground there was a long large living-room with pillared loggia on which I had put Mrs Hawksbee rattan chairs and tables for *pahits* and *stengahs*. This room had a spacious alcove which acted as dining-room for eight or ten people, also a palatial Hollywood bed and bathroom, which was given to Tony Keswick. The living-room was to be Duff's office, impressive with green lines and scrambling telephones. Upstairs was just such another long drawing-room, a large bedroom for us and a single room for Martin Russell.

Pains taken had repaid me and the house was delightful. White gardenias picked long-stalked in our own garden, a lot of clean white rugs and Oriental jars, white cushions, no glass windows or curtains, a few noble lanterns hung from the ceiling, white and painted to my order by a street-side artist with appropriate characters in red. I could not tell if they had painted the appropriate, or whether I was advertising trusses or aphrodisiacs or my own or Duff's price. White china windmills all over the ceiling did not improve the appearance, but they circulated welcome air.

A midge in the ointment was Duff's outlook. He did not really know what he was doing in Singapore. No one complained, or if they did they strangled the complaint when change loomed up. Confidence and a relaxing climate had lulled the administrators into an euphoric coma. True it had been the same in America when Japan was talked of, not least in Pearl Harbour, but at Pearl Harbour there was feverish activity. In Singapore one might have been behind the Sleeping Beauty's briar roses.

I knew I must beware of wishfully thinking all was well. There was not much for me to do; perfunctory packing of parcels; in wartime the English always turn to that activity, but there was nothing much to pack. Wandering in the Chinese streets was my delight, watching the cunning workmen carving and hammering and painting, visiting the cripples' meeting-place where they all sat resting from their labours of begging, legless and armless, with little tassels of fingers springing out of their shoulders and

suchlike. The coffin-makers' street, the models made less sinister than ours, fish-lanterns, painted candles, paper houses and shoes, roast joints and sham coins, all for pyre-burning. The native restaurant with new aromatic smells – soya? sesame? There the Chinese sit on high bar-stools, buttocks and feet gathered up on to the seat monkey-wise.

We dined one night with Mr Kao, the Chinese Consul-General, another English couple name of Scott (M.O.I.), another Chinaman, Martin, Tony and I. The meal was a *chinoiserie*, chopsticks and all. The house was a European disgrace, full of photographs of Chiang Kai-Shek and scrolls of characters, treated as Titians, not texts. 'Whose calligraphy is that, Mr Kao?' I gathered from Tony was the correct question. There was a grog-tray on the terrace bearing a hundred bottles, many of which are only seen in bars, like Crême de Violette and Crême de Cacao, besides every known spirit and aperitif. After some adventurous drinks we sat down to a table of Mr Kao's own design. It was round, and the centre of its circle (in diameter about a yard) whizzed round dumb-waiter fashion – very ingenious and well suited to Bognor. Soup first, next a very small spatchcocked sucking-pig with sly unspatched almost-human face and the crackliest of skins, eaten from the centre dish with chopsticks. The host, Mr Kao, handled an extra pair of sticks for passing delicacies to his guests. Then a fish *à la nage* in its own *bouillon*, thin shark's fins swimming in the same, followed by cabbage and mushrooms sweetly blended. Then – East compromising with West – a chicken pie very unlike ours. A delicious dish of sweet-sour something came next, and then little bags of suet containing I don't really know what – a great many eaten by each guest (Duff made a beast of himself) and we *wound up* with a nice delicate duck soup. All very good, eaten out of little Chinese bowls with sticks and all tasting, to my amateur palate, identical.

Conversation was restricted to food-subjects with occasional health-drinking. If Tony said 'You're a wonderful man, Mr Kao' in a rollicking way, Mr Kao would grin and say 'You think so, Mr Keswick? You think so?' delighted and in part believing it. Mrs Kao, a dear woman, was the fifteen-stone skeleton of the feast, having no English. She all but wept in the ladies' lu when she explained to me in pidgin how fond she was of conversation. The evening broke up in an avalanche of rare gifts – tins of green tea, four scroll-pictures of the seasons by a living though traditional artist (they will greatly ornament our house) and a book by Madame Chiang Kai-Shek. We came home laden like children from a Christmas tree. The two Chinamen trying to translate the poems on the scrolls were so reminiscent of poor Maurice. He, though, was always sure, since his were extempore, whereas they could never agree as to the meaning of the characters, let alone the translation.

Java was to be Duff's first engagement. It had been decided that I should not be taken – Hudson bombers were not suitable for women, was one excuse; joy-riding was another. I wanted to go and fought valiantly with Duff's loyal backing and the Dutch Governor's wife saying disappointment would be felt if the lady didn't come. At midnight, before the start at dawn, my battle was won.

I'm experiencing my first flight in a bomber, two-engined and a bit grim, not gadgeted like a submarine as I expected. Plenty of space for us three, and three Australian crew. We flew low enough to see the horrors of Sumatra below – a relentless jungle, alive, no doubt, with snakes and deadly animals. We wore parachutes. The harness robbed me of dignity. Straps between one's legs in a skirt are always mortifying to one's pride. What good, I thought, will a parachute do us in a sharky sea or a cobra-swamp? What

happens if, the engines stalling, one does by a miracle land, or crash in the machine through the forest, breaking one's fall in branches? One lights a fire perhaps as a signal to a saviour and as a warning to beasts not to venture. One is seen by the saviour. What then? He cannot land; there are no paths. I'm over that same jungle as I write, so I'll change the subject and get back to arrival at the Batavian airport.

'Got away with it again,' the pilots love to say to me as we bump down to earth. I wish they wouldn't. It makes each subsequent flight more alarming. I don't even like 'Happy landings' – too near the knuckle.

We drove for two hours up mountains to the Governor's Summer Palace of Sans Souci, a particularly unattractive residence, but we were shown on arrival to our own little fresh guest-house, with native bath-house consisting of an Ali Baba jar and a pannikin (much nicer than a shower). We felt independent and private and greatly exhilarated by the cold snappy air, said by most to be 'like champagne.' I forgot about India and Canada and was surprised by the official pomp, for after a reasonable interval officials arrived and said that the Governor would see us.

We sat down twelve to dine – ourselves, secretaries, aides, aides' wives and officials. Full pomp – a liveried dwarf Malay behind each chair. They serve you on their hunkers if you are sitting on a sofa or at tea, and, pressing both hands to their parts, bow from the waist in acknowledgment of an order. Guests are assembled in a horseshoe and the Governor and his wife are brought out when all is ready. The English are so dreadful, I thought, and no one ever warned me about curtseying, so when to my surprise he walked up to me, first extending a hand that I had so lately pressed, I shook it with warmth and held my full height. All the other ladies fell flat on their faces. We think no royalty exists unless it's King George. I apologised afterwards but could find no civil excuse.

Faithful Conrad had continued to write almost daily, and his letters reached me at the end of our visit.

Mells   *20 September*

Anniversary of the fall of Rome 1870, and I for one jolly well hope it will soon fall again.

I've had such a comic letter from the Milk Board. The writer called invasion 'War Disruption' in an effort at originality, and wanting to say that there is no need to be very particular about the cheese, he says: 'In this regard I suggest that an over-meticulous technique need not be visualised under the circumstances.' That's his way of making his meaning quite clear to the Somerset farmers. *Quorum pars minima sum.*

The whole day has been devoted to silage-making and I think it is going all right. The book of instructions tells one 'not to be self-conscious about trampling the silo.' Can it be at all usual for farmers to suffer from self-consciousness in kneading well on the silage?

I see the Pope has told the President's man in Rome that he is unable to 'take sides' in this war. One must find it hard not to take sides in the quarrel of Germany versus Poland, or Germany versus Czechoslovakia. Hilaire once said to me that the Papacy has always been wrong; all through history it has always taken the wrong side. When I said 'Why?' he said 'Well, what would you expect of a lot of clergymen?'

I revelled in returning safe to my quiet house, to the grinning servants, and to the cross bird that I had bought – a jade-green parakeet, fat and preened, with scarlet cheeks and nose. I would take it walks on a hibiscus branch (the Chinese take theirs in cages). It hated both me and Martin. I was glad to get back to the flowers and the golden orioles flapping about in the branches outside.

Health worsening daily – permanent headache now. Shall I try tiger-balm, the Chinese cure-all, or better shall I go to Malacca? 'I want to be alone.' Duff and his Tony and his Robbie (the Major's pet name) are off for the day and two nights by train to Kuala Lumpur. I could take two days too, but mentioning it to Duff produces an eruption. I make every thing more difficult – don't I know that I'm only here on sufferance? – I'm not to go to Chungking – I'm not to lose face everywhere by not giving official warning of my visit etc. Then I turn sulky, not surprising when you feel as sick as I do. So after twenty-four hours sweet Duff showed remorse and said I could do what I liked always – that I could go to Malacca – that he wouldn't have come without me, and by this show I was cured of my sulks, but not, alas, of the heavy fog in the head. I think that if I spend five hours in the air-conditioned train, see Malacca, sleep at the Governor's Rest House, avoid all food and drink and return next day in the same cold train, I shall mend.

En route

How will it end? Duff got off all right, asking no questions but resigned and kind. The train is dandy. It started on the wrong leg for me by the Station Master coming up and saying that the Somebody didn't like me travelling in the Number Two train, so was having his private saloon hitched on at Tamping. First blow!

3.15 p.m.

Adventure No. 1. Arrived at Tamping looking exceptionally grubby in dress that 'can't hurt,' sun-hat, bare legs and dusty dark-blue shoes instead of the Chinese-cleaned white ones. Met by an official who has shown me into a private coach for twenty with dining-table, bureau, large radio, two nice

bedrooms, shower, vast white armchairs and observation-platform. I've wandered round it like Beauty round her empty palace. It's very windowed and the Malays, Chinese, Tamils, Eurasians, paddy-workers and buffalo are staring in at this poor fish in her gilded tank.

Malacca

Next morning I hired a nice car with Malay driver (no communication possible) and after picking up enough shells to make a necklace and bracelets on the yellow sands, I started off on a seventy-mile drive to Batu Pahat ('Carved Milestone'). The country was faery. The ground is a looking-glass of water, the growing rice-fields of tender vivid green, the sweet water-buffalo pulling plough and ploughman under water and pulling also carts with long pagoda-roofs made, I think, of painted palm-leaves. We came to Mau ('Want') and crossed by ferry into a little port-town. Ten miles beyond, still in this very rural country of rice and coconut-groves and small carved wooden Malay houses, grass-roofed, stilted, each with a pompous flight of marble stairs hooked on to the front door to give grandeur, we were bowling through a bit of a village quite slowly when three Chinese children ran out. The driver, whom I was sitting next to, honked and braked for all he was worth, but nothing could save one of them and a sickening noise and bump told me that we had run it down. The Malay hated stopping, but I crashed on the brake myself and, getting out, found a green, bleeding child of three, seemingly dead, on the road and a mother baying like a dog. It was dreadful, Conrad, in one flash to be taken from happiness and plunged in such horror. The impotence too of no language. I tried the word 'doctor' but no understanding. There was none, I supposed. Then the word 'hospital' mispronounced seemed to ring a bell. The village was out by now, gabbling advice; the driver was gabbling maniac-wise, justifying the accident, I imagined, with shades of the prison-house in his heart. I

bundled the poor howling mother into the car, clinging to her broken-doll child. Quite dead it looked, with glazed slit eyes. We drove ten hideous slow miles back to Mau. All the way she bayed without tears, her open mouth filled full of gold (the mouth is the Malay Chinese's bank). The driver never drew breath trying to prove, no doubt, his blamelessness. The woman pressed the child's flat face into her flat chest. I could not persuade her by gesture to give it air, not that it mattered, as I was confident that it was dead. She kept doing such strange things to it – instinctive things – but to what purpose I could not figure out – articulating its legs sharply, thrusting her fingers into its mouth, perhaps against death's rigidity.

At last, when I felt nearly desperate, we drove up to the loveliest hospital you ever saw. Outside the town, with air and sun and gardens, roses round the door and long cool wards, a competent English doctor and two young executive Sisters. The Chinese woman had total confidence in the strange skill and gave the child gladly. She was taken away to be soothed, while the victim was rushed to the theatre. I was soothed too, given tea and Marie biscuits by the nurses, all so English. The doctor returned and said that the child was not dead and had head injuries, no more, and would in all probability recover. An officer in uniform arrived and said that he was the local bobby and took my testimony. The driver was put out of his terror but kept to be cross-examined, while I was sent off in the bobby's car with a driver without an idea of the way. The child's father arrived before I left. I felt glad that I had seen British health-schemes work so well, and the natives' confidence and lack of suspicion.

Not many weeks later we were off again, this time to Burma and India, both unbroken grounds to me. The Mission had taken shape and direction. In Sir George Sansom, Duff put all his faith and full agreement that war with Japan must come. Sir Archibald Clark Kerr flew from Chungking to confabulate, as did Sir Josiah Crosby from Bangkok. The report was worked on by Duff and his staff assiduously.

So now India and Australia remained to be probed and consulted. Of the beauty of Penang we saw what air-travel allows – the airfield – and political reasons forbade us leaving just such another field at Bangkok. We crossed jungled mountains, where for once I forgot fear and experienced an artistic ecstasy difficult to describe – almost mystical. It had to do with colour, atmosphere and strangeness. Nothing was the same as I knew it, neither sea nor land nor sky. I thought that perhaps I was dead, and how beautiful it was. Rangoon brought me to earth in every sense, a dirty beast of a port, all dredgers, oil and cranes. Still the Indians were dressed in fraise-pink which married ill with their discontented faces. There were Colonel Miller and Captain Richmond, in fact the thin end of the British wedge. We were driven through unattractive streets, dirty and modern (unpardonable combination), to the White Man's club – *Punch*, *Sphere*, tepid whisky, boiling soup, hot apple tart.

In Rangoon there is a very famous temple-pagoda called the Shwe Dagôn. It rises gold to the sky. Luncheon conversation was about it. To my surprise no one had ever been inside it. 'Footwear' was the explanation, 'You have to enter barefoot. An Englishman can't do that. People do everything there.' 'Full of lepers,' 'the stink of the place' – out rolled the excuses. I said one's feet were washable, one did much worse with one's hands, leprosy wasn't thus caught, a temple *vaut bien* a whiff. They looked exaggeratedly shocked. I've got mixed. It was tea, of course, when this conversation took place, and when it was over we drove in closed cars to have a look round. When we came to the temple door I said 'I'm going in.' There was a bit of a scene. Captain Richmond looked revolted and Pilate-ish. Duff shook his cheeks at me, but I am 'blind and deaf when I list' and in a flash I had my shoes and stockings off and was following the votaries into the great dark doorway. It was one of the most repaying sights I have ever seen. I was quite breathless with excitement. In this high dark corridor that is always ascending are congregated sleepers, vendors, priests,

water-carriers, every caste, every age, every race. Everything sold is beautiful – fantastically-made miniature white pagoda-umbrellas to offer to Buddha, bunches of ginger-flowers, lotus and jasmine, cocks and hens like Chinese ornaments, shining gold Buddhas inset with jewels. On and on you mount, the stairs are very steep, faint with the smell of exotic flowers. Burma girls smoking always their 'whacking white cheroot and (actually) wasting Christian kisses on an 'eathen idol's foot,' their hair agate-smooth, though like the White Queen they carry a comb in it (so handy!). They wear a flower in it too, and a clean muslin shirt (always clean) above their bright, tight sarong. At last you come out on to an open circular court, in the centre of which rises the cloud-high gold-leaf pagoda, surrounded by hundreds of Buddha shrines. The devotees vary from nakedish men who walk round and round, falling whistling-bomb flat between every two steps (progress is slow), and the pretty little maidens, smoking and playing with their babies under Buddha's nose. Orange and saffron priests lounge around, and little oil-saucers with floating wicks were everywhere being lit. I wished I could have stayed until dark to see the flickering, but Duff and Captain Richmond were weighing a ton on my conscience, so I hurried round. Even without pausing it took me over an hour. When I came out the atmosphere had improved a bit. My excited, radiant expression I think subdued Duff's irritation, but the Captain still looked nauseated and sulked.

I liked nothing else of the drive round except the buying of a priest's umbrella for practical use. It only differs from an ordinary oiled Chinese one in that it has a five-foot-long handle and a pagoda-ish other end. These peculiarities make packing and even getting into a car more difficult, so it wasn't a popular buy. It's Sunday morning, and I can hear an English bell calling the Governor, the Army and the white Raj to church.

We had a dreadful dinner-party of ten white men and one Burman, the acting Prime Minister, complete in sarong, black buttoned boots, native black jacket, bright pink head-kerchief, white European shirt with gold collar-stud but no collar (*de rigueur*). My going into the pagoda was talked about with bated horror. It may apparently lose us Burma because, so they say, it is a purely anti-British racket. However, Mr Baxter, Financial Adviser to the Governor, in whose house we had bathed and dressed for dinner, came to my support and said he repeatedly went into the temple and took all English visitors, Peter Fleming included, and that it was now considered the thing to do.

On the Way to Mandalay by Train

The stations and the loungers are always a great pleasure to watch, especially after air-travel. The crumbling pagodas everywhere are beautiful. The scene, which varied not at all for six hours, was quite untropical save for man and beast. The rice looked like spring grass, the distant hills might have been our Downs, and the brushland, where no rice grows, looked for all the world like a Sussex upland. Into this English scene are built the romantic, now ruined, bramble-grown shrines to Buddha in century-worn stone and gold-leaf – very ageless and peaceful, made living by browsing white sacrificial oxen.

More white Raj to meet us at Mandalay and the same hot lunch at the club. In the afternoon we were taken to the undisappointing city sights and to the palace of King Theebaw and Queen Supi-yaw-lat rising mirrored out of water-lilies. The British kicked them out in the Eighties. We were shown over this crumbling relic of splendour by an old Burman, born in the palace in the good old days. He had photographs of his official parents, and of the King and Queen. They were faded out of discernment but he saw them

still quite fresh. Most embarrassing it was, being told the story of the royal banishment, the occupation of this fabulous palace of gold and mirror-mosaic, so fairylike and splendid, by the English soldiers who whitewashed the gold to make it lighter, and broke it all up as they do today if given a chance. Even marble is shattered. Nearly all the gold has gone, the glass is unmended, dilapidation reigns. We are barbarians. It would have cost so little and have caused less humiliation if we had respected their Versailles. True the king died well-pensioned in India and all relations draw about one pound and one penny a year. If only Fathers Woodlock and Placid and D'Arcy and the rest of them could be dressed in orange and saffron togas, draped like Pompey's over a bare shoulder, shave their heads and use against the weather a six-foot-long orange umbrella, you would get some colour into Farm Street and Mells. No one ever told us about priests in Burma, and yet they are the things that overwhelm your eyes. Anyone can be a priest for the nonce. There are 10,000 in Mandalay's population of 100,000.

Up the Burma Road, pictured in our mind as dangerously con-gested with aeroplane-parts, ammunition and oil, we did not pass a lorry. At Maymyo, the summer palace, the Governor received us in a house like a Swiss hotel in the middle of glorious English parkland, lake, forests and glades, racecourses and polo-grounds, golf and botanical gardens, all laid out by a former Governor with Turkish prisoners in 1920.

Reginald Dorman-Smith was a broadminded man. It was refreshing after Rangoon talks to hear him rail against the little we had done in Burma. Still, my going into the pagoda was too much for him to swallow. He asked the dinner-table of guests and staff if any of them had ever been inside. 'You,' he said to a nice young police A.D.C., 'you wouldn't be able to go, Eric, would you, even if you wanted to?' Blushing and bravely Eric answered, 'I'm afraid I have been in, sir.'

How they governed India from this mountain-top before motors I can't imagine, when it took them three days to get up to this huge and hideous Viceregal Lodge, built by Lord Dufferin and greatly tidged up by subsequent Viceroys, I suppose. Our rooms are magnificent – real plumbing, two sitting-rooms and dining-room, no service for me. At my door stood two inscrutables in scarlet, as they did at every door down the passage, but I never got my shoes cleaned. I took them out in despair the following morning and dumb-cramboed brushing them to an old inscrutable, who shook his head at them and gave me to understand that he would fetch help. So he did, but the help gave the dusty shoes the same inscrutable look and would not touch them. Mercifully Captain Somebody appeared when I was half-crying and took the shoes.

The door of the room where we are assembled before dinner opens and an A.D.C., with the long black regimental coat that I thought was of a past age, and that goes with a black pill-box hat, walks in front of Their Excellencies with the face of a priest before the hangee. The Linlithgows, being mortals of another clay (if mortals they are and not brontosauri), fill the role wonderfully, I think. They have learnt no bad tricks and he has a lot of uninhibited charm, great seriousness, a very serviceable sense of humour and a fund of strange information, not an ounce of smugness. *The Roast Beef of Old England* is played to make one feel on a liner again, and those two immense creatures stalk in. Twenty servitors in scarlet redingotes with gold hats and daggers clap their two hands to their heads and the meal begins. Once it is finished Duff retires into a huddle with H.E. and I lie luxuriously on a Victorian couch and listened to a first-class orchestra playing such classical music as you would choose to ask for. The assignment for the first time seems to have its recompenses, and later, when Duff came out of his huddle

and told me that we were to go off next day to a shooting-camp and that I should be the only woman, I felt it had many rewards.

Calcutta has been what I liked least, the day shooting with the Viceroy what I liked best. Sleeping in the splendour of the Viceregal tents I enjoyed. I felt as on a stage set for *Julius Caesar*, or the Field of the Cloth of Gold. I had a huge one lined with printed linens, a large pole up the middle, as big as a circus. Real bed, carpeted floor, lamp-lit and romantic, a full-sized bath made of rubber in a little annexe, also a revolting Indian lu-lu (that has to be cleaned by human hands, 'sweepers' belonging to the untouchable caste). I roamed out by my tent's back-door to try and avoid using this barbarity, but there were too many native policemen guarding the precarious life of the Viceroy for me to find the necessary privacy. I loved too the eleven hundred beaters bawling their lungs out as they tore down the hills hurling rocks in front of them to arouse the game, and their thousand dogs (not retrievers – any dog does).

I love too the great, great beauty of these huge and tender hills, like a giant Italy sometimes, for there are a lot of trees of the shape and blue of vast olives, and the hills are flowering to their very tops, and water gurgling everywhere. It reminded me all the time of Dante's Paradiso – whether *my* idea of it or whether bits of Botticelli drawings or Fra Angelico's I can't say – and the distant white figures in single file going up and down the paths wherever you looked, for all the world like the blessed saints and all good souls. I should like to have spent another day and night in those heavenly heights, and I should have liked the Viceroy better still. He has remnants of the child left in his brontosaurian body. He carries for instance a 'catty' (catapult) for having a shot at a crow on a roof and he is a butterfly-fan and goes tearing after them with emerald-green net and stinkpot.

The Governor in Calcutta was Jack Herbert. His wife we were very attached to, so with excitement we accepted to spend two days under their blue-domed summer palace at Darjeeling. Once there I seemed to change my attitude towards India and found everything in those mountains that climb to the Himalayas good, clean and venerable. Kangchenjunga I could see from my bed, highest of his range, taking blood-red shape before the dawn reached the foothills. We were taken to a Tibetan monastery where old monks draped in purple blew from their roof twelve-foot-long trumpets to greet us with a blare. They held a propitiatory service for us – lamas in chrome-yellow with cockatoo-shaped hats and rows of purple chanting monks.

I never seemed to get accustomed to the flying. It was the *schwer Motiv* of all my letters. Hearing that a G.O.C. and his entire staff had been burnt to cinders taking off from Batavia had worsened my panics.

We got back through the storms and the battering that the most beautiful of tumbling Titans-at-play clouds can give, to Singapore and to the sweet, neat, clean and green house. Japan was being talked of more apprehensively, but I had no nerve left to spasm over war-clouds. Plans for going to Hong Kong and fears of my not being taken preoccupied me. I could, at a pinch, do without seeing Hong Kong, but to reconcile myself to the days of positive pain of anxiety was unbearable. The mission never eventuated; the F.O. vetoed it; for once I blessed Anthony Eden's wheel-spoking ways. Duff was fully engaged in writing his report, the first part of which was to be flown home as soon as completed. 'Counsels of perfection,' he wrote, 'must give way to imminence of war,' so the imperfect council was to appoint as soon as possible a Commissioner General for the Far East. If war came a Far Eastern Council would be set up and the Commissioner would automatically become its head. I knew that Duff had in mind Mr Robert Menzies of Australia as being a man of such standing that in conferences he could speak as an equal to Viceroys, Prime Ministers, Commanders-in-Chief, and the President in Washington.

I do not think his name was actually suggested in the report, for I remember wondering and I wrote to Conrad:

> What if it is approved of? And what if Duff is given the office? What if we stay here for the duration? It doesn't bear thinking of. Maybe Winston thinks Duff comfortably out of the way here – no necessity to find him another job that way and quite easy to stop any trouble – some act of initiative by coded cable. Soon our fate will be in the balance at 10 Downing Street. My ideal would be an order to 'stay put until the right man for the job is found, probably in March, then return.' I would then holiday with John Julius at Easter, come home to an English spring, a farm programme and my own dear farmer.

So Tony Keswick took home the report, nothing loath, for he was to rejoin the family that he had long been parted from. I was dreadfully sad to see him go. He had become an essential to our happiness and good humour. Besides, he carried perhaps our fate in his hands. We settled down for a short spell during which the Hong Kong visit collapsed, and plans were made for an expedition to Australia and New Zealand. War began to cloud the air. Vincent Sheean and Edgar Mowrer arrived – vultures assembling, but vultures I was devoted to. Ramadan came and went. I went to see *Hamlet* in a traditional Chinese production. I had daily lessons from a Malay guru, a gummy, giggling little man in a Mahommedan hat, who taught me the House that Jack Built in his language. The repetition is exceedingly helpful and to be recommended for first steps in any language. One could also learn 'Twelve for the twelve Apostles' with advantage. I learnt too that hair is grass, a train is a firecart and an express a proud firecart, that a holiday is 'eating wind' and ice 'iron water.' This is all I have retained. There were work-parties at Government House to which I went, and cut out pyjamas and talked about war. 'There are no shelters at all; they would never work, they say; you come to water

as soon as you dig.' Fighter-planes of a very obsolete make were depended upon to protect the island. No gas-masks were issued; 'the Chinese would never look after them.' The Sultan of Johore gave me a mynah bird, a loquacious talker, but only in Japanese. Duff let it escape. There were Chinese festivals to revel in, dragons and bulls made of Chinamen in pelts and scales. In the temples one could see marzipan tortoises for sale and, most surprising of all, the veritable Madame Tussaud peep-show opium-smokers – half-naked beggars supine beneath a flickering red light. I was told by a Javanese masseur that the temples gave free opium to consumptives. It proved an effective cure, as de Quincey discovered. Martin Russell was my companion for these revels while Duff pored over his report.

Before leaving for Australia I heard good news from John Julius, now at school in Canada, and all the home news from Conrad:

Ploughing is a very great new pleasure in my life. Almost everything is nice – the walking so slowly, smell of earth, solitude, communion with the horses, talking their odd language and so on. The mice are the sad part. You plough them out of their well-prepared subterranean nests and they skip away terrified and in great danger of being trodden on. Today a mother stopped in the road and took a small child out of a perambulator and held it up well above a wall for it to see me ploughing. The child was far too young to speak, but it seemed deeply interested.

Mr Rendall and Mr Pipkin came for the threshing. Mr Pipkin (72 or 73) never removed his bowler or starched collar all day and worked like a horse. He is hardly as tall as John Julius and has the shortest legs in the world. When I paid him I said 'What do you say to 8/- a day?' and they both said 'We come only to oblige you and don't mind at all what we are paid.' It was a noble answer.

We had a quiet guard, not a mouse stirring. Lady Lovat appeared and gave me nearly the whole of a red deer from

Caithness. He must have been the Monarch of the Glen by Sir Edwin Landseer. There was a huge haunch, two flanks of ribs and the umbles, from which, as you know, umble pie is made for inferiors. It was an embarrassing gift and I'm not exactly wrapt up in venison. I'd rather eat sardines, cheese or two fried eggs.

I have started a new book *The Heathen are Wrong* and the author is called Bagger, but I have not let it deter me.

Ronald Knox comes daily to work on the farm and is a real help. The men now call him 'the old Rector.' They think of him as seventy. He is in fact ten years younger than me, perhaps Duff's contemporary.

After two days of packing and prayers we left at dawn in a crowded Dutch aeroplane bound for Australia. Our first night was to be spent at Bali in the hostel of Manx, a Liverpudlian lady who ran it as a rival to the K.L.M. hotel. She had been warned that we were anxious to see the dancing, so all was prepared and the thought was like a lifebuoy to me.

Sky

At four we got to the earthly paradise, Bali, and there was no disappointment – old girl Manx, fifty, four foot high, a mop of black hair and a 'Mother Hubbard' garment, was to pop us into cars and take us to her establishment. Already the men hauling off the luggage from the aeroplane had looked different from any natives I had seen. A translucent coffee-coloured torso, sleek and strong, a sarong coloured and draped by Tiepolo, and an innocent beauty of countenance. Arrived at Manx's 'Kampong' the servants greeted us into this jungle, almost garden, on the beach, four or five of them and as many children of different sizes, all dressed as princes and princesses in macaw colours with flowers used as jewels in ears and hair. They clasp their hands as in prayer when speaking to you and all move like the

waves of the sea, for they are all highly trained dancers of a dance that is well beyond the powers of a European. In the jungle garden there were three or four little grass houses with a fresh cool native bath apiece, a grass bar and a terrace to eat on overlooking the sea. Nothing lovelier could there be. Manx took us a drive through the town and villages. The women are naked to the waist, not of course all Milos but all with the serene face. From what? No education? No driving force? No pathetic content nor yet divine discontent? They are Hindus up to a point and have dilapidated and beautiful little temples here and there, rather ungarnished and very ungarish. Dinner of roast sucking-pig and flowers, I think, and a native heady drink was improved by an attractive and beautiful young couple – Dutch but seemed Russian, and artists both. Pol was the name.

After dinner the dancing. That I couldn't describe if I wanted to – the beauty, the strangeness, the fantastic music made of sound only, not tune or time but seemingly all the better for that. The audience – all the island with their children and their shops brought along for the *festa*, incredibly artistic and sophisticated and distinguished, distinguished. (Emphasis is given in Malay by a simple repetition of the operative word – very useful!) Nothing seen ravished me more in the realms of travel, customs and art in dancing, than these Balinese rites. It ended, as it had to, and we went to our jungly grass house, only to leave it at dawn and board our Dutch 'Dodo.'

We flew to Darwin, where flowering trees outshine Malaya's. It was jammed with troops, so not until the next day, when we travelled nearly 3000 miles to Sydney, did the emptiness of the continent astound one – an arid plain, rarely a habitation, no tree or river or one town. Why I wondered were there no human beings? Why had Australia not followed America's repaying example of accepting settlers of all nations – Jews, Poles, Austrians, Russians? All for a white

Australia? A terror of unemployment? So there is no one to work or buy or make employment. All this was thought nearly twenty years ago. Today the case is, I suppose, altered. We landed at 8.30 p.m. in darkness amid the million lights of Sydney. Thousands of cruel cameras and flashlights to blind me, already deaf from the long flight. I felt inhuman. A sea of blue and green electrically contorted faces, an address from the Prime Minister, dissecting pressmen. I might have been a one-celled amoeba for all the sense I made. One night of rest at Government House and on again to the country capital of Canberra. [It may no longer be rural, but twenty years ago it was built only in mind's eyes.] We stayed at Government House.

It's really rather lovely, and the Governor General, Lord Gowrie (once Sandy Ruthven, V.C.), and Lady Gowrie are unspoilt pets. The unpopulated country is beautiful and invigorating. Looking out of my window now I might be in a tender part of Scotland – no moors, *Mary Rose* country with blue burns and blue distant hills, yellow foreground and never a fence nor a house, bigger and better roses at every step. Miles away, equally isolated in Scotch beauty, is the House of Parliament. Miles away again a bit of residential section, I suppose. A hill is pointed out where Embassies are to be built, another, miles away, where the Foreign Office is to stand. It's fascinating to see an unbuilt town, more fun than Pompeii. The English flowers are enough to make one cry – huge iris, sweet peas, gladioli, roses, lilies, catmint – all the garden let into the rooms and smelling of June. No Viceregal pomp at all. I suppose that to the Australians it would be a joke. The half was not told me about the Gowries. I eavesdropped on a conversation at dinner between her and Duff. She was saying that, when the war was over, she was going to keep pigs because she was so fond of them. Lord Gowrie next me across the table said, 'What's that, dear?' 'Only telling Mr Cooper about the pigs.' 'Horrible brutes!'

She: 'Then Sandy will keep violets.' Duff: 'What will he do with them?' 'O, pick them and tie them into bunches.' Then I had to turn back to Mr Evatt, Minister of External Affairs.

I'm lying at Melbourne as I close this letter. Then back to Sydney. The Wakehursts make it happy for us there. They are what I once heard some horror call 'very us-ish.' I want to get back from Melbourne's greyness to the dazzle of the Sydney sea and the new-found jacaranda trees, oleanders and coral trees. Letters are life, don't forget it and don't flag.

I really loved Australia. I thought it most beautiful. Its green downs, its soothing flocks of peace. The eucalyptus trees had almost flesh-coloured limbs and their movements in growth had a human sweep. While Duff visited Ministers and airfields and munition-factories I would take an occasional drive with Lord Gowrie into the country, stopping to talk to farmers coming from several hundred miles away with slow-moving sheep. We would look for and never see the duck-billed platypus, nor, alas, the lyre-bird, but the kangaroos, wallabies, koala bears and emus were fun and usually unexpectedly tame. The Australians were good to us and we loved each other. I should like to revisit Australia.

In New Zealand we landed at Auckland. We got lost in the sky on our way to the South Island. We were like souls in a grey limbo and the petrol was beginning to fail when God put us again into radio communication and we came to Christchurch. My mind must have been overweighted with new scenes and impressions, for I remember little but the fine mountainous country and the burning patriotism of the New Zealanders, the Ireland green, the fleecy sheep, the imported gorse and starlings and elder-trees which have turned to plagues, geysers, and Maoris who sang like Slavs, the charm of Wellington, and prefab houses with corrugated-iron roofs and enough wires, poles, cisterns and waterwheels to make it look like the Klondyke in '96.

I shall never let the beauty of Australia fade from my vision. I missed only the touching and safe cluster of farm, manor and

cottages round an aspiring church protecting its dead beneath the crooked tombstones, to be seen, I suppose, from Siberia to Californian mission-towns. Back to Sydney for goodbyes and Godspeeds and 'happy landings,' and up and off again for five flying-days, coming down at Gladstone and Townsville, where we slept to the uproarious noise of drunken sailors and woke to the screech of what sounded like drunken birds with Australian accents. On to Karamba and back to Darwin, to be welcomed by the Residents, Mr and Mrs Abbott, to whom we had become very attached. The heat was suffocating and the mosquitoes as dense as locust-storms. All night they bit and I was sure that the irritation would lead to something more dire. On to Timor, Koepang and Komodo, the country of dragons, over the Gulf of Carpentaria and the Arafura Sea, still like the earth before she received her name. Savu and the Sandalwood Seas already a later day of world-creation, land and sea slimily blended with islands backed like whales, lagoons for sea-serpents, simple blue and sand-coloured. Pterodactyls flying with us would not have surprised. Then Bima, civilised but for flies, Bali-like though not so innocent and old, Surabaya, and at last Batavia. Java looked watered and tended and tilled and fought-for after Australia, that wasted Utopia.

Singapore   *2 December*

Just now I went to the Naval Base to see *Prince of Wales* and *Repulse* come in and five other pieces, camouflaged to kill, a lovely sight but on the petty side. I watched them glide in. Everyone very moved and over-excited.

3 December

Just been to a dinner given by our brave new Defence Tuan Tom (my name for Tom Phillips) and Captain Tennant. Tuan is four-foot-nothing and sharp as forked lightning. I put great faith in him. Brussels ball once again. We danced on the wide decks and quaffed toasts for victory, the red-and-white awnings flapless and everyone dressed overall and

grinning with security. Tide turned, wind changed, and beneath my red-and-white dress my heart tolled.

Peladang (farmer, in Malay) darling, since writing those two words in ink I have been struck down with dengue fever. It has a sort of Kipling–Maugham–Conrad cachet but it's rather unpleasant. Like mild rheumatic fever with no aftermath. We are expecting the balloon to go up any time now.

Martin woke us at 3 a.m. to say that the Japanese had made a landing in the far north of Malaya. He drew Priam's curtains in the dead of night. I took it more calmly than a Trojan. We both turned over and slept until woken an hour later by the familiar thunder of aeroplanes, guns and bombs, followed at long last by jokey sirens whistling away unintermittently for half an hour in different quarters of the town. To my great surprise I felt nothing. Was this unusual calm due to the dengue-drugs or to an attitude I had settled to adopt when the bombing started – the veteran's 'O well, after London, you know' – having become part of me? That first raid they dropped a bomb bang in the middle of Raffles Square, a bull's-eye.

I felt, when I first saw this pretty feminine rococo town, so graceful and flimsy with its frail pink and robin's-egg-blue arcades and quays garlanded with nameless fruit and flowers and paper intricacies, that a modern world would not let it survive. Either friendly ferro-concrete or barbarian hands would get at it, so it's for the rubble-heap.

It's only 9 a.m. and we've talked to the Governor and the Sultan, a rich start. Three or four ships have been sighted, thought at first to be cruisers but now turn out to be transports. Shouldn't we have bombed or sunk them before

they could land? The stop press says that Honolulu and *Havana* have been bombed. Is it possible? Aircraft-carriers? Or have they captured Wake and Midway? Well, America is at war, but will she be at war with Germany too and throw her glove in their snout?

Now I suppose we must expect gas and parachutists, dropping of soldiers dressed as orange priests, with their umbrellas turned to parachutes, and the rest of it. I've not been in an invaded country before. There will be naval bombardment too. Lord help us! The air is loud with aircraft, ours I hope.

10 December

This morning the telegram arrives that Duff has the job of Minister for Far Eastern Affairs with much authority, enough to be able to form a War Council. My darling Duff is tickled to death. Either this answer or one to the effect that Menzies was on his way ('Carry on pending handing over, then return') he was ready to be pleased with. The dread was of 'Still considering report. Suggest you roll bandages till we say stop.' The present development flatters and stimulates him. What does it do to me? I'm curiously numb, thank God. I can see every horror – no escape, speedy and complete infiltration by Japs, Rotterdamming of Singapore town and the Base, massacre of the whites – but all in a detached, weary way. People who have been in Chungking are windier than I am. I always knew Chungking wasn't a patch on London or Bognor, caverns measureless to man and two hours' warning!

11 December

When I said that I thought of every horror, I didn't think of our two proud ships finding so early a grave. Duff came in from the Naval Base at 8.30 and used that dreadful line (first used to me by Helen Kirkpatrick when Boulogne fell) 'How

127

black can you take it?' Expecting black, it was blacker. We get no details. Did Tuan Tom, in whom I had faith, go down? O toll for Tuan Tom, poor little live wire! I should hate to be killed by Japs and I probably shall be. The Germans are legions of Anti-Christ, but missing links. No, no, not sunk by missing links. Our peninsula is yellow as gorse with them, but no one seems much put about.

A very entertaining man called Darvall came to dinner and we talked about what muddlers we were. Duff had to go off and do a broadcast on the loss of the ships, and I hung over the table, lit by two candles (all we dare show), while the fever dropped off my face and arms on to the cloth. This morning at last I'm normal. Last night I was 101. I feel like something rightly thrown away. It's difficult to remember myself as that bright dynamo in Australia so few weeks ago. I'll brighten. A nice cable from Claire Luce today advising courage in the shooting-match, an invigorating one from Tommy Stout Winston dragged me out of my well for a moment. 'Who put her in?' Sigh for poor Pussy.

I learnt coding and decoding yesterday in the office. It's what I should like best to do if there is a lot of work, but I fear there won't be and I shall have to nurse if the raids are bad.

> *O little did my mither wist*
> *The night she cradled me*
> *The lands I was to travel in*
> *Or the death I was to dee.*

12 December

If only Duff had received his orders three days earlier, the War Council, however hastily formed, would never have allowed the ships their umbrella-less enterprise. The Council meets daily and our dear Admiral Layton has been dragged off his home-bound ship to fill his old post.

Like veterans of war who expect the next one to be exactly like the last I began preparing for siege and invasion – goose-chases after poultry and a sow, hectic dibbing in of vegetables, all useless effort as it turned out. Penang had collapsed in a flash, and eye-witnesses were pouring in to Singapore with gruesome stories of panic, breakdown, idiocy, lack of defence and of discipline, native police running amok and looting whisky. Even the white Fire Service ran and had not been seen since, which had infuriated the Government. Yet even with this disaster an outcry from the press, local B.B.C. and intelligentsia seemed to be the only reaction. Suddenly Duff was expected to be the genie and build on no foundations shelters, fire-service, evacuation schemes, food-storage, censorship and rationing, every municipal service, with no approval from the Government of Singapore. It opposed everything, including the scorched-earth policy, still imagining the Japanese to be Samurai who would show honour and not destroy the reclaimable. The calm infected me for a change. A new mynah bird, gift of the Sultan, replaced the one Duff had let fly, and a lady's tame gibbon had settled in our tree. This young man on a flying trapeze was a perpetual delight as it tore across one's path with arms high to heaven.

Conrad's letters continued to reach me, although many of them must have perished on the way.

We've now reached the stage in the war when the muddle and incompetence are universally recognised. The Crimea, the Boer War and the Great War all went through this phase. This time it is our miserable production and high wages for doing little or no work. And food muddles! Of course there are the actual failures in the field too, Narvik, Dunkirk, Crete. Now Libya has turned out disappointing. How could our dear Prime Minister make that 'Blenheim and Waterloo' allusion in his speech? It was asking for it. But Englishmen never, never learn. It is always going to be Agincourt or Crecy and then it is Majuba or Kut in the end.

The relief of Mafeking was good news, and it was so unusual that the English behaved like a lot of jack-asses and the verb 'to maffick' was invented to describe what we did (me among them).

The two great ships were forgotten by people in the street who looked unconcerned, and careless of the huge shadows cast. There was faith too in the inhabitants' loyalty (true, the Japanese were a traditional enemy), but I could see no particular reason why these eighty-five per cent Chinese and fifteen per cent Indian and Malay citizens of Singapore should fight, as Cockneys do, *against* people of their own shade, *for* the dear good English, who when they hadn't irritated them with schools and demands for work had bored them with restrictions, requests for voluntary service, for blood from their veins, for rice from their stomachs. Of course they would scatter in a crisis. At one rehearsal raid 1200 coolies had left the Naval Base and had not returned. No one did much about the shelter that had been digging for two weeks in our garden. Another slit trench was cut in our office-plot, but that was filled with our Indian guard. I restrained my brag about London in 1938, the gentlemen with their coats off, the soldiers and the old girls digging away in parks and squares, and me fitting snouts and schnozzles on to gas-masks against time.

It's quite simple. I just take two cachets of amytol every night and sleep without squeaking until Duff gets up at seven. I feel quite different and have calm dreams and no dread of oncoming day or night. When I think of the mountain of morphia I consumed in the last war with no habits formed, a few amytols won't do me any harm.

Poor Mrs Reed, the young American doyenne of the typists, who came over with the Mission, cried all yesterday with homesickness. I tried my hand at comfort with fair success but she said: 'You can't really understand, Lady Diana, because you are never down.' Isn't it extraordinary? I think my gloom, despondency and great alarm stick out for

the public to be shocked at. If only I were like Eve Curie with one selfless preoccupation, that of winning the war.

Evacuation of women and children is talked of. I notice it is a subject Duff is loath to discuss with me. I am quite determined not to go and know how to avoid it, namely by not arguing but hiding at the last. No ship is going to be held up for one. My trouble would be (and it's what I greatly fear) a reasoned appeal from Duff – duty, others, his own work etc. I can't stand up to that if it comes to it, so I try, and shall to the end try, not to discuss it. I live on prayer. A lot of women are off voluntarily to Australia. Never a dull moment, now beri-beri is listed as a threatened epidemic, with cholera of course and malaria.

I made an appeal for blood. When I got to the jerry-built bungalow-building on a lake with two topless meccano-towers as landmarks, 'the real thing' was said to have started. There was a jolly gang of boys telling me we were indefinitely off the air and would I like to go and lie in the slit trench. I feebly said that one might watch the raid better from the trench and perhaps spot the Fifth Column rockets, but it was laughed off and as a sop they brought out the first-aid box, jumbo-size for splints and gas-detergents and snake-bite virus, but it proved to contain only Alka-Seltzers, aspirins, pick-me-ups and brandy as hair-of-the-dog. We came back on the air and I delivered my piece and went to the blood-transfusion place *pour encourager les autres*. There was a gratifying rush of donors, but I could not get any of my Chinese boys to go. They had promised to but thought poor relations paid out of their wages would do as well.

There is going to be an awful scarcity of women. Anyone with children is to go. Many have left already and the Naval Base is short of cipherers and typists. I deciphered an absolutely epoch-making message which may alter our plans and might bring us home or send us elsewhere. It read:

Prime Minister to Lord Privy Seal for Chancellor of the Duchy of Lancaster. Prime Minister to Mr Duff Cooper. Personal and Secret.

1. The very large arrangements which have developed from our discussions here, and Wavell's appointment as Supreme C.-in-C. South West Pacific, necessarily bring your Mission to an end. You should at your convenience, and by whatever is safest and most suitable route, come home. If possible, without undue risk, you should confer with Wavell at his Headquarters in Java, and tell him what you think and know. Pray let me know your plan.

2. H.M. Government are entirely satisfied with the way in which you have discharged your difficult and, at times, dangerous task, and I look forward to our future work together in a world situation which, with all its trouble, has changed decisively for the better.

I rushed over with it to show Duff and found him making his adieus to poor Brooke-Popham. Embarrassing. I didn't produce the telegram, and every word said about the Air in Singapore and Malaya seemed to be a reflection on the Services. Now Pownall has taken over, but I'm sure it is too late.

31 December

Last day of a full year – pain, pleasure, fear and relief. I imagine that the fateful telegram is activated by the appointment of Wavell as Ruler of the Far East. There can't be two Number Ones and Duff thinks that Number Two should be an American.

We had been threatened since the war broke out with the loss of our Military Attaché, the gallant Robbie, who had become most dear to us. His regiment was the Argyll and Sutherland, who were engaged in the north, and it was thought that he would be

promoted to command it. I so prayed that he would be left with us. It is difficult to discover what soldiers really wish for. He was of great use to the Mission. He felt that he was in the hub of things with messages from Churchill and Roosevelt, airing his sensible views to Pownall and other big shots, but he continued to say that he hoped to be ordered to the front, and to the front he went. We had a goodbye dinner and Robbie left for the firing-line, looking schoolboyish and wistful. I prayed for his speedy return like Nelson with a black eye and an empty sleeve, but we never saw him again nor do I know the end. I was so very fond of Robbie.

The epoch-making telegram was followed up on 7 January, and in the twinkling of an eye our plight changed for the better. Or for the worse? I really did not know. Singapore was at this time divided as sharply as hard sun makes a shadow and I truly hated the idea of deserting Duff's crusaders.

The more I think about it the more I feel that we shall be home as soon as this letter. It's very exciting. The journey will be alarming and via India, I suppose. They travel this first Jap-ridden Malacca Straits–Sumatra piece by night, I believe. Wavell is due tomorrow and something must then be concocted to ameliorate the condition of poor Singapore. It can't be left to the Governor and Colonial Secretary Jones or to the gentleness of G.O.C. Percival. No Pownall, no Duff, and the place is lost. True we have now a Duff-chosen dictator of civil defence and an engineering Brigadier (Simpson), but can they hold it down alone? Percival plays Trilby to the Governor's Svengali. I shall hate, in a way, to desert, but it has its compensation. Of course all these assumptions may be wrong, and we may be bound for Java next week, but Duff sees no place for himself there, in a country not his, with a Generalissimo. Pownall's nose looks a bit wonky. It's sad for him to have been Commander-in-Chief Far East for a minute, and then become Chief

of Staff and Commander-in-Chief under Wavell. A nice man.

These last days we are in a state of uncomfortable suspense. Duff is restless, with suddenly not enough to do. The War Council sits in the morning, but with Pownall instead of Popham, and the Governor a bit cowed. There is less struggle, fewer Ephesian beasts. The Civil Defence daily meeting has served its purpose in electing the despot Brigadier over the Governor's head and responsible to the War Council, so it no longer meets every afternoon. The office is slack. We all snatch at arriving telegrams but it's never the one to tell us of our fate. My mind reels. It's such a readjustment from beri-beri and the massacre of white-devils to home – loves – forgotten reading.

A second telegram arrived at noon and it's back to the arms of my farmer, I honestly do believe. I feel pleased but I have felt pretty sure of it for days. I hate in a way to leave them to it here. I loathe the idea of His Excellency rubbing his hands. I think though that they can be manacled. The Generalissimo and Pownall are downstairs now, I hope, arranging with Duff to depose him. People here had such faith and hope in Duff, and now I suppose they'll think we are hooking it while the hooking is good. Winston's personal telegram was exceedingly nice, full of praise for the 'dangers you have passed' and of his conduct and resource, and talking of continuing to work together. No question, thank God, of Duff becoming a kind of Governor of Singapore, nor yet any question of Java. I shall continue to write to you, though I shall bring this letter in my hand, I hope, across India, Arabia, Egypt and Europe. The journey will be as usual hazardous, but this time fraught with real enemy-action danger. We may go by commercial aeroplane that takes off occasionally, when it feels good, *via* Sumatra and Calcutta, or we might snaffle a Catalina flying-boat (armed) and fly direct to Colombo, travel up India by train, see my

airy-fairy Viceroy, and take the aeroplane from our old haunt Gwalior, stop perhaps a week in Cairo too. It's all frightful – but poor Singapore! I do love it so.

The two biggest shots stayed to dinner with Duff, me, Martin and Alex Newboult. I ordered a gourmet's Chinese dinner and enjoyed the evening immensely. A blanket of cloud and monsoon-squalls gave us a raid-free night. I loved Pownall. Wavell alarmed me, though I might fall in love with him if I got over my fear of his silences. His drooping eye suits me. John Julius will look just like him if he makes sixty and stays good, for Wavell might be an angel in disguise. It's early days and seen by candlelight. Pray, pray, dear God, let him succeed, at least in part.

They were both most happy and I got going and said all the truth about the situation here, which Duff had told them already but which I could make much more indiscreet and crude. The result was that for the second time Martin drew Priam's curtains in the dead of night with a letter from Pownall enclosing a draft of the telegram to be sent (if agreed to) to the Prime Minister saying how far from satisfactory the situation would be minus Pownall and Duff, and could he suggest at least postponing Duff's departure. It's a beast! And yet I half want to stay. Ambivalence has me in its thrall.

8 a.m.

I've just had breakfast downstairs. Everything glitters in the garden and country. The caged bird chatters, the others make a loud harmonious chorus, the trunks are out and airing. Duff is off to his Council, there to announce the end of his Mission. Nothing can be said there since the Governor and G.O.C. are part of it, but afterwards he will discuss this new plan with Pownall. Wavell has gone north to look at the enemy.

If Duff takes it on temporarily I have warned him that it will be for good, and not the best that can be done for Singapore. 'Good enough' however for a frenzied set-up in Java to put the subject from their overcrowded minds. Wavell said he felt like a man not expecting a baby, being suddenly given quadruplets. I'm sorry for him, and although I'm sorry Pownall will not hold *this* fort, it is perhaps just as well that he should hold Wavell's hand. They are excellent friends. In an official telegram distributed to a chosen few and addressed to Pownall, Wavell ended with the words 'Bless you, we will see this thing through, or do our best or something.' The telegram to Winston wasn't sent.

Above Ground   *13 January*

It's days since I wrote. One becomes less ready to set trifles down when one knows they cannot precede one. The last three or four days have been sad and trying. Every sound man from up or down country (newspaper men, sound *en masse*) begging Duff to stay and dictate. It's heartrending to appear callous and glad to get out. I don't know really why he is being removed, which makes it more difficult to suggest staying. It may, after all, be that the home Government think he has made an appalling mess of it. They wouldn't think so if they were here.

5
A Long Way Home

January 13 was the day chosen for our departure. We were all unhappy. I was sad, too, that the telegram to Winston asking for Duff's departure to be postponed had not been sent. It would have proved at least that Wavell and Pownall and all the fighting side of Singapore had faith in him. Deputations would call with petitions. The editor of the *Straits Times* also pleaded. It was impossible not to look as though we were running for it. I was so frenzied with packing and goodbyes and tearfully returning borrowed Ming and celadon to Chinese merchants, and generally winding up, that I missed many decisions of policy and plans. People were pouring down from the north in cars loaded with bundles, dogs, whisky, shotguns, golf-clubs and birds. They had lost everything else. They reported Kuala Lumpur as really scorched earth. They told of breaking cases of whisky and pouring it away to discourage Japanese rapine and loot. It seemed a crime. No one even now looked worried. Raids were incessant but fairly harmless.

On the eve of departure, after the difficult goodbye dinner at Government House, to my amazement a respectable middle-aged woman sitting next me on the sofa suddenly mumbled: 'Don't look up, don't start. I'm going to pass you a letter. Nobody must see.' It might have been in a Dumas novel. I smuggled it into my dress and when I got home read a condemnation of the Governor, begging Duff to stay. It was too touching, and dreadful to feel that we had a sneaking desire to be going home.

13 January

This morning has been full. Luggage had to be reduced to the minimum (44 lbs per head) so everything we both need

was dragged out of the already packed boxes and put in others for a sea-trip. I have had to jettison (leaving treasure to be sent on when a town is falling about your ears is jettisoning) my lovely scroll-pictures, my galloping horse and my three poets on mules. I shall miss them always if I ever again have walls on which they might have been unrolled. The staff is plunged in gloom to lose us, and I am plunged in gloom at leaving my Chinese staff. I've photographed them all, but only you shall see them, as who else could want to?

We were told 10 a.m. and then 11 a.m. Moaning, gnashing of teeth and many tears in the office, then Alex and Duff and I sat down to our last gin-sling. I said 'Boy, give me a last gin-sling.' Of course he thought I said 'large' and got me a *beer*-glass full. The result was wonderful, and I survived a very trying time without a qualm. The alert went as we got to the airport. Guns banged, bombs dropped. We were forced into a dangerous lift-shaft – me, Duff, Martin, Alex, Mr Kao, Mr Yen and two soldiers. It was nearly all made of glass. Hardly had the All Clear gone than the Alert started again, followed by more guns and bangs and the roar of engines, and down we went into the gleaming glass. So we didn't get off until one.

The weather two months ago would have alarmed me (rain-clouds and storm) but today I am grateful for its covering veils. It's pretty rough too, but I didn't notice it until the Captain said 'I'm afraid we're giving you a very nasty passage.' The passage is curiously enough to Batavia. From there we don't know. We are in one of the old Imperial Airways flying-boats, and I think that now I'll sleep some of that gin off.

15 January

We crept up the south-west coast of Sumatra. It has a ridge of high mountains that serves us in the office of a wall against the Japs. The night before, Batavia, now G.H.Q., had sheltered us. Wavell had left for another boistering day in Malaya. In

the Dutch-Indian capital, provision had been made against attack – glow-worm lighting, injunctions or orders on every wall. Winston's picture looked out of most windows; interlaced flags draped the little palace dedicated to Spitfire funds.

Duff's sadness lowered me. We stared at each other in the clouds, afraid now of the subject that haunted me more than him. Were we to be thought quitters? He at least knew that he had orders and that he saw no place for himself; my predicament of conscience was, unnecessarily, less simple.

16 January

Never a dull minute. We arrived at the penal settlement of Port Blair, Andaman Islands, at about three. I took a hasty dislike to it. No gentle Malays and intelligent Chinese, only surly filthy Indians and bad Burmen, criminals to a man though freed, and with their crimes written large on their faces. Another airliner came in from Rangoon and the west and disgorged three Australian officers. There seemed little plan and no action. At last we piled into two small motor-craft and spluttered off through high seas to Ross Island, some thirty minutes away. Ross is the select patch where the Chief Commissioner has a Residency. There is a barracks, a post office, a club, a church and parsonage, a village institute, and that's about all, except for an old Circuit Home lately turned into a rest-house for air-travellers. On the quay of this little settlement, now evacuated on account of the war, stood the strangest old rickshaw-for-two ever I saw, equivalent to the Irish bankrupt's buggy. It had six slutty-looking Indian jailbirds, with filthy torn white shorts and different shades of faded carmine tops and turbans, to draw it up a stiffish but very short hill. A quiet, unassuming gentleman in shabby European tropical get-up said 'My name is Waterfall. Do get into the buggy. I'll walk beside you. I thought it better to lodge you in my house. I'm not living there myself. I'm afraid the light is cut off and we'll see if we can't forage up some tea.

I'm afraid we have no kitchen. I thought we'd dine on the other island with the Colonel and Captain.' The house was indescribable, very large and wandery and shapeless, with strange devil-carvings mixed with suburban taste. A huge haunted bedroom ('no mosquitoes on Ross,' so un-netted beds), the inevitable plumbing horrors of India and an impossible trickle from a cold tap dripping into a pan-bath. We messed around and suggested looking at the flowerless garden, clinging to our hats and skirts that the wind was skittish with, while time *would* not pass. Dinner, he said, was on the other side at 8.30. One couldn't wash, one couldn't even go to the lu for very shame. I suggested dining at eight and we listened to a croaking portable wireless. I'm only interested in Singapore, and there was no news of it. We crossed over by launch. Daylight was fading. We listened to the radio again in the Colonel's melancholy house, and a brilliant suggestion was made that we should move to the Club and hear the radio there. This was welcomed as a time-killer, so we buggied over, the Chief Commissioner going as always by foot, and listened for the third time to the meatless programme of news. Still there was whisky at the Club and some boys and even a woman not yet evacuated. There are only three left.

Then back to the Colonel's house and dinner and port, and a snub from the Chief Commissioner when I said that India was an unhappy country, and he said that I hadn't seen it and was talking about things I didn't know anything about. He was right, of course, but I was only describing my impression. That got the Colonel and the Captain winking and on my side, and cheered things up a little. The excuse of being woken at 5 a.m. allowed us to beat a difficult retreat across a troubled sea in a bit of a launch at about 9.30. The Chief Commissioner waved us off with relief, and we groped our way up in inky darkness to our inky house, empty but for ourselves, two witch's cats and three speechless Indian delinquents. After a struggle with washing and a stinking

lamp we slept, but I was as usual eaten mercilessly by mosquitoes, no protection, no net, no artillery of Flit. I chucked it at four and somehow lit and tended the lamp.

At 5.30, when I was dressed and packed, the three Indians padded into the room patting their stomachs and saying a lot. No means of understanding. I knew it couldn't mean breakfast and there was a tone of alarm. Duff slept, cheek on folded hands, through this babel. At last the word Circuit Home emerged from the gibberish, so seizing my torch I ran down to the Circuit Home, to find that our pilot was at death's door, 104 temperature, swollen painful glands in the groins. The rough, tough, jolly lady-doctor Thornton who had joined our flying-boat at Batavia was well in charge and diagnosed it as something I had never heard of belonging to the malarial school. It was a body-blow. Praying that Duff would have got a move-on and be shaving, but unable to explain my absence, I went with the eastbound (already-late) Australians in the launch to their Clipper, and got all the low-down about our near future. News wasn't too bad. The First Officer of the eastbound aeroplane, in dual control with our First Officer, would pilot our ship, and a kind passenger R.A.F. boy would First-Officer the eastbound machine. Well, that's better than another day in prison, though two underlings at the joy-sticks is not my ideal. I got home at eight and found the Circuit Home people having a gorgeous sausage-and-egg breakfast after a lovely night in fresh rooms with netted beds. The Chief Commissioner, from long dealings with the punishable, must have thought up something to irk us, i.e. almost solitary confinement in the dark with three murderer-keepers and no breakfast.

A half-caste doctor, delighted to get a line from Dr Thornton, proclaimed the Captain's disease to be the same as had the first diagnoser, so he is to be got on the aeroplane somehow and left in a Calcutta hospital. A wonderful procession formed itself of passengers, coolies and luggage.

The lady doctor, quite a lot grimier and gayer than yesterday, me with my nightcap on to keep the hair from the hurricane, and in the middle the septic pink-coated bearers carrying shoulder-high the Captain on his bed. His mattress laid on the floor of the launch, he was tossed across the bay and somehow squeezed through the narrow aperture into the aeroplane. The lowest Officer and I dragged and unscrewed and pulled at the chairs and tables in the smallest compartment until we wrenched them free, and he lies there now, a sort of dying Nelson in the hold. Devoted officers fan him and I mop him with eau de Cologne, for the heat is intense when we are at sea-level. The shocking truth is that I'm frightened of infection, more for Duff than for myself, and I dare not say so. How lucky are those who don't think of every fatal eventuality.

4 p.m.

Just refuelled at Rangoon. My old Shwe Dagôn was gleaming unscathed. We made a lovely landing on the Irrawaddy. Youth at the helm, and at the prow as well, has kept me a little jumpy, and now we are over that nasty mountainous bit that divides us from the Bay of Bengal. We shan't get to Calcutta, but will spend the night at my dear little friendly Akyab, the rice-port on the coast. It has a good hospital and we can leave our perhaps dying Captain there. Thalassa! Thalassa! I feel better over water.

I must have been writing during all the flying hours. It helped me in the air to keep my small mind contained in earthly human limits, not lost in vertiginous space and elements unknown. If it was not the Irrawaddy, it was the Hooghly or the Ganges, and bemused through Gwalior and other bird's-eyed landmarks we came to Delhi unexpectedly by train.

Impressions of grandeur. Secretaries in Prussian coats, palms on the platform, Lancers by the portals of the thick

red walls, no cheer or hallos, or 'Have a drink, you must be cold.' No, but smuggled discreetly in (with as much haste as is decent) to our suite – the Viceroy's (discarded as untenable) two bedrooms, two bathrooms, two sitting-rooms and three large loggias, rather ugly and intensely cold, walls curry-coloured, plumbing, lighting and roses good, service nil. A ghastly ruffian in tattered European jacket, cotton English shirt (tail out, of course) and filthy socks out at toes, a clout for a turban, is introduced as our bearer. No rudimentary knowledge of his job. Breakfast is served by four turbaned giants in scarlet redingotes beneath which peep white petticoats. Life in the Viceroy's house is not like hotel or ship. We register our meals in or out with noughts and crosses. You might see no one all day but the A.D.C. assigned to you, who is daily changed. The aeroplane is postponed every twenty-four hours, and time drags although there are wonders of Mogul art to be visited. The air is brilliant and clear *wie am ersten Tag*. Old Delhi is indescribably squalid with half-hidden remains of beauty, a marble doorway, a delicate grill. The Viceroy's house is too big, too big for nature and its trees, too big for its height, too sprawled, too big for anything and full of faults and mischief, full of great conceptions and magnificence. Even rainbows can be laid on, Lutyens had told me, while building. We see none. The A.D.C. marches us a mile to the morning-room. There we stand, lonely V.I.P.'s whispering complaints till the Vicereine (for the Viceroy is sickly, abed) sweeps in smiling resignedly, led by another A.D.C. and two gentlemen flunkeys. These lead the three of us to an ante-dining-room where the *canaille*, i.e. staff and guests, join the melancholy procession. Lo! before each chair the scarlet-clothed Indian buries his face in his dark hands to hide his untutored mind as we sit at our assigned places. Luncheon scarce swallowed before we double back to our rooms and thumb-twiddle until four, when the A.D.C. is again at his unrewarding task of

taking us sightseeing. Forts, mosques, palaces seven, Delhi's towers and tanks, follies and shrines. The Taj, under scaffolding as usual, the Great Mogul, marble inlaid by Italian hands, colour and gold, transparent alabaster, gardens with even balance of earth and water. Home at six for thumb-twiddling until eight, when processions re-form. The broadcast of alarm and despondency fills the gap between table and the double back to one's room.

Everything is clouded because the man I love and admire has influenza, or does he not want to see us? His never being referred to is suspicious. This house is so vast that birth, death and marriage are doubtless going on within its walls without our knowledge. I see a pack of foxhounds coming out of a *porte-de-maître* outside my window. In our passage for two days we are asphyxiated by the smell of elephant. It may be a dead one in our wing somewhere; it may be dead Viceroy. The party are all Jim Crows, I think, for the Duke of Connaught, so I tear out and buy an unbecoming grey number to merge in with the weeds which may be for Lord Linlithgow.

Later

So the Viceroy is not dead, for he appears, not in glory but looking weary and ill. The next day we are at last off again. Hours and hours over that dry hag Mother India's hot plains and cold skies.

On, on to the Persian Gulf that stays in my eyes when other scenes of this Odyssey have faded – a sort of Sinai freemason picture, half-seen at Salt Lake City, cathedral-shaped rocks long-shadowed by a rising sun, a great eye with compasses framing the vision. Is it trucial Arabia? No question answered in the air, a thousand ages in Thy sight. Six becomes three in a trice, and it's Basra, and nothing to say about Basra but a bed and at misty dawn on again to Bagdad – only the tarmac of Bagdad – and down again at

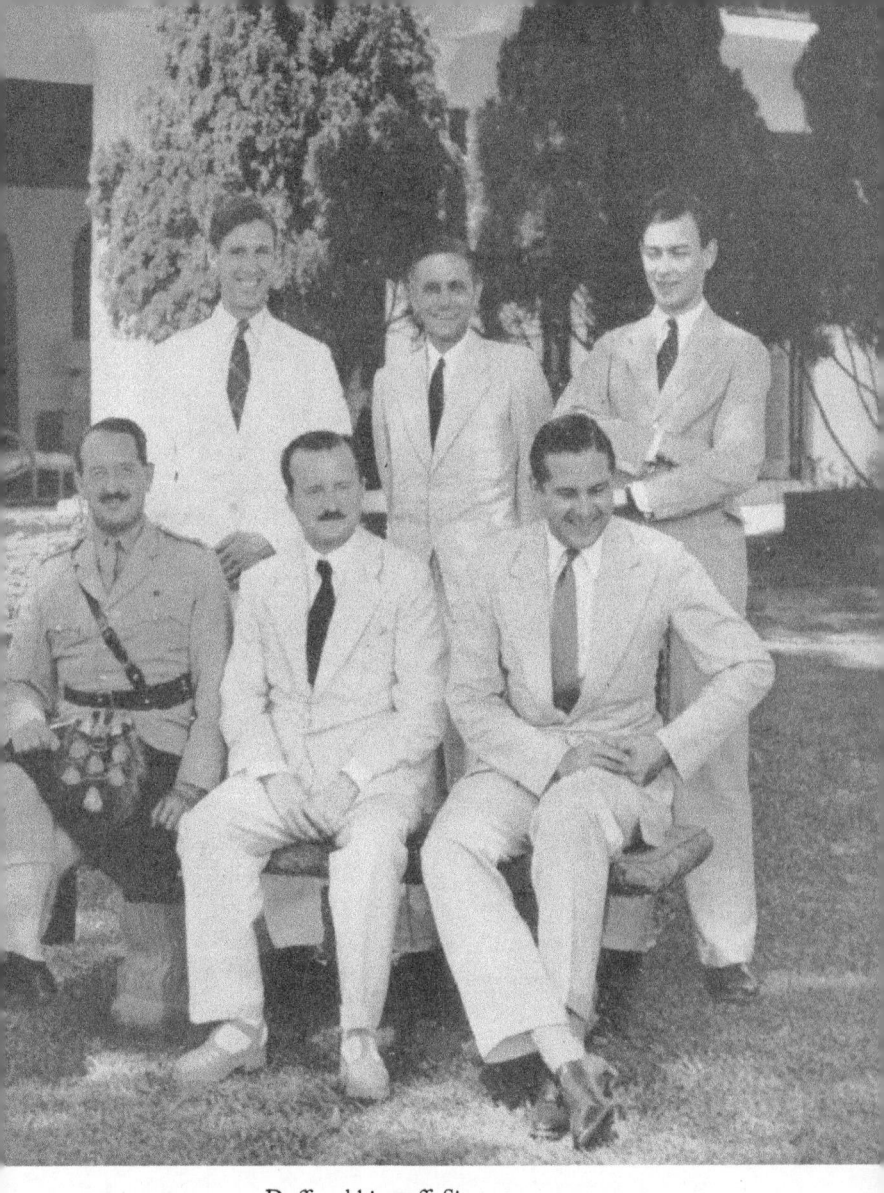

Duff and his staff, Singapore

Denis Allen   Alex Newboult   Martin Russell

Major Robertson   Duff   Tony Keswick

Minister of State in the Far East

Habbaniya, where Oliver Lyttelton, Minister of State in Egypt, is to chinwag with Duff.

'Dr Livingstone, I presume?' said Duff when he met us, only they were both like snowmen, white with cold and the silly chilled yet blazing sun not unfreezing them. Oliver bouncing and lusty as ever, his pretty wife pinched and frail.

'Shall we be back for Valentine's Day?'

Conrad must put on his thinking cap about my farm activities. He must pray Bashan and Isis and all the Hindus that Princess Cow will be functioning, and pray Baal too for the calf. Shall I have a sow this time that says 'honk'? We must requisition more arable and order fertilisers. Think, farmer, think!

Next stop Tiberias. We eat a nauseating meal in a lido and I discover (unfortunately long afterwards) that the waters beneath are those that Christ walked on – the Sea of Galilee. Over Jaffa, where they are throwing oranges and lemons into the sea, over Tel Aviv, over the Suez ditch (it's nothing more) to alight like an ibis on the Nile. Here we instal ourselves with hospitable Sir Miles and Lady Lampson, but they don't realise, poor things, for how long.

A load of trouble meets us. The Catalina flying-boat is due to leave next night for Malta, Gibraltar, Lisbon and Foynes. We buy extra wool sweaters, stockings and shawls and are all set when the sudden cry goes up 'No women on Service planes.' Duff fumes and Oliver Lyttelton, who has returned to his Cairo base on account of Egyptian crises, refuses to overrule the Priority Board, which he has the power to do, and ship me in place of mailbags. It is senseless to send me priority all round the world and impede me on the home run. Oliver is afraid of questions in the House and suggests a flying-boat being sent from England to Lagos to fetch us, and so home via Brazil and Baltimore. That extravagance should raise a louder question. 'Send Lady Diana and the luggage by sea,' I say in a voice that echoes suicide. They won't even use the inflexible-rule line, but indulge in so-called comforting reasons, 'No accommodation

for ladies,' 'War risks.' What about London Town and the Atlantic? Brendan Bracken is wired to by Duff asking him to expedite our flight out of Egypt. It is all disquieting, so are Eastern wars. This one is none too good and the Pacific one appalling. In the night we get news of the retreat into Singapore island. I can't think of anything else – Martin there, our Robbie fighting the last rearguard action, Alex Newboult, so gentle and so brave, my amah and the Chinese boys, all those good peaceful harmonious people in the delicate plaster house, bashed and crushed, crumbled and scrapped. Bernard Freyberg says that Singapore is a 'goner.' 'Once you get the fighters over your airfields it's over,' he says. We had them over ours – does he remember?

No news of departure. The Lampsons will refer to us in future as the Outstayers. Fortunately Sir Miles is oblivious of our nuisance, as he has a first-rate political crisis boiling up on him.

There have been students in the street shouting *'Vive Rommel'* and *'À bas l'Angleterre'* and *'Vive le Roi.'* These presumably are the Fascist palace-pro-Italian party, I gather a very small one. The King wouldn't see the leader of the Wafd until the Palace was surrounded with tanks and machine-guns, and a boat waiting to bear him, crownless, to Ceylon. Sir Miles went with some generals and a pistol for Pharaoh's head to insist on our advice being taken. In the other hand he carried an abdication drafted by the practised hand of Walter Monckton. Pen in hand the victim complained of the ink and then asked for another chance, so the tanks rolled home. When I came back from dining with my new favourite, Mr Alexander Kirk, American Minister here, a dear freak, at 11 p.m. I found the Embassy hall a babel of huddled groups – Oliver and Moira Lyttelton, Walter Monckton, Mr Michael Wright, lots of A.D.C.'s, Military Secretaries and unknowns. Wright and Walter see it reminiscent of Munich in not getting an abdication signed, but Oliver and H.E. were 'just certain' they had been right in the present arrangement. H.E.

came out of his den, dressed in a pearl-grey *frac*, arm-in-arm with Nahas Pasha, both grinning themselves in two. Nahas (now Prime Minister) was waiting outside for orders.

The original plan was for a *coup d'état* at seven. If the King proved stubborn the raid Alert was to be sounded and the palace surrounded. This hour synchronised with a 'few words' about the harmony of our two countries being delivered by Duff at the Anglo-Egyptian Club, where we were bidden as honoured guests. Our orders were to make for home should the siren go. I disliked the humiliation of us London veterans rushing for safety at the first alert. The clock struck seven and no wailing, so we thought all was settled. Really they had discovered that sounding the siren called all the soldiers in the vicinity to the palace, which was not a situation to suit the British plan, so the coup was postponed until nine. When the poor cowed Pharaoh slumped and agreed to send for Nahas and suited his action to the word, the zeal of the surrounding armoured divisions did not allow of the Pasha's entrance. It all sounds a bit comic-opera, but maybe will read in history as comparable to Brumaire 1799.

The Priority Board, after two weeks, has seen the light. Friday was, as usual, finally selected as departure-day, and we went down to the dock at 9 p.m. in fine fettle. I had had my whack at dinner and a final mouthful of brandy, and *three* turquoise amytols. I felt like a million dollars, hot as toast and V.C.-worthy. The Ambassador and Lady saw us into the ordinary flying-boat, the bad ship *Claire*. No stories true, no lying on bomb-racks with mail on your stomach, but the luxurious dentist-chair and to our surprise masses of inferior tough passengers instead of ourselves alone. We settled down. The lights were put out, or maybe fused, and I composed myself for a nice drugged sleep. An hour later I was rudely awoken and told to disembark as the trip was OFF. No reason given. It was like being roused in the middle of one's operation and being told to walk back to bed. We felt pretty aggrieved too. Bad. But wait until you hear this one. After a night at the

Embassy, with new sheets and apartments furbished up in the small hours, after an interminable day, we re-embarked in the *Claire*, same time, same drug-and-drink precautions. An Air Marshal to see us off. Everything honky-donk, we actually took off about 9.15, made it, and were airborne and relieved. I composed myself to sleep and was lost in a semi-calm when, at midnight, I woke to a certain unrest, a lot of vibration and a soothing Scots steward telling us, with what serenity he could, that we must get our life-jackets on immediately. He then walked up the emergency ladder, loosened all bolts of the trap-door above and took up his anti-panic position at the ladder's foot. It is difficult for me to believe that I was entirely *un*frightened. Was this unpredictable detachment due to amytol? Or is one like that in the hour of death? Duff thought that things looked desperate, and with reason. He told me afterwards that he recited to himself 'Be absolute for death; either death or life shall thereby be the sweeter.' He had learnt the *Measure for Measure* lines in the trenches and used them for such emergencies. I prayed a bit but in no great fear. I even put what trinkets and little valuables I had into my pockets for salvage. I don't know what the eight other passengers were doing because I was in the front seat and strapped in, and the chairbacks being high, I couldn't look backwards. The lifebelt is your seat and the back-padding of your seat, so one sat hard-arse from then on. After a little time a member of the crew appeared and said the situation had improved and that we had turned and hoped to land at Aboukir or Alexandria. Later another bulletin told us that, with luck, we should get back to Cairo, which indeed we did at 3 a.m., none the worse and no better off. The Lampsons had gone away to their desert home, so we had the dreary Embassy to ourselves. Clean sheets again.

We made our usual start on the 13th. The same formula, goodbye chorus, drinks, drugs, layers of wool and fur piled upon us. This time we only got as I thought about half-way to Malta when the soothing steward told us we were landing in

five minutes. 'How is it possible?' I said. 'We are not due for two hours.' 'But we're landing at Cairo,' he answered serenely, with no reason to follow. Only next day, for the third time in our bedroom at Government House reappointed with clean linen and flowers, did we learn that another aircraft was encumbering the hush-hush harbour of Malta.

On St Valentine's Day

We actually got away, nerves a-quiver. We reached Malta about five but circled around until seven. I was peeping through the black-out and seeing a bit of gunfire, but so great is my air-alarm still that gunfire doesn't seem to matter much. Malta looked as before, too beautiful. There was a non-stop raid all day. The people in the street seem completely disinterested and at the Palace you seek the roof whenever the gunfire sounds more than usually active. It is cruelly cold on the roof and you see nothing, but it is the custom. We arrived, perished with cold, to be told that there are no hot baths, and indeed as they have neither coal nor timber it is not surprising. I crouched over an electric heater and appeared for lunch. Grace, before so-called meals, and T.T. house-rules. The Governor Dobbie has the faith and heart of a saint and allows only rations on which no native can survive. Weevil-biscuits and spam is the fare offered the high, though below stairs, said a visiting chauffeur, 'I had a whole duck to meself.' Our greatest fear was to be held up in this worthy man's noble palace. God was good and sent us a flying-boat on the same evening. So good were the conditions that we by-passed Gibraltar. I saw its tall searchlight-fingers pointing from the black block of rock, isolated in Spanish flood-lighting, and at seven we landed at Lisbon. We were told that we could catch the old Dodo you saw us off on at seven that same morning and I'm writing on it now. 'Nobly, nobly' probably beneath me as I write. It is the last page of my block, and with God's good grace we should be home at 2 p.m. I'm much moved. How soon shall I see you?

6
Back to the Land

London seemed quiet, almost humdrum, after our alarums and lashing excursions. Morale seemed soaring in spite of the grue-some catastrophes that were piling up in the Far East and Africa. Conrad, older and tireder but unchanged in outlook and courage, was still my strength and my weakness.

There followed an interim, a time of indecision in ourselves and in our future. The Sussex land tugged hard at my inclinations – to return to farm-smells, routine, livestock dramas, to the idyll of last year's merry peasant life. I found, through some organisation that told you where a rush was on and when inexpert hands were needed, some work to tide me over the coming hang-fire weeks. The making of camouflage-nets seemed to have no appeal for war-hands, with its 1s. 6d. an hour and no music while you worked. This curious and useful task had dumped itself on the top floor of the Army & Navy Stores, so there I clocked in for the full working day. There were erected large open frames of wood like Gobelins tapestry equipment, on which tarred nets were stretched. To each frame were allocated two women, face to face through the trellis, both supplied with foliage-coloured strips of canvas. We would thread and knot them in roughly symmetrical patterns. I began as a time-worker opposite a calm middle-aged lady who, as the long hours ticked peacefully away, told me much of her past life and her aspirations. Older than me, she was far nobler. As war-effort she had resolved to learn Esperanto and hieroglyphs that, thus armed, she might be ready to follow the invading armies across the sea into countries where, not knowing their vulgar tongues, she could still be useful. The rest of us were a bit cretinous, dregs in fact, without zest or much morale.

Efficiency at the hand-destroying job was quickly learnt and I put myself on to piece-work. With no union this was allowed, and oh, the difference in production! The three or four of us on piece-work brought our sandwiches and pots of yoghourt and ate our snacks gaily enough on a bank of bogus woodland. Half our time was spent dodging bottle-necks, pursuing nets and strips that held us up by not appearing when they were wanted. We naturally turned out twice as many 'camouflages' as did lethargic 'timers' who gave most of the day to queueing up for cups of tea or the lavatory, and to snatching ten-minute breaks for a fag on the balcony, generally falling into a watch and thence into a weakness.

I can't remember how many weeks I threaded the sylvan green and the numberless shadows into a web to make pastoral protection for young gunners; not long, for by spring Duff, as Chancellor of the Duchy of Lancaster with little or nothing to do, was again commuting to Bognor and writing his book on King David, while I was back with the dung and the swill, the curds and whey, and the spiders. The goats roved and the sky was empty, so I re-stocked with seven dreadful little castrated nose-ringed pigs, as miserable as Alice's in Wonderland, with Sir Francis the drake, geese tame as dogs, making messes in my lap and wandering upstairs, downstairs, to and from the chamber. I also added a vast colony of rabbits. These were our meat, made succulent with pungent herbs, while their pelts, alumed and then nailed on to boards like flayed martyrs' skins, dried in the salty sun and made gloves for airmen. It was now that Enid Bagnold Jones, the torch of Rottingdean, came closely into my life and ardent affection. She too was a smallholder and most Wednesdays we two old farmwives would meet at Barnham market (by train to save our meagre petrol-ration), baskets of produce on our arms, our shoulders hung with nets and sacks, first quivering with living things to be auctioned, then carried back filled with kids and cheeping day-old ducks, often out of control, flustering free on to the platform – a rough-and-tumble harum-scarum Rowlandson-Caldecott scene of flying feathers, ourselves doubled with laughter at our obstreperous

merchandise. But the day I took my calf to sell there was no laughter – Oscar, my Guernsey, just three weeks old, proud-stepping as a prince and fearless of his butchers.

Our green lawns were littered with mobile wire enclosures in which ballets of white rabbits, with ears that the sun made luminous pink, frisked, cropped and fed on daisies. Duff would leave King David and, speculating about the Psalms, forget time, staring fascinated by their tricks and manners. He loved young animals tenderly, and old ones only a little less. At sundown the whole welter would be snatched up by their twilit white ears and thrust into their lettuced bolting-hutches.

This year too began the 'arable' waste-lands, building-plots ploughed gratis for me by a neighbouring farmer. Conrad would teach me how to plant them with Hungry Gap kale and mangels. The fly would have the kale and it would be to do again, with always the last resort of dibbing in some turnips or swedes. Hoeing filled every spare moment. The crops were bumper. No one molested us, the coast was clear. The usual mosaic of cartons, tins and silver-foil, both sides of our chestnut fence, had vanished, leaving fresh sands and in the little wood only the black pellets of goats.

I was happy, yet the news always seemed worse. Rangoon went in March. Singapore had fallen a month sooner. Conrad wrote:

> O dear! Libya and Tobruk! I feel anything may happen
> and Egypt may be lost in a jiffy like Singapore. They seem to
> be preparing us for Malta going now. I can't help wondering
> all the time if we could repel an invader. Why should the
> Home Guard fight any better than the Hong Kong,
> Singapore, Crete and Tobruk people? Why? We just believe
> in a happy-go-lucky way that it will be all right on the night.
> How awfully bad it looks! And at any moment the German
> airborne troops may arrive in Africa in thousands. There's
> not much agreeable in the world except Bognor. Bang, bang,
> bang! there goes Jerry! And we all say: 'Quite like old times.'

Tavistock writes: 'I and my friends will be wanted when the country is tired of politicians.' Wanted? I jolly well hope not, unless it's by the police.

One happy morning brought me a bombshell of a benignant kind – a suggestion that Captain Frend of the *Enchantress*, now in command of H.M.S. *Phoebe*, and shortly due to sail the deadly Atlantic from Canada, could bring my son home in his cruiser. Duff was overjoyed, but my excitement was naturally tempered by fears of the cruel sea. In September John Julius was booked for Eton and Duff was thinking of this more seriously than I was. I wrote discreetly to Kaetchen in March 1942:

> I was at Ditchley with Henry Luce. It will have given him a very erroneous picture of English country life. There's nothing lacking there, but you can't get anything anywhere else. Winston dresses night and day, and I imagine in bed, in the same little blue workman's boiler suit. He looks exactly like the good little pig building his house with bricks. On his feet he bears inappropriately a pair of gold-embroidered black slippers that I gave him – more suited to the silk-stockinged leg of William Pitt. Over all this, if chilly, he's got a quilted dressing-gown, once Pooh-Bah's of *The Mikado* fame, woven in bright spectrum colours. New neighbours dropping in think, I imagine, that it is ceremonial dress, as he never excuses its eccentricity.
>
> My farmer has lost two stone. He works too hard. I let him come here weekly because I can't live without him, and also the train and company and light chores rest him.
>
> Now for a serious topic – John Julius. A friend of ours who commanded *Enchantress* will call on you. He is due to return by sea under what sound to me advantageous circumstances, and will, if I like, bring John Julius home. In telegrams I will refer to 'the visit,' to 'Junior' and to his 'uncle.' The scheme sounds wonderful, but he couldn't of course take Nanny on a

warship. It would be a tremendous adventure for the boy and make up for the sneers of friends who have borne the blitz without him. All these plans are dependent on views about the invasion. We are so gloomy about the Orient that things nearer home don't seem so near.

Many code telegrams about Uncle and Junior's visit were exchanged, always without dates. I did not know if it would be this year, now or never. I could only importune God with prayers and try not to talk about it, even to Duff. When Wade rushed into my dairy, her eyes streaming, to tell me she'd taken the news of his arrival on the telephone we mingled our tears like two fountains in the sunshine.

Telegram to Kaetchen
  Dear dear custodian of my treasure ten million thanks for improving it and returning it bigger and better.

May 1942
  John Julius has arrived safely from the sea-cemetery and I am absolutely delighted with him. I think him good-looking and wonderfully disposed, ever happy and considerate and affectionate. He shows a sweet resolve to say everything here is good – the food, the scarcities, the lack of service. He had a wonderful crossing on the cruiser and it will be an experience to brag about when others vaunt their Atlantic flights of eighteen hours, for he has kept watch for submarines. He arrived on Thursday, and by Monday I got him pupilled to two tutors in Chichester for Latin verse and general things. Canada taught him better mathematics than he'd have got here. June 15 he has to pass, if he can, an examination called Common Entrance, which applies to all our Public Schools, and determines what form he takes. He has no misgivings and is quite confident of passing in a blaze of honours.

Don't scold me for reclaiming him (I knew you would) and don't impute selfishness to me. After two years one is used to being without a child who from now on will spend most of his years at school. The perils of the journey well out-weighed selfish desires. But for his character and his fame he must be in England now – not as an *acte de présence*, but he must be part of it, breathe the same air as his generation have to breathe, gas or no gas, fight the same fight and not be lapped in peaceful luxury. You say 'physiologically and psychologically he is better in the U.S.' I agree with neither. The food here is A1, any child with a mother worth her salt has all the eggs he needs, mountains of bread; chocolates and oranges and filthy fish-oils go to children only, thank God. Psychologically there is no deterioration here, or lack of balanced aspiration or common sense or courage, and no shade of hysteria or neurosis in any of the children I have known and now see growing to the age when they must 'take it;' Billy Wallace, the Benson boys, the Mannerses, Henry Uxbridge – the telephone rings and my chain of thought breaks. Lucky, as a bit about not living by bread alone was coming.

Now was the happiest peak in the war's black range of mountains. John Julius's English morning face lit my days. His laugh was infectious and the hard labour was lightened for me by his hands and heart. Half the day he was coached in Chichester, with the result that he took the creditable place of Upper Fourth. I wrote again to Kommer:

I took John Julius to Mr Herbert's house at Eton on September 15. He had no trepidations beforehand though the first half at Eton is considered by all a convulsion. We went there for the day a week before to buy him a top hat and second-hand trousers out of a rag-and-bone heap. His second-hand football-boots make him into a Little Tich. The place looked lovely, but no description of squalor by Dickens or Zola

can paint the 'low' of Eton. As against this, there's a room to oneself, free range of the town, freedom to go to which tea-house you please, to telephone from the post-office and no questions asked, to do your homework when you like, suddenly to be as grown-up as an undergraduate. It delighted us both, but after all it's only the liberty of all 'less privileged' schoolboys.

Conrad wrote from Mells in October:

I travelled from Paddington with a Lance-Corporal who quoted Juvenal to me in Latin and alluded lightly to Plato's *Republic*. The conversation must have continued on a high level, as he certainly mentioned the following people – Confucius, Buddha, Bernard Shaw, Bertrand Russell, Gandhi, Dreyfus, Roger Casement, Voltaire, Rousseau and many others. He told me that before the war he was a prize-fighter and acrobat. I don't think I have ever spoken to a prize-fighter before. They seem to be highly cultivated men.

My girlhood's friend Phyllis de Janzé, once Phyllis Boyd, often mentioned in these pages; Phyllis who had learnt to dance the tango with me; who had shared my room when my sisters married and with it all confidences and escapades and heart-aches; Phyllis of the coarse tongue of another age – Restoration perhaps – which suited her gusto and gave no offence; Phyllis of the flowing feline limbs and Egyptian scarab eyes that read and re-read for thirty years an unliftable illustrated volume of Balzac's entire works, was ill. Since the war began she had exchanged the *Comédie Humaine* for an enormous atlas in which to follow the grim progress of the battles. She studied our defeats with the same scrutiny as she had traced the recurring characters in the Balzac cat's-cradle. She brought both these books, her strange freehand embroidery, sub-consciously worked in bright silks, and her emaciated beauty to Bognor. Death's hand was on her, and after weeks of undeviating decline she went back to a London hospital by ambulance, her

magical eyes flowing with tears of weakness. It rent my heart to see her go, unrecoverable as I knew her to be. I put her in the care of Max Beaverbrook, in calamity of all guardians the most careful and generous. She had lived in my cramped little lodge, tended by me and her faithful-unto-death maid Ellen for weeks – a cottage delectable enough in sunny weather, but summer had been a chill winter of rain and restless winds and the perpetual moan of sirens. She resented the death she did not fear for separating her from the man she had long loved, and from the victorious end of the war she was intent upon seeing. Nothing of her that remains!

Hutchie too was ill unto death, though still able to be at Bognor for rests and change. His ending was bound to grieve his idolising family, and not least me, who had known twenty years of tender friendship and rollicking fun. Lowered by the losses to come, I wrote to Kaetchen:

> When November looms I think I'll pack up. I'm down, and there won't be enough to do here. In London I can work at munitions, motor-transport, canteen, a thousand things; here the cow will dry up, hens can lay by, pigs can go to market shrieking wee, wee, wee, Michaelmas is catching up on the geese, cheese is stocked on shelves, 60 lbs of honey are jarred, the refugees can eat what we leave of the rabbits. I feel smug with my granary full. Duff is happier, he's finished *David* and enjoys his new hush-hush job. It's hard work and interesting; he lives during mid-week in his own house under Daisy Fellowes's kind protection. Emerald Cunard cabled she was trying to get back. I do wish I could conjure her home; she'd be so much happier here. Hutchie is dreadfully ill and that is another chain of sorrow to drag. He's too ill to defend me when I come up next week before the local justice hand in hand with a baker who gave me dry bread for my animals.

Bread in these days was a dangerous commodity. I used to salvage sackfuls of stale loaves every other day in my trailer. Once I

almost cut off a mouse's tail with a carving knife as I sliced through the hard crust and crumb, but part of the haul was sometimes a little fresher. In Bognor one morning I was challenged by what was then called a 'snooper,' and ordered to show the contents of my ponderous sacks. Caught red-handed, I was summoned before the magistrate. Conrad, full of sympathy and solicitude, wrote:

You'll see by enclosed that the Frome Bench has given costs against Lord Woolton's 'snoopers.' I'm sure these prosecutions are unpopular. I think you ought to get a local solicitor to defend you and instruct him well beforehand. He must say the prosecution is a scandalous waste of time and sheer frivolity. Why in God's name should a baker *give away* bread which is edible? It's an insult to Bognor tradesmen, who certainly aren't half-witted but good, careful men of business. It is wasting the time of our respected Bench to bring such an idiotic charge – in war-time too when we are all so busy.

Then you and Wadey and Mrs King, the baker's wife, all go into the box and say on oath that only *stale* bread was used. If Duff won't go in the box, subpoena him and he can write a letter saying he never saw fresh, edible bread used. Put the two snoopers in the box for ruthless cross-examination, and on eliciting that they didn't cut open or taste the bread feign *astonishment*. 'What? You didn't *taste* it? But how in heaven's name can you judge if a thing is fit for human consumption without tasting it?' Was it the sort of bread they would be satisfied with at an hotel? Or be content to buy at the fixed price? If yes, then why did the baker give it away? Is it their experience of shopping in Bognor that the shopkeepers *give away* their goods? It isn't usual, you know.

The case ought never to have been brought. Englishmen don't like these underhand, spying, jesuitical, nosey-parker methods. Really we might be living under the Star Chamber. Is it for this that Pym and Hampden suffered? That must be your line. Plead Not Guilty. *Ask for costs*. Say your day's

farming has suffered from this most ill-judged action taking up hours of your valuable time – and the still more valuable time of our respected Justices.

I duly appeared in Court, anxiety well camouflaged by the Mexican hat and dung-laden clogs. I stood my trial and got off – I forget how. Could I have been bound over? I know that the fact that Lady Curzon of Kedleston had been caught burning her crusts and that Lady Woolton, wife of the Minister of Food, was said to have done the same in her bedroom rather than risk prison-bars by its being found in her ash-can, helped my defence. The case was withdrawn in October, leaving me without stain, to enjoy the radiant afterglow of summer, walking along the Arun river waist-high in meadowsweet to Arundel below Amberley's white cliff and the beech-crested Downs. The farm was an undreamt-of solace. I thought I had found an activity that would, as the hymns say, 'never cloy.' And so I had for war-days, but in peace-time with Plenty cheap in the markets, brought in choice to your door, I feared the incentive must go.

Maurice Baring was lying at Beaufort Castle, never to recover; and in the winter of 1942–43 Enid Jones and I went up in dark, unheated trains, to see him for the last time. Though he did not die till December 1945, we knew we should neither of us ever see him again. What an awful finality in saying 'I shall never see him again' of someone so near to one's heart and still alive and alert. Maurice was playful all his life and to the end – playful as snow, weightless as it dances down, white on a dark background of cloud. Newman said 'there were angels in disguise;' some get can-onised, some, like Maurice, don't. The budgerigar Dempsey still sat on his shoulder, chirping sweet nothings, the indefatigable nurse still dedicated her soothing gestures and words, her life itself, to his service. He was in a centre of the Faith he proclaimed, yet leaving him was so dreadfully sad that one wished he would soon win his last battle.

So ended 1942.

Emerald Cunard had arrived back before the New Year and had installed herself on the seventh floor of the Dorchester. She had been desperately unhappy in America, a country she had left in youth before it had recognised her remarkable worth, and to which she had returned (for reasons of sentiment) with reluctance and a certain hostility. Her relationship with her closest friend was foundering. The wreck was to be total, and I had had the saddest of reports from the English in New York of her dejected state. She had all but broken her last link with a past love and had succeeded in flying home *via* Lisbon.

There were great rejoicings on the seventh floor, by none more than me, since I had a curious protective feeling for this little creature whom I had known since I was fifteen, when she was still a young woman. Emerald was like a jewelled bird uncaged, perched on ormolu; hardly cut and glittering, one could not imagine her in skies or branches. She belonged to the salon. Her song was of wisdom and wit and love, sung with a lark's abandon and exuberance. For someone so rich in gifts and imagination she was extraordinarily unegotistical; she never referred to her own childhood or earliest youth in California but would tell you all about it if asked.

She had been crossed in love when very young. He was a cultivated Polish Count who had taught her the way to learn, and had encouraged her reading of the classics. She had married Sir Bache Cunard without more love than esteem breeds, and had lived for years in a historically famous house in a hunting county. Her choice of a husband, I'm sure, was directed (or rather misdirected) by a newly-broken heart, and no blind bargain could have suited her less. He was a goldsmith by hobby and, honouring her, would fashion leaves and laurel wreaths and a garden gate with – inevitably – the words 'Come into the garden, Maud,' wrought into its design (Maud was her real name). She despised it all as she did the wearisome society of 'sports.' Sir Bache was an M.F.H.

After her daughter Nancy's birth she must have gradually emancipated herself from those Leicestershire confines, to surround herself for the rest of her life with artists, writers, statesmen,

John Julius at Eton

Marjorie's drawing of Emerald Cunard

wits, beautiful women and youths of promise. She had the dows-er's gift for finding water and brought into my life many a rising man who might have blushed unseen in longer apprenticeship. Paddy Leigh Fermor was still almost blushing when I met him at Emerald's table, since when I mean never to lose the floodlight of his heart and mind.

Emerald had the hopping gait of a bird as she moved, a little restlessly, from perch to perch. You wanted to lure her to your hand, but she kept herself clear of human touch. Her hands were elegant little claws, her legs and feet of the slimmest and most shapely workmanship. There was nothing rushed about her mod-elling; everything was as finished as *biscuit de Sèvres*. Her skin and bosom were of the whitest, finest *pâte*. To my eyes she had scarcely changed in twenty-five years. The colours were the same, the out-lines remained. A few wrinkles made little difference to the prettiness that lay in widely set eyes, shining healthy teeth and infectious animation. She forced people to live and give and ask for more of the elixir she had distilled and was proffering.

Now in her war-time suite – one low, large room and a bedroom furnished a little *à la bergère* – she lived until she died in 1948. Not many years – only five – but rather happy ones. Most of her money had been dissipated in the cause of love and music and charity, and although she never said so, her possessions were slowly going to the sale-rooms to pay for her lavish entertaining. She spent little on her clothes, which were off the peg and never quite reflected her personality; her linen and scents and slippers and tortoiseshell and crystal were more illustrative of her tastes.

She had always lived in large Mayfair houses of the kind that no longer exist – houses in Grosvenor Square, Carlton House Terrace, and, once during the first war, in a beautiful eighteenth-century house in Cavendish Square with its staircase painted by Thornhill; generally they were stereotyped London houses, accepted as such and rarely redecorated. Her hotel salon was densely packed with valuable French furniture brought, it seemed at random, out of store. One's eyes boggled at the assortment – the *ad lib* eclecticism,

the unproportion, the mixed Louis's, the Buhl marriage-coffers on stands, the busts by Houdon and Mestrovic, the welter of velvet and gilt, the *objets de virtu* and the *pièces* bought in the fortuned days and chosen not by herself, who had not a collector's eye, but by the eyes and assessment of good advisers and nefarious friends and dealers, from the proffering hands of indigent artists or the houses of friends on the rocks; for, if Emerald caught me or my kind forgoing a treat for economy's sake, she would casually call, pretend to fancy a picture or a table or a rug and insist on buying it for double its worth. One's eyes, as I said, boggled at the agglomeration, and yet it did not disturb. It was so funny and characteristic of Emerald, of Emerald adapted.

This winter of 1942–43 (we must have gone back to the Dorchester for a month or two) I did some part-time work, but what I can't remember. There are no letters to help me; Conrad was up and down to London, Duff by my side, John Julius at school. Duff and I had from his birth, on which day the practice was to put a boy's name down for Eton, looked forward to the old school revisited – the Fourth of June, strawberries and cream, one's own flannelled cricketer to be watched and prayed for from beneath the shade of elms; ices, hampers of cakes and cold salmon and walks with intimate talks through fields where Waterloo was won. War-time's hammer hit those hopes on the head. Duff never had the day off; this winter I would go alone, standing up in a crowded, unheated train. John Julius would be waiting for me in his outgrown, second-hand, threadbare Eton clothes with blue hands and grinning pink face. He would ask me to come in trousers, which seemed very unusual; but he was never convention-ridden, and I suppose he liked to see me as he knew me. It was alarmingly cold. In his scrubby little room there was no fire and no comfort of any kind; even sweets were rationed; so I came empty-handed. We would walk up and down that High Street till I knew every article that hung or stood in the shop-windows. Luncheon at Miss Masters's restaurant was a bright spot, and the long afternoon we would spend mostly at the Art School because it had a minimum

of heating. The journey home again, standing up in the corridor, was blacked out and took for ever. Spring made the visits a little less austere. We both rather hated games, so we still walked the unaltered High Street and dawdled at lunch to pass the time. By summer I was too busy ever to leave the farm, except for the Fourth of June, when it poured with malevolent relentlessness the livelong day – no fireworks because of Jerry and alas, no sisters in floppy hats, no swamping of boats, no nothing. The dear boy was doing very well under the tutelage of J. S. Herbert, whom I had come to like very much in spite of my shyness with masters, and the following year he was made an Oppidan Scholar. Duff and I preened ourselves in pride.

I seem to remember we dined most nights with Emerald and the politicians, the writers, the Foreign Office, the freelances and the Free French in the shape of Eve Curie, Gaston Palewski, Guy de Rothschild and Michel Saint-Denis. Other nights Emerald would go to the theatre, half-empty because of air-raid menace. But Emerald had no physical fear of the blitz, or of anything except the police. Some Irish atavism in her blood made her tremble at the thought of the police, but bombs she defied, and she never believed they worried other people. She would say in good faith when the apprehensive sought shelter 'It's quite different for me, you see, as I don't sleep anyway.' She read all night and never forgot what she had read. Alone in the small hours, between classical and current readings she would disentangle the welter of the morrow's twenty guests culled at random for dinner or the opera, and in her mind place them in her own unconventional conjunctions. Her mind was, when not inspired by fancy, serviceable and orderly. Her erudition perpetually surprised scholars and ignorants alike; she would come out with some obscure fact in the life of Apollonius Rhodius ('he was an African, you know') or refer *en passant* to the Spintri that swam for his delectation between Tiberius's legs. She called Lady Colefax and Mrs Greville (both hostesses of note) 'the Dioscuri of gloom' and could quote with a feathery touch a chorus-ending from Euripides.

She loved me dearly for my mother's sake; my mother befriended and admired her from the earliest Maud days. And she adored Duff and spoilt him in a thousand delightful ways. George Moore, whose Grace and Muse she had been, bequeathed her a few very fine Impressionist pictures, which at her death were divided among her daughter Nancy, Sir Robert Abdy and me.

In earliest March I again restocked my farm and settled down for the third time to rusticity, to the same absorbing life of labour, while Duff commuted and Conrad came weekly. Ambition grew; increase was all-important. Mushrooms were tried, and proved my only hundred-per-cent failure. Cheeses, now that the threat of invasion had lessened, changed their austerity into frivolity. I got the recipes of Coulommiers and Pont l'Evèque among others and made experiments in temperatures and maturities; England's capricious cold-snaps and heat-waves precluded successes (and failures) on a big scale. I told the bees the news and prospects as usual, for this is as traditional a law in the apian world as is the banging of frying-pans when you follow your emigrating swarm, thus proclaiming that the buzzing treasure is yours and not your neighbour's, and I told them this season to work overtime to make me mead in September. (Duly made and bottled – ambrosial but lacking authority.) I began to worry about Conrad. Hard work was killing him – the patrolling all night, ploughing and penning sheep all day, drenched to the skin ('the rain went into my neck and ran out of my boots') was too hard a tax on his age.

I'm wearied ploughing up grass, the nicest form of ploughing. It tires one's arms more than one's legs. Virgil says '*Nudus ara*,' which means '*Plough naked*.' Triptolemus is the name of the man who invented ploughing. It was a remarkable thing to think of.

21 March

I listened to Winston, but post-war schemes don't take my fancy a lot as I shall soon be dead, almost certainly without

posterity. He seemed to imply that lazy people, including pub-crawlers, would not be tolerated in the brave new world. But he didn't say how they would be stopped. By imprisonment? I've read *David* in the *Sunday Times* – a mistake, because snippets always are a mistake. It's very good indeed. What a poetical man Duff is! The most poetical man I know. I wonder if the Germans will hear about it. They'll be more certain now than ever that Duff is really a Jew. Maurice is a poet. He is a lovable man. Would you agree he has a vein of silliness which you and I lack from not being poets? No, no – Duff is a poet and certainly is not silly at all.

2 April

My drake (he has four duck wives) is absolutely dithering for love of a large speckledy hen and pursues her ceaselessly, covering her with kisses which she simply hates. He goes to all lengths and never once looks at the thirty other hens. The men have never heard of such a thing before, which must be characterised as unnatural.

Grief, as regular as winter, came this March in a severe, gnarling way. The last time I had seen my cherished Kat Kommer, in 1941 on Long Island, a quarrel – something said, something done – clouded our leave-taking. It had not haunted me; I felt safe in my devotion to him and I am not much troubled by remorse (without which penance the God-fearing tell me one may not hope for salvation). I had written him a rough letter that ended with loved-though-worn jokes and thanks and decorations galore for all he had done for John Julius and for me.

When Duff told me of his death I remembered this last wrangle; but there was so much more to regret than one of many such. He had dropped dead. His heart had stopped as he had been warned it would, while reaching for a book in the Ambassador Hotel, New York.

His wide quantity of friends, in many capitals and countries, were shocked and sad according to the quality of their relationship

with this unique genius from Czernowitz. Iris Tree, his 'doll,' his 'derelict' of *Miracle* days, wrote his funeral oration, which was recited in the synagogue to a multitude of devotees assembled there to honour him. Of the many sad I am sure I was the saddest. Duff said how glad Kaetchen would be, did he know of the bitter tears I shed, and the darkness of the cloud I walked under.

April

Darling Conrad, I am quite quite down. I wish the God of Kaetchen's fathers would wipe the tears for ever from my eyes. Why do we always write in quotations and talk in them? Its eroticism – no, do I mean esotericism? – must irritate others.

Material things were tightening up in England but doom was relaxing its vice upon us. Rations were shorter; such noxious meat-alternatives as whale and snoek were fobbed off upon the patriotic. Clothes had become a struggle and were mostly second-hand. American friends sent stockings and nightgowns. Petrol-allowances were decreasing. Forms, controlling milk, shell eggs, poultry and pigs' balancing meal, coupons lost and found and exchanged and illegally black-marketed, cluttered our pockets and became a whole-time nightmare. The swill, once mine for the taking, now was processed and mass-produced. But somehow we carried on, with better hopes ahead. Conrad wrote:

13 May

We had a really nice day with things growing and housemartins coming back to their nests. I thought I should never see those elegant birds again. Bognor went in a flash. I never in my life knew time to go quite as fast, and a man's life is but to say 'one.'

The stallion was due to call to see if Kitty was *enceinte*. He always calls again, free of charge, three weeks after to see if

all is well. But he never came. Forgot, I suppose. The carter is sure Kitty isn't horsing.

Katharine got a note from her Aunt Muriel saying she must see her urgently. K. hurried round and then her aunt asked her to pray for the conversion of the Jews. Katharine said she would.

I've finished Chris Hollis's book. In it he says once more that you've only got to think of the men who don't go to church and you'll notice they are a degraded type. I think he means me.

What a triumph for Lord Grantley to be made co-respondent at the age of 87. I wish there were more like him. Indeed I wish I was more like him myself.

27 May

The stallion remembered and called. It seems he calls *every* three weeks just to see if everything is all right and carries on so all summer. An attentive lover, and all for three guineas.

I travelled with a clergyman and he talked of the Battle of Ethandun, fought 878 A.D. If it is his regular conversational opening he can't often find anyone as interested as I am and able to keep the ball rolling.

Changed times. I asked Mrs H. my neighbour if she minded her three children aged twelve, nine and six standing in the farmyard to watch the bull servicing my cow. She seemed surprised that I should ask. No, not the slightest objection to it, and 'Straw' (the one aged six) helped the men haul out a calf from its mother's womb one day when I was away. No more storks and gooseberry bushes.

This coming winter I resolved to remain under the livestock's yoke. We ate so well that friends wallowed and felt refreshed after two days of cream and chickens; there were still more good lobsters in Bognor seas than had ever come out of them. John Julius

was with us for the summer holidays, and the dark clouds of disastrous news that we were used to had a play of light upon them. One evening after dinner came into our blacked-out cottage a blazing Very-light. Freda Dudley Ward on the telephone told us Mussolini had fallen. 'The beginning of the end,' 'half-way home,' we said, exaggerating from joy.

Conrad wrote:

> The bull's licence has come. He had to have a licence like a motor car. There are lots of rules, e.g. what to do if the bull dies and what to do if the bull is castrated, then what to do if the owner dies, but nothing about what to do if the owner is castrated. No one seems to think that matters.
>
> Last night I heard Noël Coward explain on the wireless that 'Don't let's be beastly to the Germans' was *ironical*. It seems that lots of people who heard the song just thought it was a pro-German expression of hope that we would let the Germans off lightly. It seems incredible, but it shows they are on their guard if inclined to be a bit literal.
>
> I thought our last day's mangel-pulling was paradise – an opportunity to say '*Verweile doch, du bist so schön.*'
>
> If I had a wish I would like it to be 7 a.m. at Bognor and me just coming out to carry back your milk-pail and the whole day before me. I wouldn't mind if it were raining as we could read *Barchester* and do the crossword by the fire.

It was never again to be.

7
The Giraffe and the Duckling

In *Old Men Forget* Duff told how, in October 1943, Anthony Eden asked him to call at the Foreign Office and invited him to go either to Algiers as British Representative to the French Committee of Liberation with the rank of Ambassador and the prospect of going on, as such, to Paris in due course, or alternatively to go as Ambassador to Italy, when the enemy were driven out of Rome, which was then expected to take place sooner than it did. Duff had no hesitation in preferring Algiers, and asked only for time to consult me before definitely accepting.

My face, I suppose, could not hide the shock of aversion that his first words, walking home from the commuter's bus, 'How would you like to be Ambassadress in Paris?' gave me. Nothing I would dislike more. I expect I said so, for I generally said all. Even without the farm's loss to mourn, and the life that had soothed me into a new happiness, I shunned the very idea of such a position. I had aged. John Julius must remain in England for war and school. North Africa was far away, and only reached by skyway. I knew nothing of Algiers except that Mademoiselle's eldest brother had done his service there in 1900. I shuddered at the thought of losing independence, of wearing conventional clothes again, of my stammering nursery French, of chaperonage by chauffeurs, of leaving Conrad, friends and Wade, the centre and hub, the map-rooms and planning in London. Were my excursions and alarums never to stop?

I don't think that I gave more than a few feeble moans, and before we reached our door I was for going and Duff for staying. It was always that way, and a good way. I had remembered too that just before the war he had said 'I should like to finish up

Ambassador in Paris,' and I, hardly weighing the probability, had concurred and said 'Yes, yes.' Now on this October evening I could see how he glowed with the fulfilment of an ambition, and a wave of my own old strength for adventure came welling back to join the tide.

And so I was off again on the next alarum. No one could give me any idea of Algiers; no one I knew had been there except those who had not come back. I felt unequal to diplomatic life. The French I knew was culled from the simpler passages of *Les Malheurs de Sophie*. The last day in London wore its nervous way through, shifting its hour of departure, arranging for my head to ache as acutely as my stomach quaked and quivered, and for John Julius to be nicer than he had ever been before. Off we set by car for the deep west, with John Julius on the box to see the last of us. At Lyneham the R.A.F. boys brought us to a firelit collation, and to darken that moment of cheer a lantern-jawed pessimist delivered us a short lecture on the dangers of the flight. We were issued with boots, helmets and a nosebag apiece for oxygen.

Once in the air I could see the world below through a chink in my black-out. I couldn't tell if the silver floor were earth or water. The bright stars and the black corner of the wing seemed real enough. Strange though not to know the country you are crossing; Portugal or Spain must have accounted for the lights I saw. The dawn gave promise and soon it was day, and day showed the coasts of Europe and Africa. An hour or so of Morocco, Algeria and the hills of Atlas, every acre cultivated and rich but so wet that through the young growth one could always see the sun reflected (as mirrory as rice-fields). We were met at Maison Blanche, the airfield for Algiers, by Gaston Palewski, then Chef de Cabinet to General de Gaulle (referred to by all English-speakers as Wormwood), and by our Comptroller, called Freddie Fane, a man in appearance like a pocket Mephistopheles to whom in time I became devoted. He had been Secretary of the Travellers' Club in Paris and was therefore sacrosanct in Duff's eyes. He brought us plenty of bitter news, delivered as glad tidings. Without condolence he told us that we

were to share the house with Mr and Mrs Rooker, that there was no cooking-stove, no heating or hot water, no car, no telephone, nothing in the nature of linen, china or plate, and that he was trying to find Italian prisoners as servants but so far had not succeeded.

As he spoke we turned into a very beautiful, measureless *Belle au Bois Dormant* demesne. As far as eye could see was jungle of palm and cypress-covered hills, green as jade. We came to a Moorish door, a courtyard, hammam and tiles, cypress and arches. The home of Omar, I thought, Jamshid's palace – but inside! O dear, ugliness can produce pain and this ugliness was of a colossal kind, combined with gloomy darkness, paralysing cold and dusty, musty squalor. The style was ragged palmist – a dingy junk-shop, brass tables and hubble-bubbles green with verdigris, heavy brass beds thinly overlaid, unvalanced and equally green, exposing cracked chamber-pots, baths brownly stained, lavatory pans not describable, no looking-glasses or curtains, no washerwoman (there being no soap), no anything, sans, sans, sans.

Harold Macmillan, whose official position we were taking over, lived not far away in a desirably vulgar villa, and it was on his good grace that we were to depend for warmth, food and baths. Algiers was totally bereft of any buyable thing – not a plate, hammer or nail, not a sheet of paper could be bought. Glasses were beer-bottles cut down, with jagged lipsticked edges. Streets and streets of shuttered shops, and the few that were open closed at 11 a.m., cleared of what they had to sell. I tried those first few mornings to buy essentials – soap, electric bulbs, candles, pillows, toilet-paper, matches. Not a hope. It was very discouraging. Cold wrapped us round. It was warmer outside the thick walls than within them. North Africans cater for summer's heat and forget December's frost. I slept *in* my fur coat, shaking it out vigorously for day wear. In the morning we would heat water on a primus stove and improvise a towel. Tinned milk and acorn-coffee for breakfast, warmed by the only occupant of the palace, a skittish, greasy, not unlovable old maid called Louise, who, when winter's discontent and dearth

were over, became my friend. Duff was undaunted – he the sybarite, me the Mark Tapley; our roles were reversed. Freddie Fane, the London link (a lock of White's hair), gave him confidence, serenity and the comfortable giggles of old club jokes, while I moped on a dilapidated pouffe and wondered how I could conjure up some djinn from a bottle to produce me courage, coal, a gift of tongues, pink spectacles, a cow, some geese and goats, and most of all Wadey, my maid, to cosset my frailty.

6 January

Darling Conrad, Duff has not yet had a bath. Anne Dupree, daughter of Ambassador Chilton who was in Hendaye during the Spanish war, teaches me diplomatic ways and takes me shopping. I bought with triumph two minute five-candle-power lamps, one pink and one blue, both painted (bowls and shades) with Scottie dogs. They will help us to read and dress by. I lie awake with galloping out-of-hand thoughts, some niggling ones about ash-trays, others about British prestige and Duff's dignity. A conflict goes on as to whether to be strong or accommodating, whether to persevere with these Augean stables or leave them uncleaned, hoping for H.Q. staffs to move out in two or three months, and face uncomplaining this miserable squalor. Freddie has found some prisoners. They sleep on stone. I've got a petty-fire burning in one of the brothel-like sitting-rooms; so far brushwood is the only fuel, so feeding it is one man's whole-time job. Mrs Rooker and I sit unthawed in front of the frivolous flames.

Harold Macmillan is our saviour. He's a splendid man. He feeds us and warms and washes us. One day he'll be Prime Minister. I've put my money (nay, my shirt) on him. He's my horse. This afternoon a reception was given at his villa. I was greatly dissatisfied with its tone. It was said by most of the staff to be our introduction; it was also to be the Minister's leave-taking. We were not stood to receive with Harold but

were steered through as guests and introduced to no one. There were two hundred *invités* and one passed us to another. As de Gaulle sent a proxy, I felt that Freddie might have represented Duff. Catroux was there, and legions of Generals, Ministers, Senators, Norwegians, Czechs and Yugoslavs. I stood and sweated and struggled with my French the best I could. A 'few words' are not so hard. One develops a set piece explaining how one can't speak, and a short description of the night-flight and one's away with the next stranger. '*Comment trouvez-vous Alger?*' is a hard one. The newcomers talk only of their discomforts. The topic is as monotonous as drink was in American prohibition days. The older hands aren't the least *épatés* by one's groans and sordid disclosures. Their standards are at rock-bottom and they've none of them had butter for months.

Gaston Palewski took me to lunch at the Inter-Allied Club, where all the upper homeless eat. He made me skip while he skipped (conversation unhindered) to get warm after being three minutes in this house. He may go as representative to Moscow. I hope not, as he's good to me and takes me to the Kasbah and to palaces. I picked from some Omar garden a sprig of rose geranium and absinthe herb and felt less dejected. Colonel Warden* sends for us to Marrakesh. I talked to him on the telephone and that reanimated me. He is to do something about our lodging and a car. There are no taxis, no hitch-hiking, nothing but trams which they warn you are typhus-ridden. At Harold Macmillan's, after a welcome wash, I flung myself on someone's bed and slept for an hour to be woken by Randolph's clarion call. He had just arrived with Brigadier Fitzroy Maclean, the partisan hero, on wing to see his father.

Randy is to stoke Winston up into giving some orders in our favour. General Eisenhower, for instance, has a fine

---

* Winston's *nom de guerre* of the moment.

house which he has vacated today, and which his successor, Jumbo Maitland Wilson, hopes to take over immediately. We might, with pull, get it. Then Air-Marshal Tedder has just left a little Parisian gem, having been asked repeatedly to bequeath it to us. He refused against real pressure from Macmillan, on the grounds that he must leave it to his American successor. Seeing these civilised houses has stirred Duff into action, or anyway outraged reaction. After all why the hell should these warriors, who are supposedly fighting a war in Italy, loll in luxurious immunity, while we permanent missionaries, with orders to entertain and impress, are left nothing but sties?

The only people who live like real ladies in painted rooms and white satin feather-beds with heat radiating from every niche, indirect lighting, washerwomen and slaves, are the higher ranks of the Allied Forces. They should hie to their tents, hangars and hammocks and leave these soft delights to middle-aged diplomats. Duff's U.S. opposite number is in a gorgeous villa, the Commander-in-Chief Mediterranean and his Sparks and Flags live in a luxury palace warm as a stove; the Russians have three villas. We must be known as His Majesty's Goofs. It's the army v. civilian war, as old and strong as sex. It began in the Stone Age. All these slights and strains, plus no water, no eating in, no sofa, no scope for my job of feeding and cheering the dejected (I might as well be a Mussul-woman) make me feverish from 4 a.m. till 7 a.m. I'm sure a kettle would boil and splutter if stood on my head, as it did on Sir John Simon's in Low's cartoons.

From these first days we were welcomed and cherished by General and Madame Catroux, who lived exactly opposite our gates. His Spahi and Senegalese sentries challenged us from the doors of authority. Owning no car we could not wave our Union Jack. Once in their warm Mahommedan house, we met many of the mighty and ex-mighty; General Giraud, a more wooden

Kitchener of Khartoum, looked too young for his years. One felt his key had been lost and if one found it and wound him he would walk nicely round and round. General Pechkoff, Maxim Gorki's adopted son, I was drawn to at first sight for being Russian and poetic, for being a General in the Foreign Legion and for having one arm. (He was later to become French Ambassador in Tokyo.) There was the great General de Lattre de Tassigny, of whom much more later, and his famous Personal Assistant, Eve Curie, the nonpareil of efficient amazons. La Générale Catroux had sparks flying out of her own Ambulance's khaki while showing unexpected tenderness towards us. Two reliable khaki supporters lived at the Catroux gate – Minou de Montgomerie, the Egeria of the Free French flying like a bee over the long North African littoral in V.I.P. aeroplanes, and Elizabeth de Breteuil, equally privileged, generously built, cheerful and confident, loved greatly by her friends as by the women's military units that she trained. What leisure these redoubtable women found was dedicated to keeping us warm and cheerful. Together we cowered over their inadequate stove, sipping glasses of hot brandy and water. At the Catroux' we met many good men and true – René Massigli, René Capitant, René Mayer, Diethelm, Tixier, Emmanuel d'Astier de la Vigerie, Lapie, all resistant as the Great Wall of China.

The Prime Minister at Marrakesh was recovering from an alarming attack of pneumonia. I wrote to Conrad:

> The Colonel has never been off the line, arranging,
> postponing, advancing and rearranging our visit to him. The
> idea was that he wished to see de Gaulle first and then us.
> De Gaulle puts it off from day to day, chops and changes,
> and in my opinion doesn't mean to go – probably thinks it
> beneath his dignity – so for the moment we go alone
> tomorrow for a few days. I hope to have the Colonel's own
> wings which Randolph is borrowing to bring him back
> today.

The Colonel's telegrams to Harold Macmillan and others are ever so sharp. I'm glad, as I used to think those Duff received in Singapore were a little acid. These are much worse, perhaps due to cross convalescence, or is it waxing too great? I must get up now. We've asked Leslie Henson, Tommy Trinder and Joe Brown in for a drink at noon. It will make a change.

10 January

We're off today; de Gaulle goes in two days, so I was wrong. It's early and the sun is just rising on a clear sky. The mountains must be crossed. Oxygen perhaps? Tremors begin. I shall peer down on the snow-laden shoulders of Atlas and pray not to add my burden to his.

Marrakesh

Here I am on top of the deep romantic chasm, where Alph the sacred river runs. It's wonderfully hot; the sky is without blemish of cloud. We've just had a terrific lunch *al fresco* – stuffing ham and chickabiddy smothered in mayonnaise, fruit and *gateaux*, washed down with shandygaff. It's been a most wonderful *entr'acte* in the grim, cold misery of Algiers. We flew here in the Colonel's fine plane. Four hours it took, and I weathered them. An ample champagne collation was served, and three charming young gentlemen were thrown in for good measure.

The party is a circus. It's lodged in a millionairess's pleasure dome, all marble and orange-trees, fountains and tiles, in the richest Mahommedan style. *We* live in the hotel (two bed, two bath, one sitting-room). We are guests of the United States Army, so a tray with gin, whisky, two sherries, coca-colas and a carafe of fruit-juice, plus all the American *Lifes* and *Times*, are laid out for our delectation. At the villa there is a big set-up of decoders, W.A.A.F.s, map-room, secretaries at two a penny, your old doctor of the Yeomanry,

Lord Moran. The Colonel's wife and W.A.A.F. daughter Sarah were on the airfield to meet us and buzzed us by U.S. car, complete with immense white star on its camouflaged side, to the pleasure dome. There was our old baby in his rompers, ten-gallon cowboy hat and very ragged oriental dressing-gown, health, vigour and excellent spirits. Never have I seen him spin more fantastic stuff, the woof of English and the warp of Slang. Max [Beaverbrook] the Calvinist is here, dressed in black and utterly uncontributive to the general pool of chatter.

There is a lot of talk about our housing problems and plans for purging officials who obstruct our hopes. No sign of Wormwood yet. The meeting was due on the 12th and we were to return to Algiers the same afternoon. January 11th was to be picnic day, but it's always picnics here.

In the evening we walk in the *souks* (i.e. markets) and buy what we can. I've bought the stuff for a dress, a pair of candlesticks, two pairs of shoes, a large straw hat of native design (of course), eleven metres of white linen, etc. Bumf unprocurable, sunglasses unprocurable, but the whole place offers a thousand times more than Algiers does.

After dinner the weaving goes on until 1 or 2 a.m., interrupted by abortive plans for our flight home and sudden new veerings and *volte-faces* on the Wormwood front. Our man asked a little arbitrarily for an insufficiently starred French General, de Lattre, to be brought. This has been refused, so tonight there was an explosion followed by threats of being too ill to have an interview with the Giraffe at all. Duff is the oilman. Meanwhile the town is being beflagged and the local chieftains, smelling the news, are assembling without the city wall. I hate to leave and miss the drama.

12 January

Woken up at eight by the telephone telling us all plans were altered and would Duff go up to the villa quick, quick.

177

Later

Duff is working on him now.

Later again

We hear we are to stay till the 14th, when the *ménage* breaks up, that all is set for a reconciliatory lunch today and a super picnic tomorrow. Great fun. The streets are full of soldiers, black and white ones, spitting and polishing; tricolors and double crosses and V's for Victory are splashed everywhere. Our boy is not in a happy mood, having just heard of the shooting of Ciano and Bono. He is not to wear his romper suit, but Clemmie says we'll have a struggle to get it off. It's to be uniform, and luncheon is not to be in the dining-room on account of its gloom, but in the brighter hall. Out of doors is not considered formal enough. A lot of rehearsing is gone through of the way the General shall be brought in, who will stand where, and who will interpret. The morning's last resolution is that pleasantries shall be talked at lunch and that no 'conference' should take place, but Clemmie has given him a Caudle curtain-lecture on the importance of not quarrelling with Wormwood. She thinks it will bear fruit. As Wormwood is sure to take offence it's hardly worth all the planning. Anyway Flags bungled the arrival completely, but it didn't matter; hands were shaken cordially and down we sat to lunch.

I had my host and a new charmer, name of Rosetrees. It all went like a dinner, which it was, and afterwards the hostess, the charming Consul's wife and I went a-shopping, leaving the boys to it. When we returned some two hours later, they were still in a huddle. By five it was over and was declared first to have done no harm, and later to have been really quite a success. Duff and his master both did a quick change of coat, Duff praising the other's patience and deploring Wormwood's vile temperament, manners etc., and the other talking most indulgently about him. He has agreed to appear at the review tomorrow and take the salute

together with the General. It will be cold as charity, and he'll have to stand up for one and a half hours, and I'll feel I'm catching a new pneumonia for him.

13 January

The last exciting day. It began at nine with the review, beautifully staged in a little grandstand, the Caliph, El Glaouï, the King of the Atlas, officials, wives, Duff and me. I cried from start to finish because of the yells and shouts of *Vive*, the French's joy and pride in the token army that passed, their *avions* buzzing just over our heads, their own few guns, their own flags and courage. The sun blazed on this inspiring scene.

Wormwood said a few words, exactly right, emphasising the honour and privilege of having so great a man beside him. Doesn't it all sound lovely? Thank God the *Vives* were pretty evenly divided between them.

The final picnic is tomorrow. Talking of the last picnic, an American paper published a picture of the Big Three at Teheran with the caption 'Most Important Meal since the Last Supper.' God bless you, my darling Conrad. I think it will not be so hard to get back for school holidays. We seem in fine favour.

Later, after the review, which seemed gruelling enough on Winston in one day, we had our eighth and last picnic. The picnic consists of eight cars with white stars and U.S. drivers (the whole town is run by the U.S. exclusively) with two or three guests in each, some 'tecs distributed around, and a van laden with viands, drinks, cushions, tables, chairs and pouffes. The advance party leads off an hour before the main body, reconnoitres and selects a valley miles away, windless, comparatively fertile and green, with water if possible.

We, pioneers that day, chose Demnat. We drove some eighty miles through the country of the Dissidents, very beautiful, olive-green and fertile, with towns walled and

179

fortressed by their *kasbahs*. We came climbing to a famous gorge, or rather to the lip of it, and there we decided to pitch our pleasure. There we laid out our delicatessen, the cocktail was shaken up, rugs and cushions distributed, tables and buffets appeared as by a genie's order, and as we finished our preparations the main party arrived.

The Colonel is immediately sat on a comfortable chair, rugs are swathed round his legs and a pillow put on his lap to act as table, book-rest etc. A rather alarming succession of whiskies and brandies go down, with every time a facetious preliminary joke with Edward, an American ex-barman, or with Lord Moran in the shape of professional adviser. I have not heard the lord doctor answer; perhaps he knows it would make no difference.

I had just time to run down the dangerous steep mule-track to the cyclopean boulders, sprayed by gushing cascades that divided them. The pull up was a feat, and the sun turned the cold weather into a June day. All spirits rose to the beauty and the occasion – all, that is, except old Max Calvin, whose creased livid face is buried between a stuffy black hat and a book. A lot of whisky and brandy, good meat and salad, and 'little white-faced tarts' (to use Winston's expression) are consumed and then, of course, as I feared, nothing will quiet the Colonel (no assurance of the difficulties and the steepness) but he must himself venture down the gorge. Old Moran once mumbled a bit about it being unwise. It carried as much weight as if it had been said by an Arab child in vulgar, rustic tongue. So down he goes and, once down, he next must get on top of the biggest boulder. There were a lot of tough 'tecs along, including the faithful Inspector Thompson, but even with people to drag you and heave you up, it is a terrific strain and effort in a boiling sun when you have just had a heart-attack. Clemmie said nothing, but watched him with me like a lenient mother who does not wish to spoil her child's fun nor yet his daring – watched him

levered up on to the biggest boulder, watched him spatchcocked out on top of it. Shots were snapped, a little Arab boy was bribed to jump into the pool, and then this steep, heart-straining ascent began. I tore up for the second time, puffing like a grampus. It seemed to me that if a rope or strap could be found to pass behind his back, while two men walked in front pulling the ends, it would be better than dragging him by his arms. I could find nothing but a long tablecloth, but I wound that into a coil and stumbled down with it. Big success! He had no thought of being ridiculous (one of his qualities) so he leaned back upon the linen rope and the boys heaved our saviour up, while old man Moran tried his pulse at intervals. This was only permitted so as to prove that his heart was unaffected by the climb.

The picnic was over. While hampers were repacked, the party walked around and watched the natives tilling, or thrashing olives out of their trees with long wands, or ploughing with a camel and donkey as team. The valley rings with voices – either song or rhythm that helps labour. A man beating raw wool will shout loudly at each whack to keep the fluff from his lungs.

The drives are very long and a strain on conversation. Once I got Winston going and the Calvinist coming back, and was shy of both. This time, thank God, Clemmie acquiesced in driving with Winston.

Dinner and jaw-jaw until 2 a.m., very amusing, the loom making enchanting designs, political reminiscences and prophecies. Clemmie went to bed at 9.30. I had a curious calm and sad conversation with her before dinner that I have thought of ever since. I was talking about post-war days and proposed that instead of a grateful country building Winston another Blenheim, they should give him an endowed manor house with acres for a farm and gardens to build and paint in. Clemmie very calmly said: 'I never think of after the war. You see, I think Winston will die when it's over.' She said this so objectively that I could not bring myself to say the

usual 'What nonsense!' but tried something about it was no use relying on death; people lived to ninety or might easily, in our lives, die that day. (Winston had said that morning, when questioned about the advisability of attending the review: 'If they pot at me they'll hit de Gaulle. That will simplify things.') But she seemed quite certain and quite resigned to his not surviving long into peace. 'You see, he's seventy and I'm sixty and we're putting all we have into this war, and it will take all we have.' It was touching and noble.

It's been a wonderful bit for me, seeing so much of this Phenomenon in the middle of the war, when he has nothing to do but talk and weave and enjoy his jokes at the events. The setting, the fairy scene, the sun-bathing, the high mountains, are stimulating. He's been very affectionate to me. 'Sit next me,' 'Don't leave me,' 'Give me your paw,' 'Kiss me, darling,' so like a child. The next day, 14th, he left. We had a long egg-nogged farewell on the terrace, and then saw the party off in their plane.

Things were better on our return to Algiers. Winston's telegrams, starting as always 'Pray let me know . . .' or 'Pray arrange . . .' had done their dictator-best to clear our way to a more possible standard of living. A lot of electric heaters had been installed, so my room was warm enough for me to discard my fur coat in bed. Two fine English soldiers had been provided, Sergeant-Major Bright, cast for major-domo and Rifleman Sweeney, still a friend and now major-domo to Victor Rothschild. The R.E.'s had dragged a tank on to the roof, and jettisoned the antiquated geysers, so an occasional muddy bath could be taken. The cars were said to be on their way. I'd have been pleased with a new jeep, which could be bought at Philippeville for one bottle of whisky, but a more awe-inspiring equipage was needed for British build-up.

Duff never groaned except at sharing the house. This was an unlined and most dark cloud. He had no proper staff. He had been told that he would inherit Harold Macmillan's, but Harold kept for

himself the plum, Roger Makins, and other lights, while Duff had Kingsley Rooker (not an F.O. man) and the young and very shy Patrick Reilly. That was all. Tom Dupree was a help, but again not F.O. Unknotting de Gaullean knots was an exhausting whole-time labour. Sometimes Duff felt that he had an Orphean touch with the creature. Winston would have been deaf to Orpheus himself.

By February the spring was already whispering loudly. The mimosa burst open and most of the ills were retreating in rout. Freddie Fane's days were given over to chastising the Italian prisoners with whips, the Arab hangers-on with scorpions, and unpacking hundreds of cases from the Ministry of Works. In the twinkling of an eye we were sporting the Royal Arms of England on every utensil we touched.

Now a scream went up from English throats in sympathy for their personnel. In this military set-up the unfortunate civilians were starving and wilting. They slept in cramped bedrooms, generally shared. Were they lucky enough to get a chair in a restaurant or canteen, they might not occupy it for more than twenty minutes. They had no retreats, amenities, sports or welcomes. Their cold, waterless diggings were their recreation grounds.

Our Jamshid's palace should solve this problem. Our many shaded glades and hills should make their other Eden. The Y.M.C.A. must provide long chairs and tables, and with restrooms, garden-loggias, tea and service, a demi-paradise would be made. The gay company of prisoners with time and goodwill on their unmanacled hands would sweep, garnish, garden and soothe the weary. To this end I put my shoulder and heart. We lived on the fashionable hill at El Kalai, Rue Beaurepaire. The typhus-ridden buses would bring the weary element almost to our gates. Our house-mates hated the whole idea, fought it and, in consequence, found another villa to their liking. It was an ill wind.

O Conrad, isn't it glorious? Now we can stay on in this once-despised villa and have the Civil Servants swarming all over the garden in true Grandpapa (Lord John Manners)

Belvoir style. The place is warm now. Hideosity can be laughed off. The two English soldier-servants have made a revolution in services. Every day the house gets gayer. Anticipation blooms.

Yesterday I lunched with Harold to meet our Russian opposite numbers, Mr Vishinsky of the trials, Mr Bogomolov and his plump, pretty little wife. I sat next Vishinsky, who had an interpreter, as he has no Basic. He seemed mellow enough and Napoleonically grand. He has his own plane. He had to wait in Cairo for an R.A.F. one, so telephoned to Moscow to send one immediately for his permanent use. I said: 'I suppose it's four-engined like the Prime Minister's?' 'No, two,' his fingers admitted. Bogomolov was meanwhile being coped with by Lady Maud Baillie, *née* Cavendish, dressed in A.T.S. uniform with her tartan skirt almost ankle-length. She looked of another epoch, like a photograph of a cricketer in a top hat, but oh, she was nice. Bogo has a bit of French and a bit of Basic; Madame had a lot of both, plus pretty charm.

A splendid lecture was given in the afternoon. It lasted an hour and a half. I feared Duff must sleep, but snuff kept him going. We'd had rather a nice lunch with Pleven, but a stupefying one. I cried a lot at the courage of the Resisters, but the house clapped itself into thunder at the story of the young boy who, being visited by Pétain shortly after his arm had been blown off, was asked by the Maréchal *'Votre bras vous fait mal?'* and was answered *'Ce n'est pas mon bras qui me fait mal, c'est vous qui aidez mes ennemis.'*

All the good French I meet, the Resisters, the serious fighters, would much rather be in London than here. They say they feel much nearer France, and also the order and organisation of England impress them tremendously. They feel that the best is being done for winning, and that this country is a mess from the French point of view. We English

never saw ourselves at the top of the organisation-mobilisation-production trees, did we?

This day (24th) was wonderfully happy. Duff and I motored thirty miles out to Tipaza for lunch alone. The road followed the sea and was of incomparable beauty, a dreamer's vision of the Mediterranean, Greece, France, Nature, cultivation, colour, air to restore the dead to life. We had lunch at a bistro, not very good, but alone and unaccountably happy.

General Giraud came to pay his respects at six. His unlined, most innocent countenance is rather disarming. He had quite a stiff whisky and gave us a few beautifully enunciated anecdotes of his past. He says the terrain in Italy is worse than anything known before, worse than the worst Atlas.

Talking of Giraud, perhaps you would like to hear what the wise men think of him? Never in the history of politics has a man frittered away capital so quickly. He held everything in North Africa – Commander-in-Chief, martial law to back him, us and (even more) the U.S. to support him. Splendid appearance, romantic record, all this made him appear to be in 'an inexpugnable position,' and yet 'he has been driven, or rather has voluntarily retreated from, every bastion of his fortress.' He has been exploded by mines of his own making, he has himself dug and opened the trenches that besieged his citadel. He's just been slowly eased out and outsmarted. He's always waited to be fired, and never resigned. He's a dear donkey – I don't know how really 'dear' to his supporters.

The evening of the 22nd was the great visit to de Gaulle. It passed off without a hitch. The Spahis at the doors drew themselves into rigidity for their presentation of arms. We had furbished up a little Union Jack for the (pool) car. It was not as royal as I had hoped. I'd looked forward to the last

phase of the First Consul, but it was only 'official.' I was between Wormwood and Massigli; my heart sank to think of the amount of dinners, perhaps for years, I shall be sitting in just such a place, struggling against the beasts of Babel, ageing and wearying. I suppose we knew that our Bognor Eden couldn't last. My pick of the bunch is General de Lattre. Spirit and wit, strength and fun. Mrs Wormwood I'd called on before – a sad, colourless, gentle little creature, hating it all and longing for her pre-war sequestered ways. She must have told her husband all I had said to her, because it gave her nostalgia. Anyway his opening remark was '*Qu' avez-vous fait de votre vache?*' He's soon to dine with us and I shall sit next him. Well, I mustn't think about it now. It makes me feel too nervous – terribly, terribly nervous.

The house is getting delightfully topsy-turvy with the spirit of an inn – more beds being unearthed, blankets aired, changes and alarms. 'Where can we find a lamp?' etc. Old Freddie I'm getting to adore. My first impressions, I ought to learn, are always wrong. The result of everything being done for me, the food, the flowers, the cards, the telephone, has paralysed me. I shall be good for lolling only, if I return.

Martha Gellhorn, wife to Ernest Hemingway, a lovely-looking American character in her early thirties, is staying. I met her – just – in London as a well-known journalist and a great friend of our Virginia Cowles. A packet of fun, yellow hair *en brosse*, cool slim lines and the most amusing patter imaginable. She thinks I'm as lovable and odd and rum as I think Ethel Smyth, and I like that. She's off to Caserta shortly and Virginia takes her place; both of them in khaki, they are always in the firing line though they grouse and groan at the way the G.H.Q.'s ignore them. Virginia is another friend, but she doesn't think me as funny as Martha does.

The daylight fades, the ghastly red, blue and green fairy harem-lights are put up, whisky is lapped up greedily, roasted sardines are handed round, Virginia arrives cold from the

clouds in battledress and is cheered and kissed lustily. I don't think it looks like any Embassy I've ever seen anywhere.

The usual six-to-eight crowd of thirsty Allies, followed by a banquet here. All the King's china and all the King's glass – all the King's silver, but alas! the linen declares itself in flowing red chain-stitch to belong to the Empire Hotel, Bath. We entertained Messieurs Massigli, Romrée (the Belgian), General de Lattre, Mr Chapin (U.S.), Virginia, Eve Curie and Joyce Grenfell. Filthy food, except for the ice. No one but us serves ice. I think our Sergeant-Major steals it from the hospital.

Last evening was dinner with the Russians. Great anticipations of splendour. Asked for eight, we drove up to the largest villa here, tremendous rooms, semi-furnished, blazing unshaded electric-light bulbs, and found to our horror that the party was just the four – two Bogos, two Coos. My heart sank. We'd not ordered the car until 10.30. A *petit verre* of warm port instead of the anticipated vodka was all we were offered in the assembling room. Madame was bursting prettily out of a smart pailletted dress. Monsieur has not much style, and what little French he commands is made less intelligible by it having to come through his hand as well as his mouth. Vodka appeared with dinner, served in another gigantic room, caviar too and smoked things. Bogo drank nothing (so rude), Madame sipped, Duff and I quaffed. Conversation somehow covered the bones (a threadbare coat) but it passed. Bolshies have such a dreadful duty of denying any relations with the Russia of centuries. I got quite a snub when I said that I liked General Pechkoff so much. When asked why, up a gum-tree I stammered that Russians were interested in problems of the soul and that I was too. 'Russians have no time now for the soul. All that is altered. Now they must know reality.' We talked of what was read in Russia. They asked me what I thought were the popular English translations. I was ready for that one; Dickens, Byron, Milton, Galsworthy. Ah yes, but I had

forgotten the real favourite. Think again! I gave it up. Why, Jerome K. Jerome, of course, and as they remembered *Three Men in a Boat* they lapsed into Russian and laughed till they cried. 10.30 came at last, and the nightmare ended. I dressed in blood-red and rubies, and they took it as a compliment.

The Aletti Hotel was a source of constant jokes. A large building on the quays, it had lost all the glass of its windows. Under the rank of a Minister or a Colonel you could not hope for a room to yourself. Above that rank you could only rely on one sheet for a chrysalis-wrapping.

When at last we had a car, Duff used to send me sometimes to pick up forgotten men from the Aletti and bring them up to our circle. The Peruvian Minister was my first charge. I was over an hour tracing him, knowing only his rank and not his name. He was found at last and brought out blinking like the *lettres-de-cachet* old men out of the Bastille when it fell. He had been there for weeks. His nice eyes brimmed with tears when he found me solicitous, for he was not accustomed to living in one room, with one used sheet, and no car with which to pay his protocol calls; he had lost prestige and hope. We gave him some gin and he stopped crying, and Madame Catroux, who had dropped in, was nice to him. He enjoyed himself until I had to take him back to his particular circle of hell.

I was very fond of Madame Catroux. She had twice the energy and public spirit of anyone else, which was irritating to many. She helped me out with my good works, such as they were, and we would gossip shockingly and exchange intimacies about cosmetics and our outmoded hats. The General was surprisingly like my Algerian gazelle.

Some evenings at dusk Duff and I walk round our Arabian property. It's huge, beautiful, romantic, and the seasons will bring flowers and new fruits. The Civil Servants mooch round and tear branches off the mimosas. They get given a lovely tea, and it's quite a success.

We have a Moorish lodge at our gates, as pretty as Scheherazade's old home, romantic though dark. This also I am going to make over to the Civils, get some divans, get the R.M. to whitewash it, and fix it with curtains from my 100 white metres bought in Marrakesh (now said to be winding-sheet material, therefore controlled in price), stock it with periodicals, stationery, such books as I can find etc. It shall be my doll's house and theirs. Great, great fun!

Wormwood's day. He's to dine here. Fourteen strong we are – the C.-in-C. (Jumbo to wit), Macmillan, Mrs Wormwood, the Laughing Cavalier Palewski, perhaps a shining F.O. light called Loxley and understrappers. One of our all-day problems was finding a topic for me and de Gaulle this evening. I asked all kinds and conditions; after a lot of head-scratching and vetoing of all subjects by an unsmiling Gaston Palewski we came to a dead end: '*Enfance,*' I suggested. It had never failed me over the years; as an equaliser it is second to none. 'No, no!' they screamed. '*L'enfance! Surtout pas!*' Ancestry better. Let him trace himself back for you. Or what about escape in 1914–18. But Giraud has drugged the market with such stories, and I can't manage my own genealogy, let alone Jeanne d'Arc collaterals. So childhood it shall be. I won't try *The Miracle*; it is quite forgot and never heard of in France. When I say '*Quand j'etais sur la scène*' my listeners start involuntarily. They don't pursue it, but I'm sure they make a mental note to check my *naissance*, wondering if they've got something wrong.

The Sergeant-Major had decorated a verdigrised candelabra of Arab design with roses and smilax up to the *bobèches*, so that the table laid for le Général de Gaulle looked like a constituency wedding. I couldn't wound his pride by ripping the flowers off, so it stood, in its vulgarity, centre. The King's glass and china and the hotel linen looked *digne*,

and I had Jumbo Wilson on my left. I talked childhood with the General and also ancestors, and *enfance* went best, as it's always bound to. Madame looked most worn, practically without any '*résistance*,' poor creature, or make-up. After dinner he sat with Duff and was not very gracious or amenable. I don't suppose that Boney was either.

Duff afterwards was much depressed about his French. He certainly is very silent in it; politeness flows, but not much wit. Should I find him a tutor, I wonder? I don't believe in them much. It's nerve and brass, *audace* and disrespect, and leaping-before-you-look and what-the-hellism that must be developed. My French, quite deplorable as it is, flows and flounders and gets there. It's a steeplechase with gigantic obstacles, sometimes astonishingly cleared, and the courage is magnificent. Grand National! So that I'm surprised at my own reckless confidence.

On our rare free afternoons we explore the countryside and revisit Tipaza. At the foot of its own cloud-capped Olympus there juts the promontory, once a Roman town, its ruins still lying among absinthe herbs and rock-rose. There are caves and grottoes where the sirens sang and white foam tracing arabesques. Proteus probably lives there, his horn hung up. From the shore you can drive through ravines and vines and mountain ways to *Le Tombeau de la Chrétienne*. It was erected in A.D. 18 (such a nice date) and has nothing to do with any Christian. It dominates a wide country, is a big stone beehive with ruined facing of Roman pillars built in warm-tinted stone. Sepulchral chambers inside are shown to visitors by an old Arab with a lamp and a little Arab girl who darts through the chinks of stone like a lizard.

The Civil Servants are still a preoccupation. We thought some needed a club and I was taken yesterday to see a wrongly-situated English church library, but it has just been seized by the British Council to sing madrigals, dance folk-dances and act the 'Screen Scene' for the purpose of

showing Algerians the stuff we're made of. As a rule I leave Freddie Fane to cope with our down-and-out personnel. Not as many fetch up as I hoped would. It's a blow, as my scrounging Sergeant-Major has a sort of Gunter's buffet of cakes and tarts. 'Leave it to me. I'll make it . . . pretty.' So encouraging he is. He stands to attention and says: 'I shall be able to scrounge that, Your Excellency.'

Soon it would be spring. The wistaria buds were swelling grey. John Julius's holidays would be in April. It was going to be difficult to get home because of priorities. Whitney Straight had the power and the promise to get me a flight, but without a permit I did not stand a chance. Tedder and Slessor had both been involved in our housing troubles and were not friendly enough to break the law for my ageing blue eyes. Someone said: 'You ought to know Dawson, Dawson always flies.' I found him. He was well disposed. *'Agnosco fratrem,'* I thought, instantly recognising a brother in lawlessness. Permits for him were scraps of paper. All the aircraft in North Africa were his own, salvaged and repaired. He had two Liberators that he used for ferrying spare parts. Weather was as immaterial to him as permits, so he crashed into the Massif Central after the Liberation, killing himself and three friends of mine. His war-work, that of making old planes into new from Suez to Casablanca, was over, but he was still young and would have excelled in rebuilding the air-services for twenty more years.

My letters continued:

Brilliant blue windswept day. We had the Soviets to lunch. The Bogomolovs are the standing joke, interest, sneer (what you will) but always in the conversation. They arrived in the streamiest-lined shining car, dressed splendidly, she in a foul sulk, Bogo yellow as an egg. They had just returned from a flight into Egypt and three days in Cairo. I asked her if she had liked it. 'No,' she said; 'how could I? My husband too – he was *souffrant d'ailleurs, il est toujours souffrant.'*

(Yellowness explained.) 'What did you do or see?' 'We had to see the Pyramids.' 'Did they impress you?' '*Non, mais je ne comprends pas comment on les a bâti.*' She's got something there! So it went on, though she admitted to having bought a lot. They have squandermania.

How I miss you, farmer! No one has asked me to be their Valentine. No hearts, no darts. God bless your crops.

Conrad wrote:

Windsor Castle

The separation is like carrying a basket of stones wherever one goes and it seems to press on my heart. You will be glad to see my address. We always use Royal stationery when we can. I am well lodged with Tommy Lascelles in the Tower, a real tower with spiral stairs and wonderful outlook. William of Wykeham built it and Chaucer lived in it. He was Clerk of the Works at Windsor, and only wrote verse in his spare time, like Duff and Vansittart. Tommy is a good guide. We see everything, even the most private and intimate nooks. The good pictures are all underground. He knows his way about, dates, historical events and where to see the different Royal ghosts. How lovely St George's Chapel is! I said some prayers for you in the Rutland chapel. There's a splendid monument of Lord Rutland and his wife. I should think earlier than the one who was or wasn't Shakespeare, and do you know Princess Charlotte's tomb with the angel and weeping woman, the work (Phoebus forgive me) of Herr Fuchs?

The carter told me about his early married life on 14/- a week. It sounds starvation at first, and then you find that he had all the butter he liked at 6d per lb. and all the whey-butter he liked for 4½d per lb., all the cheese he liked at 7d per lb. (N.B. the butter and cheese were made by Mr Osborne and would be better than what they have at Sandringham.) On Sundays they were given a bucketful of potatoes and very often

one or two broccoli. They paid no rent; the corn they got gleaning supplied them with bread. And so on. The hours worked were long, but the food was much better than what they get now. I daresay 14/- didn't leave much for clothes, but they didn't have to pay £12 for a hat as you do.

When I did my Virgil I read: '*Mens immota manet; lacrimae volvuntur inanes,*' i.e. 'He does not change his mind; his tears flow to no purpose.' How terribly they fit!

The carter says to me: 'You'll plough today. You can stick it better than I can.' Considering I pay him to be ploughman, this strikes me as a bit thick. As you can imagine, I am enormously flattered by the phrase 'You can stick it better than I can,' especially as he's a good bit younger than me. It certainly looks as if England was safe for democracy when that's the way a ploughman talks to the master.

I wrote to Conrad:

17 March

Great, great larks! I've bought a cow. Fatima I've called her. She has not arrived yet. She is coming under her own milk and it's a long walk from Dely Ibrahim, where I bought her, and when I say 'bought' you can trust the old gold-digger not to have paid for anything.

The days are one lovelier than another, arums and freesias bursting into wild bloom in the garden and fields. I spent yesterday trying to get equipment for Fatima, and managed after walking actually miles through Army Ordnance stores to get four 'dishes cooking tin meat mediums' for pouring the milk into, one 'bucket tea tin large,' a plate of tin to have a cream-skimmer made from. They all have to be indented for and it may take days, and arrive after I've gone, which date depends on Dawson's whim, as the C.-in-C. won't give me a permit. I shall miss the galloping pageant of African spring but I'd rather see John Julius and you.

It won't be long now. I've been vaccinated for Gibraltar's sake. I shall be 'freight.' Mosquito-nets and bathing-shorts to be found for Duff are still on my list, for it's spring and every morning I pick armfuls of arum lilies and large bunches of freesias.

Dawson took me without permits on 29 March. There were five of us, all strangers and men only. My face must be cheerful. My pill taken, my two prayers said, I boarded the Liberator together with Air Commodore Sowrey and two jolly private soldiers with destination-labels flapping round their chins. I had flown only once alone, and I remember feeling like a bivalve without half my defence; besides, leaving Duff was always an isolation. I was lonely if he was an hour away. I was awakening too to the magic of Algiers in 1944. In spite of the two magnets in England, it was a wrench to leave the spring and the flowers, Freddie, the prisoners, and the valiant girls on their firing-line missions who swept through, the parachutists and resisters, in short the hub of the free world. The tendrils that were to become as strong as spiral bonds were beginning to twine round me.

We came down at Rabat, unintentionally, the airfield a patchwork of purple wildflowers, and again at Gibraltar with the same prognostication that we would be too big for the runway. There we were received by the A.O.C., Bill Elliot, with whom I immediately fell in love. He took me to his flowery garden; a heavenly terrace for drinks. Admiral Burrows came in from the Mount next door. The A.O.C. dreamy, humorous and probably highbrow, because the Admiral quoted Cowper (very well and at length), and the A.O.C. said 'Stricken Deer' and passed on to the two St Theresas. After dinner at Government House (the keys were on the sideboard) an A.D.C. took me for an incomparably beautiful drive, smelling of orange-flowers, lights blazing out of caves and from the summit of the Rock, and then to see us off was my dear A.O.C., an older, thinner, tireder Antony Head, with a bunch of lilies and stocks and apple-blossom which are as fresh in my memory as they were that spring night. The boys were dossed down in

the empty fuselage and, together, Dawson and I blew up my lilo. They dressed me in cotton-padded clothes and red-hot boots, and the air leaked out and the temperature fell to zero. I woke to the iron ribs of the aircraft, frozen stiff amid a crowd of stars. I was curiously happy with Algiers and all I had left, with the A.O.C., and with England, John Julius and Conrad ahead.

I spent almost a month in London and at the Bognor cottage. When I left, the sea-verge had been like a redoubtable barbican: now it was an area barred to non-residents, and, most surprising, there were the Mulberries floating at some distance from my garden wall. The townspeople and locals noticed them no longer, and would say if you asked their purpose that they thought they were some submarine defence. There were other explanations for them and for many other strange abnormal changes. None of them tallied with one another. The English were by then used to cover-stories, and accepted ignorance with relief. Personally I knew as little of the date of D-Day as the rest of the public, but, motoring through much of Surrey or Sussex, one felt that it must be imminent. Anyone who saw it will always remember the dense concentration of steel, its whole bulk open to a sky miraculously clear of the enemy.

Our house and garden at Bognor were a riot of disorder. Nothing had been wintered away, oiled, greased or tarpaulined; garden-tools, broken roofless sheds, old boots, siphons, filthy buckets, rats' bodies, rotting sacks, nothing seemed to have resisted the fifth winter of war. My car, which I took to London, was full of dung, stones, hay and goat-pellets. I felt discouraged by the decay, but the skeleton stock had no eyes for dilapidation and were crowing and calving, clucking and pigging. London was exciting and bombless, Emerald unchanged, H. G. Wells dying without resignation, Victor Rothschild earning the George Medal by de-detonating anti-personnel bombs.

I lunched at Downing Street. The butler greeted me with: 'X would like to see you before you go in.' X appeared with a warning that Adolph Berle, U.S. V.I.P., was lunching. When told I was fresh

from Algiers for my son's holidays, he had mumbled about American women not buzzing around for boys' vacations. Clemmie, in defence, had said for all she knew I had come in a freight-boat, and would I keep to that *supercherie*. I said I would stick to the freight part, but couldn't say ship for fear of being checked up, and that anyway I could easily avoid the subject, and what the hell had it to do with Mr Berle anyway? The conversation was on a very high global theoretical level. I was still as a waxwork and as dumb.

I travelled back with 'Always Flies' Dawson, still without a permit, driving to Lyneham in the west through an English spring evening with sickle moon and smells of burgeoning life and tender green, the sky alive with new constellations of aircraft. We climbed into our ferry, the fuselage cleared for freight and nothing in it but my few pounds of junk and three mattresses for the A.V.M. and Mrs C., his P.A., and me. I dossed down, quickly donning padded coat and boots, to be unobtrusive. Dawson had a more elaborate *coucher*, Mrs C. wrapping him in soft warm armour and changing his socks. The engines were revving all they could while she soothed him with unhearable murmurings. By his mattress she set out his night-aids, two copies of *Lilliput*, his torch, his clock and water-jug. I noiselessly said K's prayer and covered myself with an Australian sheep and my Bognor milking-jacket. The clock was there, the Perrier bottle of whisky to be drunk in case (or in lieu) of panic. I fell into an uneasy sleep.

At six I was peering through the window at a clear sky and a heralding glimmer from the east. The A.V.M. broke surface as the sun rose on Gibraltar, reached over to his P.A.'s dressing-case (Mrs C. still asleep), pinched her looking-glass and started shaving with Barbasol. The sun rose on the Rock. I could see darkest Africa on my right. The horses, my horses, were not even restive, but above the engine's roar I heard Dawson yelling 'Don't forget, if you want to make yourself comfortable, just go to the end of the aircraft.' It was no good shaking one's head and bawling out that one could wait. It was simpler to comply, so, after a decent pause, down the fuselage I walked gingerly to the little hygienic

contraption, veiled by a piece of ragged and tattered sailcloth, which, if held by both hands, might achieve a partial privacy. Now these planes, unconverted to passengers, have no floors to deck their keels and down at the lowest level there is a big piece of glass, I suppose for the bomb-dropper to see what the terrain is like. Each side of the glass is almost too steeply rising for one to walk upon, so I naturally assumed that the glass was as thick as are pavement plates. I put my confident foot forward on to it and went bang-slap through up to my fork; fortunately I was walking so warily that all my balance was still on my back foot and I sat down quick and pulled my leg, well protected by flying-suit and boot, back to safety. The others would never have heard me go or realised my fall until Duff noticed that I did not alight. I felt that I had to admit to the breakage, so yelled the fact to the A.V.M., who quietly answered 'We needn't tell anyone, or say you did it.' I didn't know what that meant. Mrs C. awoke and we ate chocolate and raisins.

Duff was on the airfield when we came down about 10.30. It was brilliant and warm, and a pretty tame gazelle (it was sure to die) with Victory horns, also two sneering peacocks, greeted me in the court of the villa, gifts of the Boushaga with whom Duff had been invited to shoot in the desert. The Rolls Royce emblazoned with the Arms of England had arrived. It would make our visits to the Russians less humiliating. It purred at the door on the following radiant morning to take us on a week's official trip to Algerian and Moroccan centres, but as so often happened we were recalled by telegram after two days.

The garden now was a wilderness of flowers. The days grew hourly hotter. For luncheon we sought cool dark rooms and the loggia was forsaken. All the world from Poles to Antipodes, from the four continents, must pass through Algiers (there was no other way) and every week my happiness increased, to my surprise and conscious delight. Doom was behind us. Landings in France were said to be near and were to be immediately followed by victory.

Integration as a law had made a millennium of Algiers. Lambs and lions lay together. De Gaulle was still a rub. It was a sore fatigue for Duff to get that Giraffe to lie down with our Duckling.

For refreshment we would climb to Chréa, a resort in the Atlas shaded by the glimmering magic of cedars, peopled by singing children and carpeted with flowers. North Africa became to me a brave new world. I would have liked this phase to have lasted a hundred years, and D-Day to have been postponed for as long, but the sands I knew were running out, though the last grain's date was still unknown to me.

I wrote to Conrad at the end of May:

Tonight with Bogo was worse than ever. Just the hideous four of us, no vodka this time and a dreadful piece of dehydrated caviar which I took for pumpernickel and ate a mouthful of, or rather bit and spat out. Conversation flowed like glue; so did the single bottle of white wine. Duff did not try. I tried with the devil's help and was really nasty, but they did not realise it. They don't realise anything outside the U.S.S.R. They are as smug as oysters and totally ignorant of anything European. I asked them, knowing the answer, if they saw much of the French Resistance people coming out of France. No, they didn't, nor (their faces betrayed) had they worried to enquire about it. They delight in putting one in the wrong too, making one out ignorant or outdated or frivolous. '*Chez nous, nous constatons . . .*' is the opening of most phrases. We talked of schools and of what is taught. I said that my child read well at four. They said: '*Chez nous on lit à huit ans. C'est mieux.*' To questions like: Do they teach you religion, languages, tact, manners, psychology? (really nasty questions) they answer 'No' with satisfaction and serene unconsciousness of one's dig. After dinner chess was suggested. Bogo played as fast as tennis and volleyed the pieces about. This naturally upset Duff, who lost his queen in three moves and the game in about ten. Never again do I endure such an evening!

Mornings are still taken up with parcels for the Croix Rouge. The poor imprisoned Frogs are getting nothing of

any charm or nutritive value in their parcels now – soap and chocolate both off, coffee not reliable, and this morning the dates gave out, so it's back to dehydrated carrots. It's a microcosm of the lunacy of war. Thousands of hours of energy, tons of packing-material, cases, nails, tins; a whole country (Switzerland) choking itself with stuff being sent into Germany and as much being sent out. Couldn't it be done without exchange, I mean prisoners fed well by the country of their cages?

Algiers

Beloved John Julius, it is our Silver Wedding Day, June 2nd, 1944. If you had not come to me so late in time, you might be twenty-three years old and fighting outside Rome. Thank you for being late. I wonder if you had any choice – if you chose us and the year? It's possible. I feel sadly happy. Twenty-five years gone is the sad part. I'm crying a bit as I write, but they've been lovely years with no storms for Papa and me – not one – and I love him as much as ever I did. Some strange almost unknown Frenchman has sent me a silver necklace, very massive and chased with demon motifs. It's round my neck as I sit up in bed; nightcap and common pink silk nightgown don't marry very well with its barbarity. You may see Papa before you see this. I hope you do, but I'll be miserable here without him.

He's gone! His departure weighed heavily at dinner and weighs worse tonight. Wormwood had been intolerable to the end and he finally left without any of his peers on an English York. I dared not go to the airfield.

8 a.m. 4 June

They should have landed by now. When shall I hear? There are voices in the hall that sound cheerful, so bad news hasn't yet come. I must fettle my fine joints and go chalet-hunting in Chréa as if all was going to be well. We could requisition

one – we are commissars. C.-in-C. Jumbo Wilson has taken three on this system and surrounded them with a luxury camp. But I wouldn't have the face to grab someone else's house for a whim.

It's surely strange that Browning in 'Childe Roland to the Dark Tower Came' says

> *'Such starved ignoble nature; nothing throve;*
> *For flowers – as well expect a cedar grove!'*

Yet beneath Chréa's cedars are pansies, daisies and unknown eyes springing from thick and vivid green grass.

Algiers   *5 June*

And Rome entered! What a hideous day was yesterday. By 10 a.m. I was frantic, imagining shooting down, forced landing in France, imprisonment, torture, watery graves, fiery cremations. I had to seek d'Astier de la Vigerie out for comfort. He told me not to hope until 2 or 3 p.m. He also told me that madly disappointed as he was at not being on the *Luftfahrt* he thought it made sense. If the meeting is to be sentimental, better a lone Worm broadcasting from England to France; the visit of a crowd of Ministers and nothing done but the dropping of tails, would look ridiculous. If it is to be a serious tri-part discussion, then the nobs can fly quickly to the table-talk. Ecstasy of relief (too quickly got used to) at five when news of their arrival came.

The dread of landings is upon me – so many to pray for; two Mannerses, four Bensons (all by name), Henry Uxbridge now in Italy, Daphne Wakefield's husband, Enid Jones's and Ruby Lindsay's son, Michael Tree, Rex. Rex worries me most. They can't all survive.

DER TAG indeed! Sweeney came in with the news from
the radio at nine. Not unexpected but none the less
overpowering. I had the joy of being the first to tell my
fellow-packers. They gathered round me in a ring of gasping
excitement. To them, poor fools, the war was over. They were
settling what to take home. Prisoners' parcels seemed
senseless now. I had to damp it all.

It's evening and we get no news. I don't suppose at this
juncture that you do in England either, but you get rumours
and atmosphere. We feel suddenly removed and isolated. We
thought the King's speech marvellous. Was it?

8 June

Lunched tête-à-tête with Emmanuel d'Astier. The man's a
spellbinder and no mistake. He told me the Supreme
C.-in-C.'s speech could not possibly have been more horrible
for the Free French, and that he could hear between the lines
of Wormwood's broadcast what an exploding rage he was in
and that the situation was degenerating. (Why?) Emmanuel
is an idealist and a poet, unambitious and passionate, *he* says.

Wonderful letters from the ones I love – you, Duff and
John Julius. Duckling's headquarters must be quite near from
what I hear from Duff. He stayed at Anthony Eden's house.
He tells me too that he (Duff) had great success when
ructions arose and threatened to break the whole meeting up.
Wings spread ready on the airfield – but now from the French
broadsheet it looks very black again and seemingly past repair.

The day had its heavy cloud. I never nursed a dear gazelle but it
was sure to die, and the poor pet had been true to its tradition and
lay stiff and stark among its uneaten roses and tobacco. It was to

have been its wedding day. I had found a bride and was to have brought her to the groom this very afternoon. Did he die of a broken heart? Waiting was too long. No one could explain hope to him. It had become a custom to visit the peacocks and gazelle after our meals. It filled the polite half-hour and moved the guests imperceptibly to their cars.

Algiers   *15 June*

Write me your prognostications. Three months is the general idea here. It's slow, very slow. Wormwood, thank God, has gone to France and is said to be returning on Saturday or Sunday. I pray Duff returns safely with him, or is he sure to snatch a few extra days for the sake of White's and the girls? Freddie Fane has found six bottles of good champagne to celebrate his return with, and I have the Yugoslav choir to praise him. One imagines which he will like best.

17 June

Duff due today at 7 a.m. I won't repeat the old sagas of anxiety. Suffice it to say that after hours of pain, blood, sweat and tears, at 12.30 de Gaulle's wings, gay with tricolor and Croix de Lorraine blazoned on the fuselage, touched down, amid bands of Marseillaise, Spahis, sailors and Senegalese, all the Ministers (my Emmanuel outstanding as Saul). The first words Wormwood was asked by several sympathetic-to-me Frenchmen were 'Has the Ambassador's plane left Rabat?' and they tore back from their felicitations-group to tell anxious me the good news that it was due in fifteen minutes. I was standing back on account of trouser-trouble. Sure enough the great York flew into sight a few minutes later, and out stepped Duff, followed to my huge delight by Victor Rothschild, portly in khaki and generally delightful. He took a cooling bath, fell with all his big weight on the bathroom tiles, and is now half-incapacitated with swollen

knee and bandages. Duff was in fine form. I gathered that
the mission has not been quite the failure I feared.

Elba taken with tides of blood by our Admiral 'Salt'
Troubridge and General de Lattre.

The town is gay as bunting can make it with Stars and
Stripes, fists and sickles and tricolors – no Union Jacks, no
monarchists. Troubridge returned gloriously robust. In the
evening we dined with Wormwood. He had a sweet, innocent
face, smiling with satisfaction. I had noticed this cat-canary
look at Mr Murphy's American Independence party. Was it
some trick of light? No, there it was still last evening, not that
it made the grim little party less sticky. Jumbo was there and
Cunningham (C.-in-C.), Palewski and *Miss* Wormwood,
newly arrived from Oxford. I talked about the United States
and told him how the Pallio race was run in Siena. What
makes one select the subject guaranteed to bore him? Because
one cannot learn that people's interests are totally different
from one's own. Then I tried Australian fauna, a palpitating
subject to me, the emu, wombat, koala bear, lyre-bird,
duck-billed platypus and wallaby, all comparatively tame and
probably unique in the world. He gloomily said '*Il paraît qu'il y
a des kangarous,*' proving that he was listening but not amused.

Victor Rothschild had left for Roman bomb-dispersal, so the
house was less happy. Now Randolph Churchill would gladden
my heart and make things hum.

Randy rang up from the hotel to say could he bring Evelyn
Waugh? So he's swallowed something; it must have been his
pride. Randy is thin and grey, keen and sweet. Evelyn is thin

and silent. I had to put them both on improvised beds in the unused dining-room. Evelyn came up and sat in a grey, dejected heap without a word, a smile or a nod. Later, when I was alone with him, the girls having left in disgust, I asked the knight-at-arms what ailed him. He said that he was never so happy in his life; he had just written a book that he thought a masterpiece, he had no money troubles, a wife he adored, three fine children, splendid health and now an active life calling him to Yugoslavia with his beloved Randolph. His serenity knew no bounds. I said I wished he could reflect his happiness a little more. He said that other people had said the same to him. He doesn't speak at meals. Duff has a royal time at the table's top with two gay girls beside him, flanked by Randolph and other staff. I sit at the dank end croaking in a Frog pond, watching as I flounder the gaiety on the bank.

Emerald said to Duff on the first night of the V.1's launchings that it showed how idiotic the war had made people to think they should believe in such rubbish, but the waiter had said, and so had several fools here, that unpiloted planes prove how short of men Germany is! That's the classic English attitude and I do love it.

15 July

The great *quatorze* was a bit of a flop. A 'no-women' order forced me on to the streets. Mrs Chapin (U.S.) and Madame and Mademoiselle de Gaulle 'crashed' it. I had quite a good time shoving, clapping and running madly in a crowd to catch a glimpse of Wormwood, though I was going to see him with ease at tea. I like my celebrities seen through difficulties, and I like to run for them, not sit and speak with them. My companion wasn't much of a hand at that sort of thing, and no more are you, my darling, nor Kaetchen, Hutchie, Carl, Duff or anyone I've known but Raimund. No matter, he did his best. Then there was a reception at de

Gaulle's. He looked in the pink but pretended not to be. Mademoiselle helped me to some warm lemonade and the inevitable éclair. There was an Archevêque in brilliant puce, a very big-sized White Father and the widow of the Governor of Equatorial Africa, a negress of the jettiest shade dressed in French widow's crêpe weeds.

Palewski has been to lunch to tell us all about Washington. They cannot but admit that it was a gigantic success. F.D.R. said at lunch, off the record, that it was an historic occasion when his friend Charles de Gaulle came as an ally. People had tried to oppose the meeting, had done much to retard it, but he had overcome the troubles and now all was well. The old buffer had been the onlie begetter of spanners, and seeing his Press and his State Department against him on the subject of France, and the election galloping on, he had to do a *volte-face*. That's about the size of it. Meanwhile we look a bit silly, waiting on him and appeasing him as we timorously did. He now outstrips us in recognition of the Provisional Government and we appear the laggards and obstructionists. When Wormwood went to see General Pershing (senile of course and I think in a home), the old man's first question was: 'Tell me, General, and how did you leave General Pétain?' Wormwood replied: 'Well, I haven't seen him since 1940, but his pictures show him in good health.'

25 July

Darling J.J.

On this day of all days Randolph staggered in looking like the man that was – grey-haired, ashen-faced, black pits harbouring dead blue eyes, emaciated, with perished thighs and bandaged knees. I was really alarmed. His story was horrible. The pilot had miscalculated the runway on landing in Yugoslavia, had tried to rise, had lost speed, stalled and crashed. Randy was in the tail with Evelyn and Philip Jordan. The plane took immediate fire, though Randolph

can't remember seeing flames. The door had buckled and wouldn't open; by tugging at it they made a kind of gap through which four of them slipped. Ten were killed, nine saved. Evelyn's hands are burnt, Philip Jordan is also burnt a bit. Randolph's injuries are water on knees, jolted spine and obvious shock, yet his spirits are ebullient as ever. He lies in a hot cupboard upstairs and is carried down to the sitting-room by four Wop gorillas.

Eve Curie fills another room with her beautiful face, khaki and medals, dreams of echelons and *mêlées* and *garde-à-vous*. The house is overloaded and has burst its boiler. Victor has the best room and is too big for it. I have to drive him to the docks now with a bag of ticking bombs. The car bumps and hurtles down the shelled roads, and Victor will tell me not to forget the danger-freight and I'll be thankful if we make the *Orion* and dump them.

27 July

It's like a madhouse these days. Randolph stumbles in at 8.30 when Papa is still in his bath and says: 'Can I have my breakfast here?' I say yes. A few minutes later Victor lollops in, tray in hand, and plunks it on the bed. When Sweeney arrives with Papa's tray there is no place to put it. Papa leaving his contiguous bathroom gives one look, renounces his coffee and leaves the house. Freddie Fane joins the party to make plans, but the two toughs bawl and shout so that he gives it up. *Garde-à-vous* Eve marches in in khaki. I beg her to stay, but she asks permission not to make up her mind about presence or absence at meals, and is off. The boys 'light up' and quarrel across me. I get the trays taken away, hoping that the boys will go with them. No! 'Can I lie on your bed?' Randy says. 'Yes.' They remain even when I get up (so that I have to dress in the bathroom), sprawling in bath-towels or underpants. Once I'm gone they jump into my bed and put their dirt-crusted feet on my sheets and sweat into them, cover them with ash and burn

them with butts. I love them both, but O, I'm tired and get no
moment to write or read or think.

The doctor came at noon and thinks badly of Randolph's
legs. He is not to put them to the ground for a week, and
to have electric treatment, so now we have him where we
want him.

About this time came heartbreaking tidings, the saddest that
the war brought me.

Darling Conrad, Duff rang up and said 'How are you,
darling?' and I knew at once that he was to tell me something
dreadful, and of course it was that Rex had been killed. I
minded desperately and Duff was sobbing like a child. Rex
was one of the few younger men I really loved, and I'll miss
him, his charm and his art, his sympathy and affection.
There is pathos about it that compels tears. Rex was like
Fortinbras – fair, dedicated and physically most refinedly
made. His spare figure and pale face, the texture of his skin,
the fit of his finger-nails, his shining well-set teeth and
sweeping hair were those of a delicate and tender prince,
making mouths at the event. I have heard no details, only a
telegram from B., who likes to be first with news, however
bad. What was touching was his fervour, his frame too frail
for so much armour but wearing it erectly though it was
much too heavy. He'll be mourned indeed, sweet Rex. He
was entirely Christian without pride or envy. Injustice
enraged him.

Chréa   31 *July*
I feel too wretched. I've come up here in consequence –
left the noise of Randolph and Victor and sought this
seclusion. It's a good deal cooler, but pretty hot though it is
5000 ft above the Sultan's palaces. There is a gorge nearby
where monkeys live. You can go to the sordid little inn, and

the monkey-apes come out with their babies clinging to their flat chests, take food, gibber and scoff at you. They sit on my mudguards like heraldic supporters and cover the windscreen with their inquisitive finger-marks. The little restaurant is equally sordid, but one bribes the cook with a cake of soap to make an omelette with one's own butter, and they dig out a bottle of French wine (Chablis). In every gorge there is a wealth of pink oleanders. Figs fall from the trees. For symbolism you may see olive-trees under whose boughs are piled shells, bombs, ammunition of all kinds and sizes. Waking up here yesterday was like being in a magnifying bubble – the most distant objects brought within your grasp, unknown distances declaring themselves for the first time; a new world where the backgrounds became foregrounds. The hill-tops each carry their protectively-coloured village and *kasbah*. The more you look the more of them emerge from the lion-skin dryness, like stars that appear after staring at the heavens, or praying mantises only found on their sticks by chance. Sometimes it is cold, blankets and furs, and rolling icy mist. I walked through these strange ghostly conditions with Duff. A still steam everywhere, primaeval cedars looming through the white, sometimes a peep-hole into savage black mountains. If I could take my mind off the bombs in London and Windsor, which I can't, or if the news of Rex was false, this quiet spot in the silence of the cedar grove would have been like peace. But generally speaking my zest has gone. Rex's death contributes. My thoughts are of him mostly these days. I remember once his passionate advocacy for fighting one's war, if necessary without hope. 'What has victory to do with it?' I felt ashamed as I had not seen it quite like that.

6 August

Doggiest day of all – 100 degrees in my bedroom. We eat in the windowless Arab-pillared hall. We get all the hair possible cut off our heads without looking like lamas, and

when night comes it will be a scramble for cooler spots. The earth is baked and yet the trees blossom and reblossom as if their feet were in water. I tread the many paths in the garden watching the deprivations of summer, but always some new thing bursts into colour out of what seems scorched earth; red pomegranate flowers now, the vivid jacaranda tree and another acacia-type that drops scrambled-eggs generously. The vines are green as English spring.

We dined with General de Lattre de Tassigny, the new Commander-in-Chief French Forces in this theatre. He is a romantic figure. One pictures him with Flemish lace laid on his armour. Such intrepid gallantry, such bold effeminacy. Then again he is as modern as a streamline. A local Monty? I think he's more the local Hitler, not for tyranny but for getting things done. The house had been a sty without light or water. He has made it in two months into a floodlit palace. His wife and son Bernard were there, also the Belgian Ambassador. The rest were staff. The mulberry-skinned guard of honour were late. We could see them tearing into position as we drove up, stumbling over bayonets, their faces almost blanched with panic. We prayed that the General would not hear of it. Duff went with de Lattre to see some flag-and-sunset rites which lasted an hour, executed by the military school of four hundred *militaires* which he has created in the grounds. Meanwhile Madame gave us the most magnificent description of her husband's *évasion* from his prison near Vichy, which was conceived and carried out by her and her son. Then came dinner. Perfect: milk-fed fowl, fresh and tender salad, the right whiff of garlic. The *nappe* was right (coarse and chic), the chairs covered with interesting canvas (all stuff is unprocurable here). After dinner Nubians in white and rigid sergeants conducted us with torches beneath a sky blazing with stars to a floodlit court where basket-ball was being played (*un match en votre honneur*). It lasted a very long time, but what a beautiful

game to watch – at least it was last night with these highly-trained young men, all but naked, leaping from the ground like feathered Mercuries and as silently. No scuffle of boots – *espadrilles'* softness and an occasional *'Merde!'* was all one heard. Like some beautiful Greek game with a bit of ballet, played in a grove of pines that freshened you with their hot mountain-smell.

The game over, we made a tour of the apple-pie-order camp. The boys were marching off to their canvas quarters at Bersagliere speed, each detachment singing a different song as it strode – *Auprès de ma Blonde, Sambre et Meuse, Madelon*, and others. The place was like a pre-war exhibition with a floodlit hospital and a lecture amphitheatre in the most exquisite classic Moorish style, the foundations of which were not laid six weeks ago, and tents open-flapped, electrically lit, neat as models, each with its enclosure and gravel design of regimental badges at the entrance.

I don't know how much all this faultless organisation of chic, discipline and capacity for getting the difficult done is worth. The dictators had it, and it didn't do them or their countries much good, but it certainly impressed me last night, just as the Berlin Sports-palast impressed Lord Londonderry.

8 August

The whole place has become a little Dead-Sea-fruitish. People leave daily never to return, no others of interest take their place; understrappers step into strappers' shoes. There is a feeling of *fin de sasion*, and that *saison* the last. No one makes a plan or arrangement of life or work or pleasure, as it is not worth while – not time now. The few left are boring and talk only of Paris. I can no longer put over my act about Algiers being *'palpitant.'* It isn't any more. This toy is no longer new. A.F.H.Q.'s departure has slackened and dimmed things. The boiling humidity enervates. I want to come home and see you, and for the bombs to stop, and for my sisters'

Marrakesh, January 1944

Winston S. Churchill   C. de Gaulle

Paris, 11 November 1944

sons to be saved. The only soldier I cared for and prayed for nightly is killed. The pain of Rex's death is still with me every hour. My hair will soon be as white as yours. I look so old that I shall feel shame even before your tender eyes.

The exciting news is that Duckling is due here at 8 a.m. today (top secret). I'm so excited. It's 7.30 now, like Christmas morning when one gets up too early in childhood and hardly knows what to do till stocking-time. He'll only be here for three or four hours and (hush, hush) Wormwood has refused to see him, not rudely but firmly. I must go and distribute soap and towels, bumf and stationery, and try to make order of chaos. Lord Gort and the A.D.C. arrived last night and we've just packed them off.

Duckling came yesterday. Such preparations! 'Perfume the chambers' with jasmine. Due at 8.30. Everything topsy-turvy and exciting. Duff and Randy for the airfield, me left to put the ship in shape. Duckling's telegram announcing his arrival added a message to Wormwood to the effect that he would be happy to shake his hand. Duff went to deliver this invitation, explaining that for security reasons the how-de-do would be better *chez nous*. No good: Worm would rather not. No persuasion moved him, so after dinner Duff and a Frenchman started concocting a letter of advice and appeal which was sent as a last hope.

At 8 a.m., when I was waddling round the house dressed as an Arab straightening the divans, putting white wine on ice, Palewski arrived with a sealed answer. I asked him what it said inside. He said he didn't know. I said wasn't it maddening? He said wasn't it. I asked had he (Gaston) done his best? He said indeed he had. The conversation continued

in this vein for a bit, then he left and it dawned on me that perhaps he was quite ignorant of what I was talking about. This theory was rather underlined by his saying as he left: 'I think on the whole this letter is satisfactory.' So I handed it to Duff with a certain confidence when he arrived. The envelope only contained another addressed to Duckling. It said that as his stay here was only for a few hours he thought it more considerate not to disturb his rest – blah, blah, blah. Silly idiot! Why must he carry on so, just as things seemed much better and after the bouquets in D's speech? So snubbing for Duckling. Such a flop for Duff. Now when he, Duckling, returns via Algiers, which he speaks of doing shortly, the invitation will not be extended; in fact I don't suppose Charlie will even hear of the visit.

So Duckling arrived and walked across the beautiful morning-lit court in khaki with harlequin chest, heavy and weary, a little infirm and unsmiling, but in ten minutes the talk began to flow and, with the flow, the grins and fun, the youth and strength. Randy all smiles and love, shouting him down, abusing his colleagues, especially Anthony. We four sat for an hour or so jawing while the others had baths. No one had the Louis XIV breakfast prepared; they had all eaten on the plane. Our staff behaved unnecessarily tactfully, Freddie doing a total disappearance for the morning, God knows why. I meanwhile was feeling iller and iller. Your old doctor rolled in after his bath and Duck was nannified off by his valet to have his. Then it was iced white wine and off at noon, and I went giddy and couldn't focus and retired to my bed, miserable.

20 August

I'm off to Rome. Suddenly last evening at Chréa the exciting news was telephoned. All was set for 6 a.m. Monday. What to take? How correct in dress to be? How military? How naval? How English eccentric? The valise I had relied on had unaccountably disappeared. Randy or the Arabs have

won it, I suppose, so I'm reduced to a piece of luggage bought in Algiers, guaranteed to break or ruin by *chiffonage* anything put into it. I like it despite its shortcomings, for it belongs to a Sir Richard Burton or a Mameluke or a Kinglake and appears to have been made by the unskilled of Abyssinia.

Dawson's assistant, little bright Squadron-Leader Boucher, appeared at 6.30, and after hurling back an amytol and weighing my handbag down with half a bottle of whisky, we got away. Here I am on a Liberator (old tried model) *without* a glass oubliette piece, thank Goodness. The sanitary bin is there with no veils, but the journey should not last more than four hours.

Rome

It was six when we arrived in Rome, by jeep, yellow-red in the setting sun and looking more beautiful than I remembered. There is little traffic, horse-fiacres for the rich, trucks for the army; priests and populace all look as they did. I do not see the rich elegance, the fine clothes and fashion I was warned of. At the Grand Hotel there was a flutter of messages from Randolph, Evelyn, the British Embassy and a letter from Lady Charles saying that, as Winston was staying, she couldn't put me up and would I dine that night, and a lot of panicky messages from Security and staff members over getting me there.

Evelyn appeared, quite recovered, and well-meaning, though his ownership of Rome and its churches is going to end in a spot of trouble, I fear. Then Randy blasted in full of gaiety and affection, and I forgot his tricks and his manners, and met him with a glad, full heart.

The Grand Hotel is an old-fashioned sort of Ritz translated for the nonce into a kind of Kremlin, men with tommy-guns at every door, because all the big-wigs, with the exception of Duckling, were staying there. Like the Kremlin too there seemed to be no charge for anything – rooms free, and if I

signed bills for breakfast or drinks for Randolph or Evelyn, nothing more was heard of the item.

At the Embassy dinner there was Jumbo and U.S. Generals and Admirals, and a jumble of *bouts-de-table*. I didn't do at all well with Duckling because my face reminds him instantly of de Gaulle. This gives him apoplexy, so I turn from him to Ambassador Kirk, who tells me that he can't bear eyes, mouths or any orifices ('mucus, just mucus-holes'). I turn with a new subject to Duckling, but again my face transports him back immediately to de Gaulle, and apoplexy envelops him. It's made our meetings impossible.

I pretty well hated the evening and it dribbled on till midnight. Duck was in his state ducks with my slippers on his webbies. I've written to him and said *it* must stop or he'd best not see me.

I saw the Pope carried shoulder-high through two throngs of Allied soldiers, blackamoors, Poles and ordinaries, and he touched one per cent of the rosaries held up to him.

I'm to go back by U.S. Naval plane. (It's not true that Dawson always flies.) I expect half the feathers will be out of its wings and it will have the gapes, but I must get back.

Dining at Ambassador Kirk's I heard on the wireless that Paris was liberated. I should be with Duff. 'My sense is with my senses all mixed in.' Destroyed with dread I feel.

This morning a message from the Chancery. Can Colonel Fane be ready to start for Paris tonight? Freddie didn't bat his devil's lid. Now it's after lunch and I can't bear myself at all. It's record heat. I have a stye i' the eye, I'm soaking, tired and ill inside. I can't breathe.

I feel dreadfully about Dicky Cecil's death, and now a Lansdowne boy, and David Wallace, and Rex, O Rex!

29 August (my birthday)
Darling Conrad, This is the last letter of this batch. Things move very fast. Saturday, 2 September, is chosen as day of

departure. Freddie Fane, Teddie Phillips, Holman, Reilly
and some typists left this morning for England, then Paris.
The Government has gone. I feel sad – a lump in the
throat – because it can never be again, and because it has
been sunlit and strange and unlike real life.

Those who were left were straining to be gone, to be free and to
be in France. Duff was glad to leave North Africa. It had not held
for him, as it had for me, the same beauty nor yet the relief, for he
had never envisaged defeat and he now looked forward eagerly to
the struggles and demands of Paris reclaimed. I alone dreaded
departure from this temporary yet vital, substantial yet dreamlike,
domain. Algiers possessed me.

Black doom was retreating and the Powers of Light ever on the
march, scattering the enemy before them. This rich pagan earth,
after our five years of war's austerity, was a promised land.

The once-hated house in which we had slunk around,
unwarmed, unwatered and unfed, had become a palace of two
worlds – of earth and of heaven. My heart felt more than ever
before open, generous, almost selfless. It could offer all it had to
the thousands that rushed or wandered through our courts, to the
great men and women of five continents, to the smiling prisoners,
to the humble and meek who had learned with rejoicing and ease
to integrate. Where rats had scuttled now shimmered a gazelle's
ghost, two disdainful peacocks, a little silver cat, great Fatima the
cow and a nuzzling donkey. Goodbye to them all; goodbye to the
flowering trees, Judas and jacaranda, to the Valley of *La Femme
Sauvage*, to the Marabout's shrine, to the white domes, the Arabian arcades. Never more . . .

The last night, my mind a little disordered by imminent loss, I
found intolerably hot. I walked the moonlit paths of our wide garden and noticed that, as in shallow waters on the beach, the
temperature was patchy, and colder pools could be discovered. Like
an unhappy somnambulist I was subjected to the fearful labour of
dragging my mattress, pillow and mosquito-net down flights of

narrow stairs, through impeding doors, over park, over pale, thorough bush, thorough briar, to my marked oasis. The net I tied to the limb of a frail tree. Beneath it I stretched my mattress, and there I composed myself and slept, to be woken within one small hour by a frantic cloudburst whipped into arrows by a hot hurricane that disbranched my roof-tree and streamed my net up into the semblance of a white witch. I fled whimpering to the house.

Next day we took off from Maison Blanche bound for London. I should see my son and Conrad, my sisters and many friends in a few hours. This comfortable thought mitigated the sadness but could not dispel it.

We flew over Tipaza's ruins, syrens silenced now by the engine's roar. Goodbye! Chréa's cedars fast vanishing behind us. Never more . . . A long farewell, *Tombeau de la Chrétienne*, the last hive on our bee-line towards home and victory. My tears could not be stopped, and they had to be silent ones, for they were out of place and hysterical on so happy a day. They would not stop and for many years talk of Algiers would summon them back in my eyes to everyone's amusement.

Re-arm for Paris. No need to worry about *trop de zèle*, but *surtout pas de faiblesse*.

I remember very little of London. There are no letters, as Duff, Conrad and John Julius were all three in hugging distance. The flying bombs had been blown to bits, so I was spared that horror.

Emerald held her court at the Dorchester. Nothing was worse materially. Spirits were gladder, not higher. We seemed tired and no longer spurred by menace. John Julius still wore his open expression; his hands and feet were outsized and his hair recalcitrant as a pony's. The nephews were all alive and whole. I stayed long enough to order some clothes suitable to Paris, not to me – what we called 'like other people' dresses and some humourless hats. No more clowning. I must try not to swell the list of mad English ambassadresses.

8
Winter and Journey's End

I come now to my last chapter. I recoil from it not because it is the end – I am thankful to have done with the labour, though it was of love – but because I know even less than I knew when I wrote the first one, how to tackle it. A little time ago, crippled with despondency, I dreamed of a way out of my slough. 'I'll write no more,' I told John Julius. 'You were there, you remember the Embassy in Paris, the Liberation, the war's end. You shall write this chapter. After twenty years, when these sensitive players have left the stage, your pen can flow with less impediment than mine. You can blow your parents' trumpets to the skies, and tell the stories of their deaths.' John Julius would have none of it. He called me a coward and a malingerer, so, driven by shame, with tired hand, tired memory and an avalanche of tired repetitive letters all clamouring for life through print, I will begin my end.

Paris – in diplomats' eyes 'the crown' – loomed in mine as the *coup de grâce*. It was the crown for Duff, whose favourite season was autumn. He saw through the mists and golden rays of autumn rest after work, with books to read and write, nature to love, the harvest home. I, disliking age and holding it at bay, yearned always for the promising, adventurous spring, and this particular October, after my Indian summer in Africa, chilled me with its evening damps and cold heraldings of winter and journey's end. Falteringly I will lead the reader into the golden house of the Faubourg St Honoré that was to be our Embassy during our short mission to Paris as the King's representatives.

On 13 September 1944 we watched Beachy Head fade away in the morning light, and soaring over France we stared with pent-up

interest and curiosity at the earth of this long-occupied country. The traveller's bird's-eye that makes molehills of mountains saw nothing extraordinary except for nests of bomb-craters concentrated in fields; the land looked normal, orderly, its villages intact. We seemed to hang motionless in the high air, between the Eiffel Tower and the Sacré Coeur, while our impressive escort of forty-eight Spitfires weaved and dipped like swallows round our arrival. I don't remember who was with us, and, but for the recognisable lump in my throat, I did not feel it could be me, dressed like other people in sober conventionality, arriving with all this circumstance in Paris.

A little knot of diplomats and staff – Victor Rothschild included, thank heavens – stood in a welcoming group on the airfield. At a snail's pace we drove the twelve miles to the capital, a dozen policemen on their ear-splitting machines protecting us – from what? The streets were empty of traffic. The people by the roadside, hearing the clatter, mostly stopped and waved, many lifting their hats, while workmen in groups, recognising our loudly conspicuous Union Jacks, sometimes raised a cheer.

As we came to the centre of this unfamiliar, unjostling city, I remember being diverted by gay merry-go-rounds of bicycles pedalled by Parisians, coats flying in the speed, panniers on their back-wheels, as likely as not carrying a poodle, trimmed to kill, on their rack. These undauntable women, if not sporting the highest and most shapeless hats ever devised, hats to out-caricature the *incroyables*, dressed their hair like their dogs', and stuck it with roses, bows, feathers or fruit. The Champs-Elysées boasted a few old horse-drawn fiacres which warmed my cold heart. The Allied flags on the lamp-standards and floating from windows warmed it too, but there was little gladness or gaiety in the atmosphere. There were no restaurants or cinemas, no cafés with pavement-tables: lack of electricity, scarcity of food and coffee had dealt with them.

The official *gerbe* that had met us automatically at Le Bourget was placed without detour or hesitation on the Unknown Soldier's

grave, where, considering the luncheon hour, a fair-sized crowd had collected. Thence we moved on, not to the Embassy but, to my surprised delight, to the little doss-down hotel that had sheltered Duff and me so prettily and cheaply for fifteen years or more. This home-from-home, by chance only, had been requisitioned to house the Ambassador and his staff until the Embassy could be habitable. So we found ourselves in our own suite, whose faults and taps we knew, our Marie Antoinette still priding herself on the chimney-piece. This gave my sagging face and spirits a needed lift, as did the flowers that made it difficult to move or open the door. Baskets of orchids, long-stemmed roses, satin bows on golden wicker from the few old friends, officials, from shops solici-ting custom and from collaborationists working a passage home. I remember thinking the first day that Embassy life is a life apart, a fool's paradise, for here already was all the light, the steaming water, the steaks and butter we were warned not to expect in Paris.

The Embassy itself had been for five years the British Empire's furniture-dump; it was stuffed to its closed doors with all the paraphernalia, the treasure, the chattels and junk of Common-wealth diplomats' families and exiled Parisian residents: pianos, hatstands, bureaux, bath-mats, sponges, bottles, good and bad pictures, boxing-gloves and skates, clouds of moth, powder of woodworm. Nothing of the house's beautiful proportions or dec-oration could be seen and nothing could be done until the owners, the dividers, scrappers and cleaners took over.

The comfort I found in the little Berkeley Hotel was within a week or so snatched from me. Our friendly staff in the restaurant, the friends who dribbled in and out of England on missions, were making my difficult transition easier to bear. '*Vous êtes trop mal logés, celà n'est pas digne,*' said the busybodies, so we were translated to the Hotel Bristol, G.H.Q. Corps Diplomatique, all for the sake of a private dining-room and private staircase, two bathrooms, four basins, one for each hand and a third, at chest-level, that could, I thought, only be for vomiting. Indeed these weeks were my nadir; the gloom and cold and officialdom throttled me, then

suddenly the new brooms swept the Embassy clean of its flea-market, and things looked up. Pauline Borghese, who had owned the house, and had left her silken walls, her sphinxes and laurels, her eagles of Empire, her complete furnishings, and above all her ox-blood bedroom giving on to the *salons*, inspired me out of my sullen misery. Hers was the most extraordinary bedroom I had ever thought to lie in; it had rarely been used by our succession of unusual ambassadresses. Walls, curtains, sofas and chairs were upholstered in the richest Lyons silk which bore a design of caducei and laurel-leaves. The tables and the tall *psyche* (or full-length looking-glass) were signed by master-makers. The bed, supported by Egyptian caryatides, rose to a high curtain-hung testa, crowned by a heroic golden eagle, so perched as only to be seen by one in bed through the soaring looking-glass on the opposite wall. Sir George Clark was the one Ambassador I knew of who had made this room his own; though doubtless there were others who had slept in its magnificence since Napoleon's extravagant sister.

The autumn sun slanted through the ten high windows which looked out on to a garden, not of flowers, but of fine trees, sward and boscage, gilding the yellow silk walls of the first *salon*, the white-and-gold *pièce de cérémonie*, and flattering the green, undecorated room, to become familiar to many as the *salon vert*.

The airy country-house bedrooms above were quickly refurbished to hold a succession of V.I.P.'s and friends, who could find no room in the requisitioned hotels of Paris. On the ground floor, connected by a Victorian glass marquise, were the vast reception-rooms, darkened by the verandah, and without the charm and brilliance of our living apartments; they struck cold fear into my heart and manner. Fortunately they did not come into use until later, when I was hardened to the life.

Our D-Day was November 11, when Winston was to make his first appearance in Paris since the Liberation. We had prepared to house the party, but at the last moment the Churchills and the Edens were invited to the Quai d'Orsay. It was warmer than the Embassy, which was cruelly cold, though it gave a lambent glow. I

went to inspect the suites. They had been blazed up in 1938 to receive our King and Queen. I liked the two bathrooms, one of silver and one of gold – mosaic, crystal and fiddle-de-dees rampant, and the dressing-room Goering had left, with its cupboards for a hundred uniforms, walls raying out infra-red and ultra-violet beams, everything in it from bath to boot-jack too solid, too massive for any bulk to break.

For the great victory review I sat with Mesdames Churchill, Eden, de Gaulle, Catroux and Massigli in the Ladies' Tribune. We trembled with anxiety as we watched our two heroes drive to the Arc de Triomphe in an open car – the one so cherubically pink and benign, the other so sinister and elongated. After the inevitable wreath was laid, we held our breath as together, and in great danger, they walked half a mile down the Champs-Elysées, to join us in the Tribune. Paris went mad. The bands played, the Garde Républicaine champed and clattered and the *pompiers* who had played a big part in the Liberation played it still.

On the last evening of the visit, our Embassy opened its doors for its first dinner-party. The Sergeant-Major and Sweeney, still in khaki, were in their appointed places, and André Bonnot, the elegant *huissier*, who had announced the guests for twenty-five years, called out le Général et Madame de Gaulle, Mr and Mrs Churchill, Monsieur et Madame Bogomolov, Mr Caffery (from Washington), the Canadian General and Madame Vanier and Monsieur et Madame Georges Bidault (Foreign Secretary). The house looked as I hoped it would and better, for Madame Annie Beaumel, the genius of Hermès, with whom I had become most friendly, took over the flowers and festal ornamentation, surpassing herself in taste. (She helped me in all my efforts of this kind, once for Field-Marshal Lord Montgomery wreathing the pillars and pilasters with laurel, and giving the house panache with faded silken flags that had survived battles. Another time she brought me models of frigates from the naval museum to dress the table overall for Admiral Cunningham.)

In Paris Winston's was a name to waken the dead. Wherever

he walked – and he liked to walk if time allowed – his way was dense with cheering enthusiasts. It made him happy to give them his **V** sign and to bask in their love and gratitude. After two days we waved him off with *le grand Charles* for the front at Besançon.

We knew no one in Paris, and that was one of the rubs; we had never lived there and only passed through occasionally on our travels to mix with English pleasure-seekers, to junket in Montmartre and cry in Russian night-clubs, to wander through the museums and then push off for the delights of the open road with Michelin as guide. The Parisians were warm and welcoming; Duff had the Travellers' Club, where all men are alike and good, but I had no real friends, save those who had tagged along from Algiers.

One night Princesse Jean de Polignac, the daughter of Madame Lanvin, who sang like a syren, asked us to dine. In those early days, without fuel or much food, meals were huddled round the only fire, which might be in the bedroom. She invited to meet us two or three people whose names I knew, including Drian, the artist who had influenced my taste since childhood and whose friendship I had never quite lost. There was also a lady who hardly spoke a word and seemed to me, though beautiful, a little colourless. The Polignac champagne warmed us all into a less pompous mood. The unknown lady laughed a little, but contributed, as far as I can remember, nothing else. Next day I learnt that she was Louise de Vilmorin, a serious poetess of high worth, who lived with her three brothers in a suburb of Paris called Verrières-le-Buisson. A week later she asked us to dinner. Christian (Bébé) Bérard, Jean Cocteau, Marie-Louise Bousquet, Cecil Beaton, Edouard and Denise Bourdet, Georges and Nora Auric, and many others were there. Louise opened all her petals as suddenly and gloriously as a nightflowering cereus, and driving home that night Duff and I both felt that our life in Paris would now be completely different.

It was. '*La Bande*,' as we called this Comus-crew of artists, drew and grew closer round us, building our confidence, easing our work and filling our relaxation with gladness. Our dear stand-by

from Algiers, Elizabeth de Breteuil, belonged to this delightful company, so did Minou de Montgomerie. Louise was the hub and heart of it. It was Louise who let in the light to an Embassy that might have been as drab as Embassies often are. From the day of her entrance the place sang with laughter and song, wit and poetry. The winter was icing our bones; there was no heating anywhere. Louise was very delicate, and the alien occupiers of the beautiful Verrières house had left it in a sad plight, so she often stayed with us. I had never seen her like before, no longer silent or colourless; one wondered if it was her beauty or the poetic and roaringly funny conversation that seduced one most; the songs, the Hungarian clothes or the extravagant schemes. To us she was an acquisition of the first water, for new diffident French Ministers and hardened old English ones came to the Embassy more often than they needed to, in quest of Louise.

Now I began to work with a will; now there was light and shade, and not unadulterated officialdom. Duff was having a very difficult time and I rarely saw him, except across a ceremonial dinner-table. De Gaulle and Winston were playing battledore with Duff as the shuttlecock. The daily programme was densely packed with cold and depressing engagements. My bad French handicapped me, but I was intent on the growth of Anglo-French amity, and would have stopped at nothing to further it. The Germans had left dreadful traces behind them. Hospitals and hostels must be visited; rooms where prisoners had been tortured, their walls scrawled with last messages from those who had been shot, had to be shown us, people's relations must be traced and, if possible, warmed and fed.

The cold was appalling. One of the joys of the *salon vert* was its crowds, for crowds and shouting generate heat. *La Bande* were coming daily and so were the S.H.A.E.F. contingents (the organisation known to the cynical as V_3). The war was not getting on very fast or very well; in fact by Christmas there was a minor panic. Personally I had no time to worry much about it and was horrified one evening among a group of Anglo-American journalists to hear Knickerbocker say that Antwerp would be gone in a

week. 'Good God,' I said, 'that means goodbye to the Channel ports and D-Day to do again.' 'Oh, we'll never do it again,' he said. There was even talk of a second exodus and advice given not to bring John Julius to France for Christmas, but I do not remember its affecting me at all. Our great favourite in S.H.A.E.F., Charles Peake, brought the awful news that Strasbourg, the beloved town, liberated after seventy years of occupation, was to be abandoned. Duff put his life's blood into saving the French this humiliation and persuaded Winston to fly over to Versailles, where the Council of War agreed to leave the French divisions to fight for their city and win their battle.

Conrad wrote on Christmas Eve:

Quiet Guard. Weather mild, nights wholesome; the bird of dawning sings with leathern lungs all night long, yet the state of the world hardly bears thinking about.

I like penning the sheep on Christmas Day; there is a sort of continuity of tradition about the task. If Christ and his disciples came by they would just say 'Oh, there is a shepherd doing his sheep,' but if they saw a man filling up the tank of his car with petrol they would be flummoxed and would not know what on earth he was up to. Last year you were at Ditchley. Ever since that it's been separation. The light of my life is extinguished. The farm chores I do we used to do together, shall we ever again? Everything is the epitome of sadness now. I don't know where to find a pleasant thought.

The German success is bad enough; I suppose we were caught napping. But it's not like March 1918. A whole army was not disintegrated. We have not lost 100,000 men. I remember March 1918 as stunning and thinking 'The Germans have won after all,' and sobbing. I could show you a little wood about two miles from Longpré les Corps Saints where I sobbed alone after seeing the English routed – a disorderly rabble in flight. I don't think anything like that has happened. What you tell me about C. is a thumping lie;

The British Embassy, Paris

Faubourg St Honoré and garden side

Pauline Borghese's bed

The Embassy library

Cecil Beaton in the library

it's untrue like Kitchener still being alive, and Percy being killed in a duel, and Alexander the First having become a monk, and Winston having broken his parole, and Queen Victoria having married John Brown, and Mr Druce being the Duke of Portland, and Uncle Bedford being Jack the Ripper, and the Duke of Wellington having said Up Guards and at 'em, and Dreyfus being a traitor, and Lord Dufferin being the son of Dizzy, and Brendan the son of Winston, and a lot of other queer nonsensical rubbish which gets about.

I was learning for the first time in my life a little of the joy of power. It was amusing, when all the lights went out at a Palais Royal restaurant where Bébé Bérard and Jean Cocteau were entertaining us, to send the car round to the Embassy for twenty candelabra and priceless Price candles. It was good to dole out these candles to people without light, to beg blankets from the army for the shivering French civilians. Best of all I could have unprocurable penicillin traced to Rheims and send a scout on a motor bicycle to fetch it in time to save a girl dying of septicaemia.

Another time, when Louise was nursing a brother at Châteaubriand who was very near death, I motored through the night with penicillin, for which light labour of love the Vilmorin family gave me my treasure of treasures – a Colonne Vendôme in gold and silver. It was made by a madman called Poujade. A silver Napoleon stands on top with three changes of uniform and boots, hung in a royal-blue velvet closet in the pedestal. Its silver door bears the words '*La Vestière de S.M. Napoléon.*' In his Roman classical robe he carries a pistol and in his Marshal's dress a kind of fishing-rod and line with a hooked Légion d'Honneur.

One day a letter came from a solicitor in Geneva informing me that the Count de Luzarraga, a man I had seen for three minutes in my life, had died and bequeathed me £28,000. This astonishing announcement left me cold. I knew it could not be. Twenty years

before I used to receive letters from one who signed himself Manuel and wrote sometimes three times a day in violet ink on transparent stationery. He wrote of the anger he felt for his family who kept us apart, of our three children, and of the happy days at Newmarket. From Biarritz, Geneva and London these letters fluttered to me daily for five or six years, then less abundantly but without pause, until the war, when they ceased. Nineteen out of twenty I put unopened into the wastepaper-basket, scanning the twentieth to see if the plaint was still the same. It always was. Once, when the correspondence was at its height, I was politely accosted in Gower Street by a little gentleman, aged about seventy, wearing a black coat, a sombrero and a trim white beard, who, uncovering, said 'I am Manuel.' Now was my moment to clear up a big misunderstanding. With distaste I faced up to the situation and told him that he had certainly confused me with another, that we had no past and no children, and please he must stop writing to the wrong woman. He stared into my face, a little stunned and incredulous, and then, bowing with courtly Spanish grace, said he was sorry that I had had to suffer from his importunities but that I should never hear from him again. This meeting, the only one, made no difference to the flow of letters signed Manuel. It was no misunderstanding but an illusion that he clung to passionately, one that he could not let go.

In Geneva after his death I called on the solicitor, who must have concluded that I was the dead Count's mistress. He found my story as surprising as I had found his news. Mr Martin had known the old gentleman intimately, known him as the sanest of men, a devout Catholic, a philanthropist, one who had made a good end and was mourned by the Church and all who knew him. He showed me the will that left all that he died possessed of to me, or, should I predecease him, to my son. During the war he had added a codicil leaving a few thousand pounds that lay in another bank to orphan children and re-emphasising that no member of his family should touch a penny of his fortune. The story is strange and rather moving. I wish I had never met him.

Naturally by law his two old sisters inherited part of the sum. The Swiss and English Governments grabbed most of the rest. I would have loved to thank him, more for his dreams than for the little residue that ultimately came to me. I will, if I get to Heaven, for he is there I am sure, trying to evade his sisters.

How bitterly cold it was in Paris. I felt warm only in bed or in the car. There was little other than official transport. Our dinner-guests might walk several kilometres in rain and slush. In England we had not suffered in this way. If one went to the theatre in Paris one took a hot-water-bottle for one's lap. At concerts the orchestra wore greatcoats, hats and mittens, and the pianist had a brazier of glowing charcoal beside him to keep his hands usable.

Our satanic Freddie Fane of Algiers days, of whom I was so fond, slipped on the icy pavement, broke his frail thigh and died of subsequent pneumonia. Very sad; and sad too that Edouard Bourdet, the director of the Comédie Française and brilliant star in the constellation of *La Bande*, should die suddenly. I remember sitting up in my gilded bed, the red silk counterpane scattered with sprigs of bay torn from a shaped tree in the garden and wiring them into a wreath for his obsequies.

Economy again had me in its grip; the money exchange was grotesque. Everyone except the British Embassy used black-market rates, but I had to pay thirty pounds for a pair of shoes and seventy pounds for a lunch for eight.

I was made the godmother of the First Regiment of Chasseurs d'Afrique. It meant supplying the soldiers with cigarettes, rugs, raincoats and other comforts, plus spirits for the officers. Luckily we had our arch-scrounger, the Sergeant-Major, to diminish the cost. A visit to them at the front was to be undertaken as soon as the great cold had passed. I hoped it might coincide with John Julius's Easter holidays in early April and it fortunately did. General de Lattre was the First Army commander, so we would be in his reliable charge; and de Lattre had endeared himself to me in the glad days of Algiers.

I wrote on 8 April to Conrad:

I am going to dictate this letter to you, as I only got back last night and am leaving again tomorrow morning for our wearisome provincial tour, but I must tell all about going into battle.

John Julius, Teddie Phillips and I left at nine in the morning in Teddie's smart Bentley car. I looked awful in a tartan coat and postman's cap. John Julius wore his O.T.C. khaki battledress and forage-cap, Eton College ablaze on his sleeve. Teddie's seven foot of good R.N. tailoring gave us tone. Behind sat a useless Marine; he couldn't drive and he chain-smoked.

Hardly an hour out of Paris this famous Bentley broke down, but I had a nice time picking cowslips while the others fiddled with the valves. Off again to a place called Ligny-en-Barrois, which my old Michelin told me had a 'table renommée.' We ate a not bad meal, and when we asked for the bill the first ray of the sun of General de Lattre fell upon us, for Madame said we were the guests of the General and brought out her *livre d'or* for signatures. How de Lattre could have known that I would choose that hotel to lunch at is incomprehensible.

On again, the motor spluttering and limping a bit till we reached Strasbourg. The villages had been getting more and more demolished, and Strasbourg itself was quite a mess – worse than Bristol – the cathedral untouched, and yet every house around it flat. We were taken by the General in command to a nice little villa, which was ours for the nonce, and, it being then half-past seven, we washed and went to dinner with General Schwartz at eight. This was a fairly gloomy little affair, because the real General – du Vigier – in command at Strasbourg had been called away to consult with General Patch. Shells were falling not very often – in fact, I never heard one because I took a blue scarab and slept like a log – but there were three or four in the night.

Early next morning we were off again – this time in a more reliable army car – to Kandel, the Headquarters of the French First Army; guards of honour wherever you looked. We were conducted to another villa for us alone. Sentries at the door, but no de Lattre, who did not expect us till mid-day. To fill in time we were taken off to the Siegfried Line, which had become the popular kind of Cheddar Gorge excursion. Deep down we walked under the blockhouses into room after room of bunks, and baths, and dispensaries, kitchens, passages. The darkness was complete, and nobody seemed to have a torch, so it was a case of striking matches and looking for loot. The loot was perfectly ridiculous – tin helmets, an electric globe, a rifle, some beer-mugs, and roll upon roll of highly prized bumf which we packed into as many tin hats as we could carry. After this collection was made it was mid-day, and we returned to Kandel to meet the General. Villages round here completely broken; very few civilians; what men there were cap in hand, clearly frightened. Difficult not to feel sorry for them, but as our car had a siren exactly like the London alert, it kept me reminded how much they had made us suffer. De Lattre is a dynamic man; glints of Winston and Max, and Monty; more streamlined than any of them; everything done full speed ahead. A lot of troops were lined up, which he told me to inspect immediately. This was very embarrassing for me, as I had no idea how to do it. Duckling once told me he looked every man full in the eyes. I tried, but no eye would meet mine. One feels one ought to say 'Bravo' or 'Well dressed, sir.'

We lunched with the General Staff, which included a jolly tartaned Colonel called Aitken, and Bill Bullitt, former U.S. Ambassador to France, now a French staff-officer. John Julius became the clue and mainstay of this alarming lunch, for the General got interested in public-school systems, and turned the machine-gun on to him. John Julius rose to the occasion, plunged into limping French, and really did very

229

well. De Lattre couldn't hear enough about whipping, fagging and calling 'boy.' In fact he was calling his staff 'boy' for the rest of the trip. John Julius he called '*Mon vieux*,' paradoxically enough.

At two o'clock we started for the Rhine – me, John Julius, and de Lattre on the back seat – Teddie in front. We drove north to a place called Speyer, where the French had built themselves a bridge across the Rhine independently of American material – a great pride to de Lattre, who had the pontoon bridges built secretly in a forest, and put up in two days. We crossed it on foot with tremendous fanfares. Everything seemed to stand to attention – men, guns, labourers, spades, oars. The river was running very swiftly, and I was much moved. The little *génie* who was responsible for its building was glorified by de Lattre and told to lay everything on for our return at nine o'clock that night.

On again, at eighty miles an hour on these narrow shell-torn roads, with alarming notices saying 'Roads clear of mines up to ditches.' As we were always on the very edge of the road, and perpetually had to leave it to make a detour on account of a truck having blown up, this knowledge might have been alarming: but somehow everything went at such a pace that life and death seemed of little account. Often we would meet a General, who would jump out of his car, maps fluttering in his hands, and show de Lattre how the battle was going. We would stop and get out when we passed French prisoners tramping home with their bundles on their backs. The General would ask them how long they had been prisoners. It was always five years, and they all said '*C'est le plus beau jour de ma vie*.' It is a victorious army, and, in consequence, everything is beaming and tremendously exhilarating. Paris is my battle-front. The western front was a holiday by comparison.

Eppingen was on the fringe of the battle, and we stood like Generals in *War and Peace* on a little knoll, watching the

village (less than a kilometre away) being taken; bombers and fighters overhead, and a good deal of Generals studying maps on what I like to think were drums, white puffs of smoke as shells exploded and a lot of artillery noise. I did not like to ask from where they were firing or at what, but fear wasn't present that day. We moved on to a village still nearer – in fact in the battle. Houses were still flaming, prisoners being rounded up, hands held high in a Jewish gesture. I was fascinated by the prisoners. They looked a bit scared, but, I am sorry to say, in splendid condition. In this village we were supposed to find my Premiers Chasseurs d'Afrique, but the entire regiment was *'engagé.'* They had left one token officer behind to explain, so perhaps I saved somebody's life. From here we motored for two hours south, calling all the way at divisional headquarters. Absurdly like a picture it was – Generals muttering *'C'est très dur'* and *'Ici nous sommes en pleine bagarre;'* their fingers on maps, tracing the life and death of regiments.

We came to Karlsruhe as the light was waning. Very little of that rich town was left and the houses were still blazing. No light; no water; no gas; but the Headquarters brought its electric plant with it. We were all getting a bit hungry by nine, but food was never mentioned by the General and we continued to call on lesser Generals in little half-ruined German houses, sweeping maps, and changing orders, cutting the coat for the cloth.

Crossing the Rhine at midnight was the most theatrically beautiful thing I have ever seen. The Rhine was illuminated by the strongest, bluest possible floodlight, the kind of light that shone in Green Park in the blitz days. Silhouetted against this blaze was the broken skeleton of the blown bridge – enormous deformity. The swirling water itself was as bright as molten silver, and across the new bridge, almost level with the waves, we walked as though on the water – a Wagnerian scene. All the soldiers, engineers, oarsmen, in a state of frenzied

salute – trembling hand and glazed eye. Midstream the chief engineer asked me to baptise his pennant. He called it '*fanion*,' a word I didn't know, so that when I said '*Bien volontiers*,' I had no idea what I was going to baptise. It turned out to be a pretty little silk flag on a long wand, which I solemnly dipped into the Rhine water and so baptised it. I thought it was nice of de Lattre, who was very 'France-conscious,' so obviously delighted that no hand but a French hand had touched the bridge, to allow an Englishwoman this gesture.

We drove back at 80 m.p.h. to the H.Q. through a forest, to the accompaniment of a siren, and a C.-in-C.'s *fanion* fluttering above us, all lights up. 'It won't be safe in another ten days to drive this way,' said the General. 'Why?' 'Because it's thick with Germans and soon they will lose their fear and organise themselves to resist.' We got home at 12.45 to find the staff very long-faced, Bill Bullitt's rosy smiles quite gone. I attributed these altered expressions to hunger but discovered them to be caused by alarm. They had given us up for dead or kidnapped; they guessed we had taken the forest road where in the last few days two staff-officers and *five* other officers had been taken and not heard of again. What a dreadful thing to have happened to us at this stage of the war. Everyone at the supper was exhausted. The General's half-face had dropped with one closed eye. Teddie, in spite of sleeping in the car, was falling, face-down into his plate. John Julius, flushed with success and excitement, seemed, I thought, a little tight. It came to its weary close at 2 a.m. and we got to very comfortable beds, and a high-spirited waking on April 6. The blossoms and the ruins together were stirringly sad – the weather was sublime. At ten the General was to come for leave-taking; he was half an hour late, so I reviewed a guard of honour to fill in time. When he ultimately came, he said he couldn't find the house. I think he had overslept. He worked till 4 a.m., and claimed he was up at eight.

The Marshal's tent

Lost on the Golden Stairs

Louise de Vilmorin

Inspecting the troops with General de Lattre

Back at Strasbourg, we sat down to lunch with the General who had been absent two days before – du Vigier, a man of great charm. The lunch was purely staff and towards its end, in the course of conversation, he asked me with an unchanged voice, '*si je voulais bien lui faire une commission,*' which developed gradually, imperceptibly, into a three or four minute speech. One by one the guests and staff stopped talking to listen and mop their eyes. He spoke in burnished French of the gratitude Strasbourg (he is the Governor) owed to England and what Winston had done to save the town, when in early January the Supreme Command's plan had been to evacuate it, and he had come over to Paris to pep them all into courage again and to persuade them to hold out. (Duff had pepped Winston, incidentally.) He spoke of England's glory in not having tasted bitter shame (I thought of Singapore!), and poor France's *honte*, and would I convey Strasbourg's gratitude to Mr Churchill. Really excellent it was, and done in such a civilised way, without gavel or 'Ladies and Gentlemen,' or on hind legs.

The Embassy looked like the spring. The Verrières orchard in blossom had marched in to welcome our arrival. We were laden with amusing loot, for at Strasbourg a pretty French AT, accompanied by an A.D.C., arrived panting from H.Q. with a letter from de Lattre, apologising for having kept me waiting for *les adieux*, and with it a magnificent German axlet to hang on the waist, gleaming and smart (must have been Goering's), also a bright red flag with swastika imposed, so we made a brave entrance to the Embassy with rifle and helmets and toilet-paper and beer-mugs. J.J., Raimund and I dined at Victor Rothschild's and looked at his museum of concealed bombs – wonderful. Bombs in bits of coal, in turnips, in logs; one cannot imagine how they were found or how Victor dared open them.

Then, as so-called relief, our duties took us on provincial visits. These were no less exhausting than the Paris grind. The first took us

to Lyons. We might have been the King and Queen. Even the Cathedral bells had been taught to chime 'God Save the King' as the Cardinal Archbishop received us in his sanctum. At Lyons Duff was made a Doctor of the University, as he was in several other of the great towns of France. On to Bordeaux, Toulouse, Avignon, where we heard to our grief that President Roosevelt was dead; to waterish Burgundy that runs with wine for innumerable tastings, to Lille and Tourcoing in the north, to devastated Caen and Falaise, to Strasbourg again, where fine girls, red-skirted beneath the vast black bows on their heads, marched in the Triumph beside the victorious Generals, to St Malo, to Poitiers, to the Bravade at St Tropez, to Angers, where I carried the flag alone and scored a hundred shining marks. Roses, roses, and laurels all the way, and National Anthems and *garde-à-vous*, tears of emotion, *que Dieu vous garde.*

At Marseilles John Julius and I fought military vetos and nonsenses till they broke with boredom and allowed us to fly for a few days to Algiers that I had so fondly loved, alone in an aircraft for sixty that plied twice daily to and fro to no purpose whatever. Ghostly, and the ghost of old Louise opened the creaking door of Jamshid's palace. The lion and the lizard in possession. The court, once flowery, now choked with unswept leaves of that vast busy, sheltering tree, the garden unfrequented. To this day that white town rings its *glas* in my heart. Ichabod!

The cold increased and so did the work, with a nervous heart and a toothache thrown in. It was the most gruelling life I had ever led. Harder than being a hospital nurse or an actress or a farmhand. Far, far more exhausting and difficult. There were investitures of our King's Medal for Courage. There were the Salvation Army and world-scientists and the princes of the Christian Churches (Rome excepted) donning their canonicals in the ballroom for a convention in the Embassy church. Football teams, academicians, the Nuncio (now Pope John XXIII), S.H.A.E.F. (who had their own clock and were therefore always an hour late or early). The B.I.F., E.N.S.A., W.V.S. – queues of alphabetical representatives; there were African consuls, Gertrude Stein and

234

Alice B. Toklas and their poodle, Colette swathed in woollen shawls with naked feet, and eyes like her own idolised cat.

There were our eminent English writers, actors, composers, conductors. Stephen Spender, Cyril Connolly, T. S. Eliot, John Lehmann, his sister Rosamond, Harold Nicolson and Raymond Mortimer must be given their own cocktail parties at which to receive the literary and musical world of Paris. Freddie Ayer lived in the house, though I did not know it for weeks, and there were Arabists and Freya Stark our dearest friend, Isaiah Berlin, Julian Huxley, Solly Zuckerman and Beatrice Eden, good and beautiful in her S.H.A.E.F. uniform. There were the Oliviers, Noël Coward, Donald Wolfit, Margot Fonteyn and our theatre Dames to be merged with Madeleine and Jean-Louis Barrault and Louis Jouvet; M.P.'s of two or three parties floated round most of the time, a bishop or two on his beat, and a steady flow of V.I.P.'s must be given receptions – lavish or homespun. Dinners must be spread for Ministers of the Resistance Government from Bidault to Thorez and also for the Corps Diplomatique.

Dining with the Russians was the most gruelling of all evenings. Their orders were to invite their colleagues separately, so we were doomed to the same awkward square of four. Madame Bogomolov was dressed richly while I was more gaudy. We were received in the sumptuous eighteenth-century rooms, ablaze with raw electric bulbs, announced by a comfortable, rather scruffy charwoman in a cardigan. No vodka for the bad quarter of an hour. That standby arrived after we had sat down to dinner. With the hope of making us talk, toast after toast was given – the King, General de Gaulle, Winston, the Red Army, other armies, and when one said 'no more,' the Ambassador would try to start us off again with 'To your husband,' 'To my wife.' Nothing would have drawn an indiscreet word out of Duff. He scarcely opened his mouth. On such sticky occasions I can babble and squeak *ad nauseam*. We used the well-worn subjects, dinner after dinner. Education, Ukrainian Universities and synthetic rubber (Madame's speciality). I think they were just as bored as we were, and as

familiarity took hold they took to speaking Russian to each other across my momentarily mute body. 'What's he saying? what's he saying?' I'd scream and she would reply, 'I tell him not to talk when you talk' or *'Je lui dit* – not to *agacer* you with his toasts,' followed by contortions of laughter as they quoted passages from *Three Men in a Boat*.

Once I had the temerity to tell the Ambassador that my son, after leaving school, would have a year to fill in before our National Service claimed him. I said that the boy had taught himself a little Russian and was anxious to spend a year in the U.S.S.R. I asked how we could arrange for him to work there? On a communal farm? Perhaps in a factory? Better, could he not live with a Russian family? *'Chez nous cela n'est pas la coutume'* was all the encouragement I got, and advice to send him to the British Embassy in Moscow. 'But there he would never hear or see a Russian,' it was my delight to answer.

Another time when I sat between Molotov and Vishinsky I laughingly said to the former 'I must complain of your Ambassador, M. Bogomolov, who, when I offer him my son, a young Russian enthusiast, will have none of him.' The interpreter answered, *'M. Molotov dit que chez nous cela n'est pas la coutume. Pourquoi ne pas envoyer M. votre fils à l' Ambassade d'Angleterre à Moscou?'* I wound this conversation up with the same reply and the same delight. I was fond of Madame Bogo; she was pretty, had a hero-worship for Winston, and laughed when one of our Embassy ladies whom I had taken to tea with her said of somebody: 'He was an absolutely awful man – a regular Bolshie.'

Duff had been separated from his books ever since we had sent them to Belvoir in makeshift cardboard boxes during the bombardment. Now the time had come to unpack them in peace. There was no library in the Embassy and Duff had the generous idea of establishing one by giving his collection when his mission as Ambassador ended. The Office of Works agreed in exchange to instal elegant shelves on which to range it. The lofty room in which he worked was ideal in size and position, and the decoration

must naturally be worthy of the rest of the house. Charles de Beistegui, whom I had known for twenty-odd years, volunteered, with the help of Georges Geoffroy, to design a library which all agreed became, with its deep cornice, its slender pilasters, its busts and vases and green-fringed shelves, perhaps the most perfected room in the Embassy.

Duff and I and Mrs Walker (long may she live to see our Ambassadors come and go) and a little Polish refugee of ten who swarmed the pillars with books for the topmost shelves (he was the only one of a thousand Catholic children Auberon Herbert, in his quixotry, had determined to rescue from the Communists), spent many ecstatic hours arranging them.

Bébé Bérard chose the colour of carpet and curtains and arranged the placing of furniture. These suffered vicissitudes after our departure, so I have added gratitude to my great affection for Gladwyn and Cynthia Jebb for restoring the library to what it was, and beautifying it with commemorative words that run round the cornice:

AD FRANCOS FELICITER LEGATUS TACITAE
LIBRORUM AMICITIAE HUNC LOCUM DEDICAVIT
DUFF COOPER UT LECTORES INTER AMICOS
SUOS NUMERARET. SALVE AMICE ET LEGE.

An Anglo-French alliance was what Duff – through all the maze wrought by two absolute, redoubtable, inflexible men – was determined to see a signed reality. I can see his tired face when he would quote 'I often am much wearier than you think' – words I could not hear without feeling my heart grow cold within me, and I would think two millstones too good for Winston and de Gaulle. Duff's memoirs tell of these convulsions; this hideous game with Duff the shuttlecock, that had to be played to its inevitably successful end. I should write of peace coming at last and yet curiously enough I cannot tell of that either. Duff says I broke down when he told me through his own tears, but I don't remember that

particular breakdown among so many. I remember the announcement was bungled, the day and hour unpointed. I remember the siren shrieking its last All Clear, the church-bells pealing, the Champs-Elysées in an open car, hood and mudguards crawling with pick-ups, and generally a sense of bewilderment. As in 1918, when war-fortitude is laid aside, when prayers are answered after five years of supplication, expecting to be elated and flushed by glory and victory and a sense of ineffable relief, one is overcome instead with the miseries, the senselessness, the dreadful loss. This is perhaps what the Duke of Wellington meant when he said that nothing was worse than victory except defeat.

It was now, exploring at Chantilly, that I walked through open iron gates (an ingrained and irresistible habit) to an eighteenth-century house clearly built for the retirement of a scholarly English lover of life and his doting wife. The garden window yielded to my hand, the place was furnished and seemingly uninhabited. I found an American Lieutenant, who told me it belonged to Bill Bullitt, and was temporarily requisitioned by the American forces, that no one was home and I could look into every nook and cranny. It was the house of my dreams set perfectly on a slope *à l' anglais* within the park of the Château de Chantilly. Tall trees were reflected in a little lake fed by the much bigger *pièce d'eau* into which gushed a snow-white vigorous cascade. A willow wept away over some leisured swans, and beyond in the forest were as many glades and avenues, statues, vases and obelisks as I required. Duff was as enthusiastic as I was, and so began the light but long struggle, the candles lit in churches, the medallions of saints planted surreptitiously with a prayer at the threshold, the pleadings and the threats that made it ours, first as tenants and ultimately as leaseholders from the Institut de France. This retreat would be a mitigation of our sorrow if before our time we were to be fired; and fired we were, not unnaturally and not unkindly.

The D (for dreadful) day of the General Election dawned, and by evening we heard that Winston Churchill, saviour of the free world, was no longer Prime Minister. There was something magnificently

English and something cold-hearted and ungrateful about this result. I failed to see the magnificence, but many far wiser than I admired the unsentimental independence of the voters. 'A blessing in disguise,' some said. 'It's very well disguised,' said Winston. To us it meant in full probability dismissal. Duff had been appointed by a Conservative Government, and why should the new Labour Foreign Minister not replace him by a career-diplomat or assign this Embassy – this plum of plums – to his own political nominee?

Nothing to be done. Yet the sack did not come for two and a half years. Instead came Ernie Bevin to see and conquer us all. Massive, rude and strong as a Stonehenge cromlech, he was as tilled, as fertile and generous as his English fields. Proud of his lowliness and of his achievements, he loved his fellow-men with as much fervour as he admired himself. It was said that General de Gaulle had asked our Foreign Office to leave Duff in Paris as England's representative. My letters say confidently that he did, but in *Old Men Forget* this compliment is referred to only obliquely. Duff must automatically have offered his resignation and I think the offer was never referred to by Ernie, who came to us frequently as the most friendly and loved guest.

The work and speed and crowds did not decrease with the new régime. They became even more hectic. The *salon vert* seemed more crowded with the new Ministers and new M.P.'s, with the Massif Central of *La Bande* to give me confidence. At 6 p.m. they would arrive, at 7.30 I would slip noiselessly into the Borghese bedroom, take my bath in the Marshal's tent to the murmur of their voices next door, and return to sweep the dear remnants down the back stairs that they might not collide with the dinner-guests. What a lark it was! Louise de Vilmorin was the most faithful, the most loved.

The last two years in Paris have become telescoped in my mind – a palimpsest of events. I could recover dates and details by reading my last letters to Conrad, but my memoirs are already ridiculously swollen and I must gallop to my end.

My idea of Tiepolo's idea of Cleopatra

Bidault and Bevin sign the Treaty of Dunkirk

I remember, as who doesn't, the comic incidents most vividly. Two flit through my mind as I scribble. The first a flamboyant review in the Place de la Concorde, General de Gaulle, myself and others on the tribune, dense crowds, crowds too on the laps and shoulders of the allegorical statues – Strasbourg and the rest. Crowds had also filled to the brim the dry basins of the fountains, three tiers of them. We never knew who turned on the taps, was it a *mauvaise plaisanterie* or an order forgotten and too late remembered? Anyway, the jets beneath the cheering people's feet, so long in disuse, spurted out their gush with pent-up pressure and gusto. The consequences can be imagined.

The second was on a night of Embassy revelry, particularly democratic revelry in the pompous galleries below. Ernie Bevin and A. V. Alexander were both present. At a reasonable time they went upstairs, to our private apartments, and left me to hold the fort and speed the revellers. While I was talking to a young man in uniform, I asked him to put out my cigarette. It was summer, the windows were wide open on to the garden, the room had marble consoles between the windows holding ash-trays galore, and yet this poor Yahoo trod this cigarette out on the crimson pile carpet. 'You mustn't do that,' I snapped at him. 'Don't you know this is the King's carpet, not mine – or yours?' He all but cried with remorse: it was the army's habit, he said. The last guests to go were lovers – I had to shoo them away and as I bade them goodnight I removed from his arm an unopened bottle of the King's whisky. He apologised for that too: he thought it was the Government's, he said. Upstairs I found a sing-song going on (Ernie's parties always ended that way), A. V. Alexander and John Julius taking turns at the piano, the detective logged in an armchair. I thought he should be woken by force since our songs failed to wake him, but his detectees wanted him left lying. At long last he was slapped awake, made a dash for it, was sick in the ante-room and vanished. 'Another time we won't take him to parties,' was all they said. Ernie, A. V. and I were a splendid trio for Victorian songs: 'Whatcher,' 'After the Ball was Over' and 'Two Lovely

Black Eyes.' We knew all the words and could caterwaul away for hours.

We grew fonder and fonder of Ernie. I took him in an open car, with the faithful Bob Dixon and a new detective, to watch the open-air dancing in Montmartre on 14 July. He loved to see people enjoying themselves and, wanting to be amongst them, he suggested having a drink on the densely crowded pavement. Bob Dixon looked dubious, the detective looked sober, and out we got. Ernie was immediately recognised by his bulk and bonhomie and the current cartoons, a table was found for us, and the crowd gave him the cheer of his life. He thanked them in a well-expressed little speech which was simultaneously translated and relayed by amplifiers.

Ernie was fond of me, and used to ask me not to think of him as a big bad wolf, but our fate was in his hands and I knew that one day he would be forced to gobble us up. I told him this in extenuation. We bore him no grudge when the grim day came. To Duff he never once referred to the dismissal and we continued as friends till his lamented death. 'He was a good man' was the highest praise Belloc could give as an 'envoi' to eventual heaven. I can say it of Ernie.

In all this sweetness, light and devoted work there were clouds gathering in England, clouds that were to shower bitter tears upon me.

My letters from Conrad grew ever more depressed:

I took my temperature tonight after ten days of whisky, medicine and cream, the doctor's orders. I wanted to see what the effect might be, result 94 degrees. What kind of a disease can it be? I go to bed at eleven feeling all right and wake aching in my legs as if I'd run six miles, utter exhaustion and deep depression. When I'm up I sit wondering if I should go back to bed; one must fight against going back to bed. The doctor has packed up; he isn't interested. I've had the carter up to cut my hair. It's nothing to a man who can cut eight acres of wheat before

dinner-time, and much nicer than waiting one's turn at the stinking local wig-fixer.

P.S. The Bath specialist, called a cardiologist, will see me Wednesday. I wonder if I've got a 'nervous breakdown' or 'neurasthenia'? It seems so unnatural. I notice nearly every day that Mr So-and-so has been ordered 'a month's complete rest.' Don't make yourself unhappy about me; it's only what happens to people all the time, over and over again. I don't read much; it's as though my mind was tired like my body. I think of you a great deal but that's a permanent habit, ill or well.

At last he gave up the farm and went to hospital in London, but not for long. His heart was ill, broken. I went as often as I could to see him in England, where he divided his days between his two sisters in Surrey and at the Manor House, Mells. There he died, a convert at the last to the Catholic faith. Farming for the war, combined with the Home Guard fatigues, killed him as surely as an enemy's bullet. Katharine Asquith was there to reverence his parting soul. No one better could he have desired. I was prepared for his end, but preparation makes calamity longer. I was prepared too for my sister Marjorie – who had meant so much to me in youth – to die too young. I was in part what she made me and I felt that part of me died with her. Her husband scarcely survived her. Their children are now my dearest support.

Even Emerald must die – her lightly pitched voice still echoes in my ear. She died gracefully without fear, or faith. I once heard her say 'I think Jesus Christ has the most unpleasant face,' as she might speak of a picture of François I or Hitler. 'And,' she mused on, 'John the Baptist's is very little better.' She had an instinct for good and she could animate sticks and stones into glistening gems. So many of her circle of luminaries faded out with her setting, but many remained strong and beaming and constant to her as fixed stars.

With Emerald's death I felt that 'all my friends are lapped in

lead,' but Paris fortunately allowed me no respite for grief, so I began with broken nerves to think that work and frustration would kill Duff. The Anglo-French alliance was making haste very slowly. Generally there was a crisis. De Gaulle had resigned and was to remain, as Winston had been, for ten years a voice crying in the wilderness. There was the Ruhr, and Syria (Duff's most barbed thorn), and more changes of government and the Council of Foreign Ministers, followed by the Peace Conference. One event succeeded another. For me this meant redoubled entertainment on a sumptuous and lugubrious scale.

It was after one of our receptions that François Mauriac wrote in the *Figaro* a piece that I would blush to publish had not Duff forestalled me. All the more reason not to reprint it, one might think, yet I am so flattered by the sentiment and so admire the impeccable French that I cannot resist doing so:

> À une fête de ces derniers jours, où les visages fermes des Slavs glissaient, tous feux éteints, à travers les groupes, j'observais l'ambassadrice d'une nation amie, cette figure de Pallas Athénée qui épandait sur ce troupeau sombre et méfiant l'inutile lumière de ses yeux; statue encore intacte, témoin des époques heureuses, sa beauté adorable se dressait en vain, comme un dernier appel à la joie de vivre au dessus d'une humanité sans regard.

Duff said he could write *Nunc Dimittis* (disturbing words for me) once a firm treaty with France was signed and delivered. And signed it was on the last day of February 1947, under rainy skies at Dunkirk. The historic seaport, so present in our war-memories, was chosen by our imaginative Ernie. He was splendidly to represent England, while little M. Bidault signed for France. I don't remember much more about the ceremony; it was a laurelled victory for Duff after all his pains, and I should have been exultant; yet *Nunc Dimittis*, those words of ending, weighed like lead in my mind, treading down jubilation. Within six months came Duff's

dismissal. As I have said before, it was natural and not unkind. Just as Ernie had never answered Duff's letter offering resignation when the Labour Government took over, so not once did he refer to this dismantling, although they had many an interview before the end of the mission. He never again came to the Embassy; perhaps he had no cause, or perhaps he did not want to show the furry ears and sabre-teeth of the big bad wolf.

I felt much older after the dismissal. I don't think Duff did; although he had expected it, it came as a shock, but he had unusual balance and serenity for the big events of his life and could always look forward. Now he would write his memoirs and enjoy the seasons and his autumn at Chantilly. For my part, I felt unusually incapable and tired. We gave a last ball – my own Waterloo. Winston was there to lend lustre to the feast; I lent it a skeleton. We went to San Vigilio, our happy haunt on Lake Garda. As always it consoled, with its beauty, my troubled mind. I began to count God's blessings. I had new friends to walk beside me on the sad road of age – Louise de Vilmorin, Paul-Louis Weiller, who had come into my life two years before and would, I knew, stay to the end, and many other reliable wayfarers. I had Chantilly to cope with, and its proportions and peaceful atmosphere would offset the effort that must be expended. Another blessing – a very old friend, Benjamin Guinness, had made us a present for life of a little flat in the Rue de Lille. I had John Julius, always a Sunday's child, who had gone from strength to strength at Eton, and after a year at the University of Strasbourg had just started his National Service as a naval rating. I liked that. Then, above all blessings, there was Duff – never sick, never tired, never cold, to me ever turning. Before we married I used to ask him if he felt equal to the heavy task of keeping me happy. He never doubted it for a moment. 'As long as Duff is there,' I would think, 'it is shameful to give these spectres of melancholy a triumph.' His thoughts as the sands ran out in Paris were of the future – work, sport (he was sometimes *Roi de la Chasse* at the Presidential shoot at Rambouillet), clubs and club-bores, lovely women, walking in the forests,

reading to himself even while dressing, shaken to tears with laughter if the book was funny, reading aloud to me, walking up and down the lawn at Chantilly refashioning a phrase before he wrote it down in his clean, scarcely-corrected manuscript. Though not liking picnics he had vowed to enjoy them for my sake, and himself bought the basket. I still had Duff, and together we left the Embassy with what *hauteur* we could muster.

I don't know how the go-up, go-down came so dramatically. We must have left our fools' paradise and gone to the new flat instead of going directly to England, for I remember a winter evening's rain, both of us clinging together under an umbrella, and looking, on the left side of the Seine, for a place to dine. Every place we tried was shut – a Monday, I suppose. With no car and no taxi to be hailed we tramped on, dejected orphans of the storm, till at last we came to Porquerolles, a favourite restaurant far up the Boulevard St Germain; and there Madame Zick must have been touched and understanding of our plight, for she welcomed us and fed us with her best and gave us comforting claret and showed us no bill.

So this was the end of Career. They wished us a happy retirement. I could not see the words compatible, but good things were still in store for us. First and foremost, John Julius's bride. He was twenty-three when he left my wing for her arms. I had no jealousy to overcome because Anne was fresh as April, as tall as a lance and because he loved her as I had been loved. They called their daughter Artemis, which is Greek for Diana.

There were sunlit days at Chantilly. There Duff wrote his last book and there I gave up keeping old age at bay. Although the change from youth is slow and regular, it comes yearly as a defeating shock. Enthusiasms wilt; the sands running so quickly through the hour-glass bury schemes and plans. Clothes lose their lure; elegance must give way to the 'funny old thing.' It would be better to look redoubtable and stump around with a stick to brandish. I look rather pathetic and still surprised. There will be no photographs of this slippered stage. Cecil Beaton, whose eyes are more dissecting than

his flattering lens, must close his shutter. It opened last to portray me as Tiepolo's idea of Cleopatra at the famous Beistegui ball in Venice. The frontiers still let me through with that picture on my passport. When they won't I'll stay at home.

I'll write no more memories. They would get too sad, tender as they are. Age wins and one must learn to grow old. As I learnt with the loss of a nurse to put childish things behind me, as I learnt when the joys of dependence were over to embrace with fear the isolation of independence, so now I must learn to walk this long unlovely wintry way, looking for spectacles, shunning the cruel looking-glass, laughing at my clumsiness before others mistakenly condole, not expecting gallantry yet disappointed to receive none, apprehending every ache or shaft of pain, alive to blinding flashes of mortality, unarmed, totally vulnerable. More faith is my first prayer; the others are chiefly propitiatory. There is one of thanks, even one for this poor book, one for benediction and reunion. I want no monument, nor to live longer in memories than the heartbeats of those who are young and who love me and protect me today. I cannot end with words as courageous as Duff's. The long custom of living disinclines one to dying, but great loss makes death less fearful. Besides, before the end, what light may shine?

Château de Saint Firmin

Saint Firmin, the salon

Saint Firmin, the library

Anne

Artemis

Index

Isobel (author's niece). *See* Manners, Lady Isobel.

James II, King, 32
James of Sutton, Mrs, 14, 15, 84
Janzé, Phyllis de, 56, 156–7
Jebb, Gladwyn and Cynthia, 237
Jerome, Jerome K., 188, 236
John (author's brother). *See* Rutland, Duke of.
John Julius. *See* Cooper, John Julius.
Jones, Enid Bagnold, 151, 159, 200
Jordan, Philip, 205, 206
Jouvet, Louis, 235
Jumbo. *See* Wilson, Sir Henry Maitland.

Kaetchen. *See* Kommer, Rudolf.
Kao, Mr, 105, 106, 138
Katharine (*née* Horner). *See* Asquith, Katharine.
Kennedy, Joseph P., 39
Keswick, Tony, 95, 97, 98, 103, 104, 105, 106, 109, 119
Kilvert, Francis, 28
Kirk, Alexander, 146
Kirkpatrick, Helen, 51, 128
Knickerbocker, H. R., 1, 62, 223–4
Knox, Ronald, 121
Kommer, Rudolf, 4, 6, 21, 27, 39, 40, 42, 43, 44, 45, 59, 93, 153, 154, 155, 157, 165, 166, 204

Lampson, Sir Miles and Lady, 145, 146, 148
Lanvin, Madame, 222
Lapie, Pierre-Olivier, 175
Lascelles, Tommy, 10, 192
Lehmann, John, 235
Lehmann, Rosamond, 235
Leigh, Colston, 12

Leigh Fermor, Paddy, 161
Leigh, Vivien, 19, 235
Lindbergh, Col., 94
Lindsay, Ruby, 200
Linlithgow, Marquess of, 116, 117, 135, 143, 144
Lloyd, Lord, 64
Londonderry, Marquess of, 210
Lothian, Marquess of, 6, 63, 64
Lovat, Laura Lady, 54, 120
Loxley, P. N., 189
Luce, Claire, 95, 97, 98, 128
Luce, Henry, 5, 153
Luzarraga, Count Manuel de, 225–7
Lutyens, Edwin, 143
Lyttelton, Oliver, 145, 146
Lyttelton, Lady Moira, 146

MacCarthy, Desmond, 52, 79
Maclean, Fitzroy, 173
Macmillan, Harold, 171, 172, 173, 174, 176, 182, 189
Magellan, 99
Maitland, Col. Mark, 2
Makins, Roger, 183
Manners, Lady Isobel, 33
Manx, Miss, 121, 122
Mary, Queen, 9
Marjorie (author's sister). *See* Anglesey, Marchioness of.
Marks, Simon, 80
Massigli, René, 175, 186, 187
Massigli, Madame, 221
Maugham, Somerset, 62, 126
Mauriac, François, 243
Maurice. *See* Baring, Maurice.
Max. *See* Beaverbrook, Lord.
Maxwell, Elsa, 19
Mayer, René, 175
Menzies, Robert, 118, 127
Miller, Col., 112

VINTAGE CLASSICS

Vintage launched in the United Kingdom in 1990, and was originally the paperback home for the Random House Group's literary authors. Now, Vintage is comprised of some of London's oldest and most prestigious literary houses, including Chatto & Windus (1855), Hogarth (1917), Jonathan Cape (1921) and Secker & Warburg (1935), alongside the newer or relaunched hardback and paperback imprints: The Bodley Head, Harvill Secker, Yellow Jersey, Square Peg, Vintage Paperbacks and Vintage Classics.

From Angela Carter, Graham Greene and Aldous Huxley to Toni Morrison, Haruki Murakami and Virginia Woolf, Vintage Classics is renowned for publishing some of the greatest writers and thinkers from around the world and across the ages – all complemented by our beautiful, stylish approach to design. Vintage Classics' authors have won many of the world's most revered literary prizes, including the Nobel, the Man Booker, the Prix Goncourt and the Pulitzer, and through their writing they continue to capture imaginations, inspire new perspectives and incite curiosity.

In 2007 Vintage Classics introduced its distinctive red spine design, and in 2012 Vintage Children's Classics was launched to include the much-loved authors of our childhood. Random House joined forces with the Penguin Group in 2013 to become Penguin Random House, making it the largest trade publisher in the United Kingdom.

@vintagebooks

penguin.co.uk/vintage-classics